Forensic Psychology

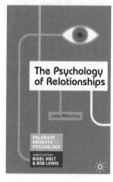

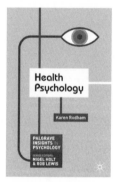

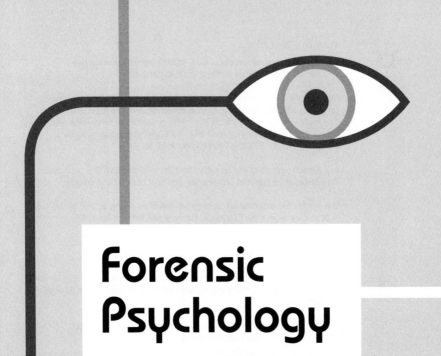

Forensic Psychology

Adrian J. Scott

PALGRAVE INSIGHTS IN PSYCHOLOGY

SERIES EDITORS:
NIGEL HOLT
& ROB LEWIS

palgrave
macmillan

First published 2010 by
PALGRAVE MACMILLAN

Palgrave Macmillan in the UK is an imprint of Macmillan Publishers Limited, registered in England, company number 785998, of Houndmills, Basingstoke, Hampshire RG21 6XS.

Palgrave Macmillan in the US is a division of St Martin's Press LLC, 175 Fifth Avenue, New York, NY 10010.

Palgrave Macmillan is the global academic imprint of the above companies and has companies and representatives throughout the world.

Palgrave® and Macmillan® are registered trademarks in the United States, the United Kingdom, Europe and other countries.

ISBN: 978–0–230–24942–4

This book is printed on paper suitable for recycling and made from fully managed and sustained forest sources. Logging, pulping and manufacturing processes are expected to conform to the environmental regulations of the country of origin.

A catalogue record for this book is available from the British Library.

A catalog record for this book is available from the Library of Congress.

10 9 8 7 6 5 4 3 2 1
19 18 17 16 15 14 13 12 11 10

Printed and bound in Great Britain by
CPI Antony Rowe, Chippenham and Eastbourne

Contents

Acknowledgements

I would like to thank Karine Hamilton, Pam Henry, Nikki Rajakaruna, Lizzie Slade and Greg Stratton for reading and editing draft chapters. Your help was much appreciated. I would also like to thank Nigel Holt for his patience, editorial help and good humour.

Note from series editors

Psychologists find a role wherever we find people. Forensic psychology is just such a place. Its popularity shows no sign of abating and with writers like Adrian Scott finding their way onto our shelves it is easy to see why. Forensic psychology is at the crossroads between all aspects of the law and psychology. As such, it is of interest to lawmakers and breakers, and all those with a role in working with people who find themselves within the criminal justice system.

Adrian Scott works in Australia, researching and teaching this topic. His teaching and skill at explaining and delivering forensic psychology have been highly praised and we are delighted to see that he has been able to translate these great skills into writing. The temptation with forensic psychology is to make it sensational, to constantly refer to the big and well-publicized examples where psychologists have been called on for assistance. The danger in doing this is that the theory is left behind, where really it should be first. Scott has done something quite special in this book. He has delivered a strong theoretical approach while maintaining an energy and lightness that bring out the characteristics that make forensic psychology so hugely popular.

- *This book may be part of your preparation for university study.* It may be that forensic psychology forms part or all of the degree you hope to study. Adrian Scott is enviably energetic and hugely enthusiastic, and this comes from his total emersion in the topic and in his teaching. The book is written carefully to allow reading at a number of different levels, and it will provide the essential foundation for further study at university level.

- *This book may be read as part of a university course.* Adrian is extremely familiar with all textbooks available for those studying forensic psychology at university. He reviews them regularly and chooses material from them for his own courses. His book is written from this strong and knowledgeable perspective and can form either your core reading or additional support should you need it.
- *This book may be read as part of your A-level.* We are extremely familiar with the requirements of the A-level student and teacher, and have worked closely with Adrian to make sure that his book will fulfill the demands of those studying forensic psychology at this level. The book is written with readers at different stages of study in mind and, as a result, it provides stretch and challenge, but maintains the accessibility we all strive for in our writing. The Reading Guide at the end of the book tells you where different A-level specifications appear.

Whether perused by psychologists, sociologists, criminologists and lawyers, social workers, legal-support or representatives of the media, we are certain this book will provide the solid academic bedrock this often-misrepresented subject requires. You may well, of course, be reading this book out of interest and we hope you find it interesting and, perhaps, stimulating enough for you to take your reading and study of the subject further.

NIGEL HOLT AND ROB LEWIS
Series Editors

Chapter 1

Introduction

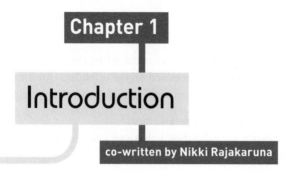

co-written by Nikki Rajakaruna

The criminal justice system exists to serve two purposes. First, to serve the instrumental purpose of responding to crime in order to secure society, and second, to serve the symbolic purpose of providing a system that is capable of taking action against those who break the law (Daly, 1996). Each stage of the criminal justice system involves different people, practices and procedures that aim to ensure a fair and just outcome. As such, important questions arise regarding the people involved and the practices and procedures employed at each stage of the criminal justice system.

The process of criminal justice begins when a crime is committed by an offender, and may raise the following questions:

- How should crime be defined and measured?
- What are the underlying social, psychological, biological and cognitive causes of offending?

Once a crime comes to the attention of the police, various procedures are used to identify the likely offender and obtain information from victims, witnesses and suspects. Questions that arise during this investigative stage of the criminal justice system may include:

- What type of person would have committed a particular crime?
- How should identification procedures be conducted to increase the reliability of eyewitness testimony?
- How should police interviews be conducted to ensure the collection of accurate and truthful information?

Once a suspect has been identified and evidence has been collected against him or her the case is brought before a court of law, and may raise the following questions:

- How do jurors arrive at decisions of guilt or innocence?
- What factors influence the process of jury decision making?

If the suspect is found guilty of committing the crime then a punishment (that is, a sentence) is imposed on the offender. Questions that arise during this final stage of the criminal justice system may include:

- What is the purpose of punishment?
- How effective are offending behaviour programmes at reducing the risk of reoffending?

Forensic psychology has the capacity to answer these and other questions relevant to the different stages of the criminal justice system.

Although the term 'forensic psychology' literally means the application of psychology to law, the term is increasingly used to encompass the broad application of psychological theories and methods to crime, criminal behaviour and the legal system (Bartol and Bartol, 2006; Howitt, 2006). This book adopts the broader definition of forensic psychology and considers aspects of human behaviour at each stage of the criminal justice system. It is separated into four sections, each focusing on a different area of forensic psychology:

Section One: Theories of Offending
Section Two: Psychology and the Investigative Process
Section Three: Psychology and the Courtroom
Section Four: Psychology and the Penal System

Chapter 2 considers definitions of crime and methods used in the measurement of crime. The chapter begins with problems associated with defining crime, and acknowledges that crime is socially constructed and that legal definitions vary over time and between countries. The chapter highlights that despite these issues, there is international agreement regarding the unacceptability of certain types of serious crime. The chapter continues with a discussion of the measurement of crime, with specific reference to **official statistics**, **victim surveys** and **self-report surveys**. The strengths and weaknesses of each method are discussed and it is argued that all three measures should be used concurrently in order to provide a comprehensive understanding of crime.

Section One: Theories of Offending

Section One includes three chapters that describe some of the prominent social, psychological, cognitive and biological theories of offending. *Chapter 3* provides an overview of social and psychological theories. The chapter begins by outlining two founding theories of offending (the classical and positivist schools), both of which located the cause of crime within the individual. The chapter continues with a discussion of social theories of offending which propose that criminal behaviour is a social, rather than an individual phenomenon. The social theories outlined include strain and subcultural theories, social disorganization theory, differential association theory, social control theory and labelling theory. Psychological theories that have been used to explain criminal behaviour are then discussed: specifically, psychodynamic theories and the maternal deprivation hypothesis. The chapter then offers a description of social theories that incorporate psychological processes in order to explain the learning of criminal behaviour; namely, differential reinforcement theory and social learning theory.

Chapter 4 provides a detailed overview of biological and cognitive theories of offending. The chapter begins with a discussion of biological theories of offending, including early explanations that looked for physiological characteristics that separated offenders from non-offenders. More recent biological explanations are then considered, including those that examine the role of heredity, genes, brain dysfunction and conditionability in relation to crime. Sociobiological theories of offending (that is, evolutionary explanations), which relate criminal behaviour to the process of natural selection, are then discussed. The application of sociobiological theories to sex differences in criminal behaviour, and rape and homicide are considered. Finally, attention is given to cognitive theories of offending and the decision-making processes associated with criminal behaviour. Specifically, dysfunctional thinking patterns, rationality, moral development and the attribution of blame.

Chapter 5 considers the development of integrated theories, the identification of risk factors that are associated with criminal behaviour and the relationship between media violence and violent crime. The chapter begins with a discussion of theory integration as a means of increasing the explanatory power of traditional theories of offending. It is highlighted that theory integration is limited because it often ignores the fundamentally different underlying assumptions of traditional theories. The chapter continues by outlining a number of risk factors associated with criminal behaviour, including family, peer, school and socioeconomic risk factors. The role of developmental processes in the onset, continuance and cessation of crime is then discussed with reference to Moffitt's life-course-persistent/adolescence-limited theory, Sampson and Laub's theory of age-graded informal social control, and Loeber's pathways to crime theory. Finally, the relationship between media violence and violent crime is considered. Although research indicates that there may be a weak relationship, media violence is likely to have a greater impact on some people than others.

Section Two: Psychology and the Investigative Process

Section Two comprises three chapters, each considering a different aspect of the investigative process: offender profiling, eyewitness testimony and investigative interviewing. *Chapter 6* considers the role of offender profiling in the investigative process. The chapter starts by outlining the assumptions of profiling before describing three prominent approaches to profiling: crime scene analysis, investigative psychology and geographic profiling. The chapter continues with a discussion of typologies of serial murder and rape. The various criticisms regarding the use of typologies are also presented. The chapter concludes with a critical discussion regarding the effectiveness of profiles in police investigations.

Chapter 7 considers the role of eyewitness testimony in police investigations. The chapter begins with a discussion of factors that may influence the accuracy of eyewitness testimony with particular attention given to the effect of emotional arousal. The chapter continues with a discussion of police interview and lineup procedures that have been implicated in unreliable eyewitness testimony, together with ways to improve the accuracy of descriptive and identification evidence. The use of facial composites in criminal investigations is also considered. The chapter concludes with a discussion of recovered and **false memories**. It is argued that forgetting is the most likely cause of recovered memories while unconscious fabrication is the most likely cause of false memories.

Chapter 8 considers issues relating to the interviewing of suspects. The chapter begins with a discussion of **false confessions**, which occur when an innocent suspect admits guilt for a crime that he or she did not commit. The major causes and types of false confessions are discussed in detail and the role of suspect vulnerability is emphasized. It is highlighted that false confessions are common when police officers use deception and trickery during interviews. The chapter outlines the nine-step procedure (that is, the Reid technique) and presents a discussion of recent advances in investigative interviewing in the UK. These advances include the progression from the **Police and Criminal Evidence (PACE)** Act 1984 to the **PEACE** interview model and the recently implemented 5-Tier interview training strategy. Finally, recent developments in detecting deception (that is, lies) are discussed along with techniques that help police officers accurately differentiate liars from truth tellers.

Section Three: Psychology and the Courtroom

Section Three contains two chapters that consider jury decision making and factors that influence the jury. *Chapter 9* considers the nature of decision-making processes in the context of the jury. The chapter starts with a discussion of research methods that are typically used in jury research. The use of case studies, mock jury studies, shadow jury studies and post-deliberation studies are discussed. It is argued that a combination of methods should ideally be used to investigate any given area of jury decision making in order to overcome their respective strengths and weaknesses. The chapter continues by outlining the different models of jury decision making with specific reference to the **story model**, **predecisional distortion** and **source monitoring errors**. The chapter concludes with a discussion of majority and minority influence. Research is presented which indicates that in the context of jury decision making, **majority influence** has a much stronger impact on verdict decisions than **minority influence**.

Chapter 10 considers the factors that bias jury decision making and the effectiveness of methods of countering these biases. The chapter begins with a discussion of the main procedural and case factors that may influence jury verdict decisions. Specifically, how strength of evidence, inadmissible evidence, pretrial publicity and expert testimony can influence jury decision making. The chapter continues with a discussion of defendant, victim and witness characteristics that may influence jury verdict decisions. Finally, three procedural safeguards that aim to reduce the influential nature of non-evidentiary information are discussed. These safeguards are **voir dire**, **judicial admonitions** and **jury deliberation**. The relative ineffectiveness of these safeguards is considered together with a number of ways in which they can be altered to reduce the likelihood of biases influencing jury decision making.

Section Four: Psychology and the Penal System

Section Four consists of two chapters that consider the different justifications offered for the punishment of offenders, as well as the effectiveness of offending behaviour programmes in reducing the risk of reoffending. *Chapter 11* considers the punishment of offenders and the effectiveness of various types of punishment. The chapter starts by outlining three justifications for the use of punishment: retribution, deterrence and confinement. The roles of rehabilitation and restorative justice are then discussed. Restorative justice was developed as an alternative to traditional approaches to punishment, aiming to resolve crimes in a manner that is acceptable to the offender, the victim and the community. The chapter continues with a discussion of prison and probation (that is, custodial and non-custodial sentencing) and the introduction of the National Offender Management System (NOMS). NOMS was introduced to provide the effective management of offenders as they progress from prison to probation. A range of alternative punishments are then considered, including compensatory penalties, punishment orders, intense supervision programmes, shock incarceration, scared straight programmes, and electronic monitoring. Finally, attention is given to the Stanford prison experiment and two aspects of prison life: prison officer stress and prisoner suicide.

Chapter 12 considers the various types of offender treatment programmes and the effectiveness of these programmes at reducing reoffending. The chapter begins with a discussion of the **what works** debate with reference to the **meta-analysis** of treatment programmes, The principles of 'what works' are then outlined, together with recommendations that programmes should target offender risk and need, as well as treatment responsivity, delivery and integrity. The chapter continues with the discussion and evaluation of general offending behaviour programmes. These programmes target the maladjusted thinking and behaviour of offenders by teaching a range of interpersonal skills. The effectiveness of specific offending behaviour programmes, designed for particular types of offenders, is then considered. These include violent offending behaviour programmes and sex offending behaviour programmes. The chapter concludes with the discussion and evaluation of token economy programmes and drug and alcohol programmes.

Chapter 2

Defining and measuring crime

Introduction

There is little consensus regarding the definition of crime while different measures of crime often produce contrasting information (Israel, 2006). It is not appropriate to simply describe some measures of crime as wrong, however, as different measures provide alternative perspectives of crime (Howitt, 2006). It is important therefore to consider the **validity** of different measures of crime in relation to various types of crime.

This chapter will consider definitions of crime and the relative strengths and weaknesses of different measures of crime. It will first outline some of the problems associated with defining and measuring crime. The utility of **official statistics**, **victim surveys** and **self-report surveys** will then be discussed. Finally, attention will be given to the comparative validity of these different measures of crime.

This chapter will examine:

- Defining and measuring crime
- Official statistics
- Victim and self-report surveys
- Comparing different measures of crime

Defining and measuring crime

Defining crime is a complex issue and no single definition is totally satisfactory (Andrews and Bonta, 2006). One argument is that a crime comprises any act or omission that violates the law and is punishable by the criminal justice system (Crowther, 2007; Feldman, 1993). However, this approach to defining crime is limited because legal definitions are not universal or stable over time (Andrews and Bonta, 2006). As such, a particular act or omission may violate the law in one country or at one point in time but it may not violate the law in another country or at another point in time. An alternative argument therefore suggests that crime is a socially constructed phenomenon that varies according to the dominant beliefs, morals and values of a particular country (Crowther, 2007; Daly and Wilson, 1997). Consequently, it may be impossible to ever have a clear definition of crime.

Despite the variability of legal definitions of crime, there is considerable agreement in the unacceptability of certain behaviours internationally. For example, virtually all countries disapprove of murder, rape and theft (McGuire, 2004). Thus, a degree of international consensus exists regarding certain types of serious crime.

Concern with the control and prevention of crime led to the introduction of official statistics (Blackburn, 1993). Unfortunately, **crime rates** produced by official statistics are a product of the **prevalence** of crime (that is, the number of people committing crimes at any one time) as well as the **incidence** of crime (that is, the number of crimes committed by these people) (Farrington, Ohlin and Wilson, 1986). Consequently, it is not possible to determine whether changes in crime rates over time reflect variations in the prevalence of crime, the incidence of crime or a combination of the two. Attempts to compare crime rates internationally are also problematic because of variations in the definitions of some crimes and the use of different police recording practices (Howitt, 2006).

Summary

It may be argued that any act or omission that violates the law is a crime, but legal definitions vary over time and between countries. As such, crime may be viewed as a socially constructed phenomenon that reflects the dominant beliefs, morals and values held at a particular time in a particular country. Irrespective, there is international agreement regarding certain types of serious crime, including murder, rape and theft.

Official statistics

The Home Office has collected and published criminal statistics in England and Wales since 1805. These criminal statistics were initially restricted to court-based data, but information concerning crimes recorded by the police was added in 1857 (Smith, 2006). In the US, the Federal Bureau of Investigation has produced annual Uniform Crime Reports since 1929, which record violence and property related crimes reported to state and local law enforcement agencies (DiIulio, 1996). Most western governments now publish official statistics annually, although these are limited to crimes that have been reported and recorded by the police.

Reporting crime

Victim surveys have revealed that less than half of all crimes are reported to the police. For example, only 42 per cent of crimes experienced by victims of the 2005/06 British Crime Survey were reported (Walker, Kershaw and Nicholas, 2006). Comparable figures were also evident in the 2005 US National Crime Victimization Survey where only 47 per cent of violent crimes and 40 per cent of property crimes were reported to the police (Catalano, 2006).

There are a number of factors that influence the reporting of crimes, including the seriousness of the crime, the nature of the victim–perpetrator relationship, the characteristics of the victim, and perceptions of the police. For example, Skogan (1976) found that the seriousness of the crime was the most important factor in determining whether or not it was reported to the police. Crimes were more likely to be reported if the victim felt threatened, received an injury or experienced financial loss. While the nature of the victim–perpetrator relationship was also important for certain types of crime, the characteristics of the victim were only weakly related to reporting behaviour. Reasons for non-reporting included 'it wasn't important enough' and 'nothing can be done'. Similarly, Gove, Hughes and Geerken (1985) argued that the perceived seriousness of a crime, as defined by the victim and determined by the police, had the greatest influence on whether it was reported. Characteristics of the victim only had minimal effects. In relation to property crime, MacDonald (2000, 2001, 2002) found that reporting was more likely if the crime involved financial loss, occurred at night or resulted in injury. The age and sex of the victim were also found to influence reporting behaviour (young men were the least likely to report a burglary) along with the perceived efficiency of the police.

Sexual offences are particularly at risk of underreporting due to the negative stigma associated with being a 'rape victim', together with the loss of privacy and risk of recrimination during the legal process itself (Allen, 2007). Men who experience rape are particularly unlikely to report the crime to the police due to embarrassment (Dobash, Dobash, Wilson and Day, 1992). As National Crime Victimization Survey data revealed, women are one and a half times more likely than men to report their experience of rape (Pino and Meier, 1999). The seriousness of the crime is also an important factor. For example, men are more likely to report their experience of rape if they can demonstrate that they were unable to protect themselves (Pino and Meier, 1999). In contrast, women are more likely to report aggravated rapes (that is, when the assailant is a stranger, there are multiple assailants, or violence is apparent) to the police than simple rapes (Clay-Warner and Burt, 2005).

Recording crime

Not all crimes reported to the police are officially recorded (Wittebrood and Junger, 2002). Influencing factors include police discretion, variations in recording practices, and changes to recording practices over time. O'Brien (1966) considered changes in the rates of low-ambiguity crimes (homicides) and high-ambiguity crimes (all other violent crimes) on the understanding that high-ambiguity crimes offer the police greater discretion regarding the recording of the offence. On this basis, O'Brien argued that the increase in 'all other violent crime' rates outlined in Uniform Crime Reports between 1973 and 1992 partially reflected changes in the recording practices of the police, as homicide rates had remained relatively unchanged. This perspective is based on the assumption that fluctuations in low- and high-ambiguity crimes are similar over time.

Variability has been found in the recording practices of local police departments (DiIulio, 1996) and regional police forces (MacDonald, 2002). When technological advances designed to improve the consistency of police recording practices across local departments and regional forces were introduced, there was an increase in the overall proportion of reported crimes recorded by the police (Federal Bureau of Investigation, 2006a; Home Office, 2006a). Other changes to recording practices over time reflect the interests of government agencies and the introduction of new legislation. For example, the category of arson was first included in Uniform Crime Reports in 1979 (Federal Bureau of Investigation, 2006a), and definitional changes in 1998 led to the widening of the **notifiable offences** category used to compile official statistics in England and Wales (MacDonald, 2002). Furthermore, crimes previously excluded from official statistics, such as less serious crimes, frauds and drug offences, are now included (Home Office, 2006a).

The reporting and recording of rape victimizations in the US increased after the introduction of rape reform legislation in 1974. Although there was variation in the extent to which individual states enacted the reforms, the most common changes included the following (Horney and Spohn, 1991):

- The redefinition of rape to include a series of offences graded by seriousness.
- The elimination of the resistance and corroboration requirements to shift the focus away from the behaviour of the victim towards the actions of the perpetrator.
- The implementation of rape-shield laws to restrict the admissibility of the victim's sexual history to cross examination.

The development of special rape units also led to an increase in the reporting and recording of rape offences in the US (Jensen and Karpos, 1993).

The validity of official statistics

Questions concerning the validity of official statistics have been raised since their introduction. As Tibbitts (1932) highlighted, the publication of Uniform Crime Reports by a government agency does not guarantee their accuracy. Similarly, Maguire (2002) discussed how official statistics in England and Wales continue to be treated as an accurate measure of crime despite warnings to the contrary by criminologists and government statisticians. For example, agencies recording crimes in England and Wales other than the Home Office, such as the British Transport Police and the Ministry of Defence Police, do not have their data included in official statistics (Maguire, 2002). Furthermore, official statistics are particularly poor at indicating the prevalence of minor crimes, as demonstrated by two direct observation studies of shoplifting (see 'thinking scientifically' box for further details) (Buckle and Farrington, 1994).

Thinking scientifically → **Measuring shoplifting by systematic observation: A replication study**

(Buckle and Farrington, 1994)

The research investigated the nature and prevalence of shoplifting in two department stores in different counties in the UK. The research used direct non-participant observation.

A total of 988 customers and potential shoplifters were followed from the time they entered two small department stores to the time they left. The customers were selected at random and were watched by two observers. The observers recorded various customer details including their sex, race and estimated age. The research was conducted during the summer months of July and August. None of the shoplifters was stopped or detained.

Between one and two per cent of customers were found to shoplift, with a greater proportion of men shoplifting than women: two and a half percent of the 320 male customers shoplifted compared to one per cent of the 668 female customers. Relatively young (estimated age below 25) and relatively old (estimated age over 55) customers were also more likely to shoplift. Shoplifters tended to steal low-cost items and to purchase goods as well as steal them.

Although the research was only able to provide a rough estimate of the prevalence of shoplifting, it demonstrated that there is a clear discrepancy between official statistics and reality. The estimated number of shoplifters in one department store (over 26,000 per year) was over three times greater than the number of shoplifters recorded by the police in the two counties where the research was conducted combined (about 7000 per year).

Evaluation

Despite the utility of this research, it is unknown whether the apparent sex and age differences would remain if a larger sample were used, if other types of store were included, or if the research were conducted at a different time of year. Furthermore, it is unlikely that this type of research could be managed on a large scale. Direct non-participant observation is highly labour-intensive and expensive in comparison to other research methods.

Summary

Official statistics are now published annually by most western governments, but they are limited to crimes that have been reported and recorded by the police. Consequently, crime rates are dependent to the reporting practices of the victims and the recording practices of the police, which are particularly sensitive to the seriousness of the crime and the nature of the victim–perpetrator relationship.

Victim and self-report surveys

During the late 1960s American criminologists experimented with an alternative measure of crime, utilizing large-scale population surveys, to uncover the **dark figure** of crime (that is, the amount of crime that is not officially recorded) (MacDonald, 2002; Zedner, 2002). The National Crime Survey was first introduced in the US in 1973 and was later redesigned in 1992 when it was renamed the National Crime Victimization Survey (Kindermann, Lynch and Cantor, 1997).

Thinking scientifically →

Redesigning the National Crime Survey

The National Crime Survey in the US was generally considered to provide a more accurate measure of rape than Uniform Crime Reports (Jensen and Karpos, 1993). However, while the National Crime Survey represented an improvement on Uniform Crime Reports, it still underestimated the prevalence of rape (Gove et al., 1985).

A fundamental problem concerning the measurement of rape by the National Crime Survey was the use of an ambiguous screening question – 'Did someone try to attack you in some other way?' – and the use of follow-up questions that repeatedly used the term rape (Koss, Gidycz and Wisniewski, 1987). The ambiguity of the screening question meant that victims had to interpret its meaning, while the use of the term rape in the follow-up questions required victims of sexual offences to conceptualize their experiences as such.

When the National Crime Survey was redesigned in 1992, an enhanced screening section was introduced to reduce the ambiguity of screening questions, to sharpen the recall of criminal victimizations, and to reduce the problem of nondisclosure (Kindermann et al., 1997). The screening question for rape explicitly asked about 'any rape, attempted rape or other type of sexual assault' while follow-up questions were phrased in terms of unwanted sexual activity rather than rape.

In 1982 the National Crime Survey was deemed reputable enough for the Home Office to set up its own version, the British Crime Survey.

Although different in their administration, these victim surveys provide information concerning people's experiences of crime, irrespective of whether they reported them to the police (MacDonald, 2001, 2002). Scotland and Northern Ireland have also introduced victim surveys to supplement the information provided by official statistics: the Scottish Crime and Victimisation Survey, and the Northern Ireland Crime Survey.

Self-report surveys developed in response to a general dissatisfaction with the ability of official statistics to 'open-up' issues relating to the incidence of crime (Elliott, 1994; Junger-Tas and Marshall, 1999). The National Youth Survey introduced in 1976 is probably the most well-known nationwide self-report survey in the US. In the UK, certain sweeps of the British Crime Survey have included self-report elements, while the Offending, Crime and Justice Survey introduced in 2003 focuses on the self-reported offending of young people (aged 10 to 25).

Despite the obvious challenge of getting people to admit to their involvement in delinquent or criminal activity, self-report surveys have been found to provide valid and reliable data (Thornberry and Krohn, 2000). Furthermore, they have shown that the majority of people have engaged in delinquent or criminal activities at some stage in their lifetime, while only a minority are caught and punished by the criminal justice system (Junger-Tas and Marshall, 1999).

Scope, sampling bias and accuracy

Victim surveys are useful as they enable the examination of the reporting and recording of crime (Levitt, 1998). The National Crime Victimization Survey arguably provides a more accurate and reliable measure of crime than Uniform Crime Reports because it is able to identify the proportion of non-reporters (DiIulio, 1996; Jensen and Karpos, 1993). Similarly, the use of self-report measures of offending are common because they are able to overcome some of the problems associated with police discretion regarding who to arrest and which crimes to record (Crisanti, Laygo and Junginger, 2003; Maxfield, Weiler and Widom, 2000).

However, the types of crime recorded via victim and self-report surveys are restricted as a consequence of their respective methodologies. Victim surveys do not account for victimless crimes (for example drug and weapon possession), crimes against businesses or institutions (for example shoplifting and fraud), or crimes where the person is no longer able to participate (for example manslaughter and murder) (Wittebrood and Junger, 2002). Furthermore, the British Crime Survey excludes anyone under the age of 16, while the National Crime Victimization Survey excludes anyone under the age of 12 (Finkelhor and Ormrod, 1999; Smith, 2006). Self-report surveys, by comparison, are biased against more serious crimes, as people who commit these types of crime are more likely to be in prison and therefore excluded from the surveys (Howitt, 2006).

Aside from the restricted scope of victim and self-report surveys, their main limitations concern **sampling bias** and accuracy. Sampling bias is of particular importance because the 'most interesting' people tend to be the hardest to find (Buckle and Farrington, 1994). Consequently, if the sample is not carefully controlled there is the risk that the true level of crime will be underestimated (Farrington, 1995). The problem of non-response is particularly apparent in the Netherlands where the response rate to their victim survey fell to 60 per cent in 2002 compared to 70 per cent in 1980 (Wittebrood and Junger, 2002). Although the response rate for the 2005 sweep of the British Crime Survey was 75 per cent, the sample was still limited because it did not consider the experiences of people living outside of 'normal' households, such as halls of residence and nursing homes (Smith, 2006; Walker et al., 2006). The National Crime Victimization Survey also has the added risk of non-response over time as residents who participate are interviewed at six-monthly intervals for up to seven interviews (Rand and Rennison, 2005).

With regard to accuracy, **concurrent validity** is often used to compare survey data with external records to gain an indication of the level of false or inaccurate responses (Farrington, 1995; Kirk, 2006). Babinski, Hartsough and Lambert (2001) found a relatively high level of agreement between self-reports and arrest records for 7 of the 12 crime types included in their study, although closer inspection revealed that about two-thirds of young adults arrested for high-frequency less-serious crimes failed to report them, and one-third self-reported committing public order crimes when no arrest record existed. Similarly, Lab and Allen (1984) found that there was substantial agreement between self-reports and police records overall, whereas Kirk (2006) discovered that a sizeable number of youths self-reported being arrested without an official record and failed to self-report when an official record existed. Research utilizing victim survey data has also shown that some women with abusive partners did not disclose any police contact contrary to evidence provided by police records (Fleury, Sullivan, Bybee and Davidson, 1998).

Issues concerning the accuracy of victim surveys are particularly important with respect to the disclosure of non-stranger victimizations, as interviews are often not conducted in private. Consequently, certain child victimizations might not be disclosed in front of family members, and victims of domestic violence may not disclose information because they feel intimidated by the presence of their partners (Finkelhor and Ormrod, 1999). Issues have also been raised with regard to reliance on one person. For example, domestic violence research utilizing **dyads** has reported a distinct lack of agreement regarding incidents in which both partners are involved (Dobash and Dobash, 1984; Dobash et al., 1992). Both people tend to report that their partners are more violent than themselves (Browning and Dutton, 1986). Consequently, there is a danger that two contrasting literatures will develop; one based on victim-reports and the other on self-reports.

Although victim surveys are designed to avoid the problem of variation commonly associated with official statistics, differences in the attention afforded to certain types of crime can impact upon victimization estimates (Jensen and Karpos, 1993). For example, elements of the British Crime Survey vary from year to year, and changes made to the 1984 sweep resulted in a substantial increase in the number of self-reported offences, which was unlikely to reflect a real increase in crime (Mayhew and Elliott, 1990). Alterations to the sampling method and the introduction of computer-assisted personal interviewing in 1994 also affected victimization estimates (MacDonald, 2000). Moreover, the questions included in the National Crime Victimization Survey have not been the same each year, and the redesign of the National Crime Survey (in response to criticisms over its capacity to gather information on certain types of crime) led to an increase in victimization estimates (Kindermann et al., 1997; Pino and Meier, 1999).

Summary

Victim and self-report surveys were introduced as alternatives to official statistics in order to uncover the dark figure of crime. Victim surveys have revealed that only a minority of crimes are reported to the police while self-report surveys have shown that most people have engaged in delinquent or criminal activities at some stage in their lifetime. However, victim and self-report surveys are often limited in scope, and suffer from sampling bias, nondisclosure and accuracy concerns.

Comparing different measures of crime

Crime estimates from victim surveys are often very different compared to official statistics. For example, official statistics in England and Wales reported that crime is increasing, while the British Crime Survey reported that crime is in decline (Smith, 2006). Similarly, annual Uniform Crime Reports showed that all rates of violent crime except homicide had increased in the US between 1973 and 1992, while the National Crime Victimization Survey showed that levels of violent crime had remained relatively unchanged or had actually decreased (O'Brien, 1996). Differences are also apparent when the volume of crime is considered. National Crime Victimization Survey estimates of crime consistently exceed comparable Uniform Crime Reports estimates (Catalano, 2006; Federal Bureau of Investigation, 2006b).

Despite these contrasting findings, official statistics, victim surveys and self-report surveys often reveal similar victim and offender characteristics in relation to certain types of crime, including delinquency, robbery and aggravated assault (Chilton and Jarvis, 1999; Farrington, 1995). Furthermore, crime rates produced by official statistics and victim surveys have become more similar in recent years, suggesting that the gap between the number of reported and officially recorded crimes is steadily decreasing (DiIulio, 1996; Levitt, 1998).

According to Smith (2006) there can never be a measure of 'overall' or 'total' crime. Instead, measures of crime should be understood in terms of their relative strengths and weaknesses. As such, it is essential that official statistics are collected in a consistent manner to improve the accuracy of variations in crime rates over time (Simmons, 2000). It is also important that victim and self-report surveys are maintained so that the data can be compared to that obtained from official statistics.

Summary

Official statistics, victim surveys and self-report surveys provide alternative perspectives of crime. Consequently, all three measures should be used in order to gain a more complete understanding of crime. It is also important that the different measures gather information in a consistent manner to improve the accuracy of crime rate comparisons over time.

Further reading

Blackburn, R. (1993) *The Psychology of Criminal Conduct: Theory, Research and Practice*. Chichester: John Wiley & Sons.

Maguire, M. (2002) Crime statistics: The 'data explosion' and its implications. In M. Maguire, R. Morgan and R. Reiner (eds), *The Oxford Handbook of Criminology* (3rd edn, pp. 322–75). Oxford: Oxford University Press.

Section One

Theories of Offending

Chapter 3

Social and psychological theories

Introduction

Social theories of offending (that is, criminological theories of crime) assert that criminal behaviour is caused by external factors (for example the environment). Psychological theories, by comparison, contend that criminal behaviour is determined by the interaction between internal and external factors (for example between the individual and the environment) (Curran and Renzetti, 2001; Farrington, 1994). Although social and psychological theories of offending developed in relative isolation, certain social theories have been extended to incorporate different psychological processes.

This chapter will provide an overview of social and psychological theories of offending. It will first consider two founding theories of offending that dominated before the development of criminological theories. Some of the most influential social and psychological theories of offending will then be discussed. Particular attention will be given to social theories that incorporate psychological processes.

This chapter will examine:

- Founding theories of offending
- Social theories of offending
- Psychological theories of offending

Founding theories of offending

Although exceptions exist, most early theories located the cause of crime within the individual. For example, **spiritualism** stressed the internal conflict between good and evil, and regarded offenders as being possessed by evil spirits (Lilly, Cullen and Ball, 2007). Guilt or innocence was determined by subjecting the accused to extremely painful or life-threatening situations. Typical situations included placing huge rocks on the accused, or binding the arms and legs of the accused before throwing them into a river. Innocence was demonstrated if the accused was able to survive the ordeal.

The classical school

The classical school, associated with the writings of Cesare Beccaria and Jeremy Bentham, developed in response to the primitive and inconsistent nature of punishment utilized during the 18th century (Lilly et al., 2007). The classical school believed that criminal motivation was 'a given'. People were assumed to be **hedonistic** (that is, motivated to maximize pleasure and minimize pain) and crime was considered to be the natural consequence of an inadequate punishment system (Curran and Renzetti, 2001).

According to the classical school, people consider the relative benefits and costs of their actions when deciding whether or not to commit a crime (Lilly et al., 2007). As such, the role of any punishment system should be to deter people from engaging in criminal behaviour through the provision of swift, certain and proportionate punishments. This range of punishments should provide just enough pain to outweigh the pleasure associated with the criminal behaviour (Curran and Renzetti, 2001).

The classical school proposal that the punishment should fit the crime is integral to the current criminal justice system (issues concerning the punishment and treatment of offenders are included in Chapters 11 and 12). Aspects of the classical school also continue to influence modern theories of offending. For example, the notion of rationality is an integral part of rational choice theory and is discussed in Chapter 4 (Lilly et al., 2007). Nevertheless, the classical school did not consider why some people commit crime and others do not, and alternative theories developed in an attempt to identify the 'criminal man'.

The positivist school

The positivist school developed during the latter half of the 19th century and in contrast to the classical school asserted that offenders are inherently different from other people (Lombroso-Ferrero, 1911). The **anti-social behaviour** of offenders was thought to be caused by biological and/or psychological factors that could be studied scientifically (Lilly et al., 2007). For example, Cesare Lombroso and William H. Sheldon studied the physiological characteristics of offenders based on the assumption that they represent a particular physical type that separates them from non-offenders. The research of Lombroso and of Sheldon is discussed in detail in Chapter 4.

With regard to punishment, the positivist school criticized the deterrence approach adopted by the classical school on the grounds that criminal involvement is determined by forces beyond the control of the offenders themselves. Instead, it argued that the punishment system should focus on the treatment of offenders with the goal of rehabilitation (Curran and Renzetti, 2001). Issues concerning rehabilitation are discussed in detail in Chapter 11.

Summary

Founding theories of offending located the cause of crime within the individual. The classical school assumed that criminal motivation is a given and that crime is a natural consequence of an inadequate punishment system. In contrast, the positivist school asserted that offenders are inherently different from other people and criticized the deterrence approach to punishment on the grounds that criminal involvement is not determined by the offenders themselves.

Social theories of offending

During the 20th century, biologically oriented theories of offending began to diminish while theories drawing on sociology emerged (there is now renewed interest in biological theories of offending and these are discussed in Chapter 4). By the end of the 1930s two major criminological theories based on a sociological perspective had developed in the US: strain theory and social disorganization theory. Although the two theories held contrasting views regarding the specific causes of crime, they agreed that criminal behaviour is a social phenomenon (Lilly et al., 2007). Other social theories of offending include subcultural theory, differential association theory, social control theory and labelling theory.

Strain and subcultural theories

Proposed by Robert K. Merton, strain theory rejected the idea that antisocial behaviour is determined by biological and/or psychological factors. Instead, it argued that deviant behaviour is the result of pressures exerted by the social structure, specifically the culturally defined goals of success and the legitimate means for achieving them (Merton, 1938). While most people accept the culturally defined goals of success and have access to the legitimate means for achieving these goals, others do not and it is these people who engage in deviant behaviour.

Merton (1938) differentiated four types of response to situations in which the culturally defined goals of success exceeded the levels of achievement possible via legitimate means:

- *Innovation*. Innovators accept the culturally defined goals of success but use illegitimate means for achieving these goals.
- *Ritualism*. Ritualists reject the culturally defined goals of success and use legitimate means to achieve self-defined scaled-down goals.
- *Retreatism*. Retreatists reject the culturally defined goals of success and the legitimate means for achieving these goals.
- *Rebellion*. Rebels also reject the culturally defined goals of success and the legitimate means for achieving these goals, but seek to replace the existing social structure with a new social order.

Subcultural theories of offending were influenced by elements of strain theory, sharing the view that criminal behaviour is the result of pressures exerted by the social structure (Newburn, 2007). According to Richard A. Cloward and Lloyd E. Ohlin, delinquent subcultures develop when discrepancies exist between the culturally defined goals of success and access to the legitimate means of achieving them (Cloward and Ohlin, 1960). Cloward and Ohlin described three types of deviant subculture that are typically encountered by youths in working-class areas:

- *Criminal*. Criminal subcultures involve gangs that commit crimes as a means of securing income. They generally develop in organized areas where material gain and power are achieved by illegitimate means (for example burglary and robbery).

- *Conflict*. Conflict subcultures involve gangs that commit violent crimes as a way of acquiring status. They are more likely to develop in disorganized areas where scarce resources are obtained through displays of toughness and fearlessness in the face of danger.
- *Retreatist*. Retreatist subcultures involve the use of drugs as a means of 'getting a kick'. The retreatist subculture represents a 'double failure' as youths have not been able to achieve success by legitimate or illegitimate means.

Although these subcultures represent contrasting lifestyles, Cloward and Ohlin (1960) pointed out that all three are similar in that the norms that guide them counter those of society as a whole. They also recognized instances when subcultures develop in a 'mixed form' (for example is predominantly 'conflict' oriented, but occasionally engages in crime as a means of securing income).

Social disorganization theory

Social disorganization theory was developed by Clifford R. Shaw and Henry D. McKay during the 1920s and 1930s. Its development was heavily influenced by the **Chicago School**, particularly the writings of Robert E. Park and Ernest W. Burgess. Park (1984) argued that cities develop in a relatively uniform manner, which reflects the habits and customs of the people who live in them. Meanwhile, Burgess (1984) observed that cities tend to expand radially from the centre in a series of concentric zones, with each inner zone extending its area by invading the next outer zone (that is, a process of succession). The five zones are:

- *Zone I*. The central business district.
- *Zone II*. The area in transition where residential areas are invaded by business and light industry.
- *Zone III*. Working-class residential areas occupied by workers who have escaped Zone II, but want to live close to work.
- *Zone IV*. Middle-class residential areas on the edge of the city limits.
- *Zone V*. Upper-class residential areas located outside the city limits, 30 to 60 minutes' ride from the central business district.

Shaw and McKay (1971a) examined the distribution of delinquents' home addresses across three seven-year time periods between 1900 and 1933. They observed that delinquents were most likely to live in Zone II, the area in transition, with relatively few living in Zones IV and V. They also noted that the proportion of delinquents in the area in transition remained relatively constant despite changes in the composition of its occupants across the three time periods.

These findings led Shaw and McKay (1971b) to make two assertions: (1) that 'delinquency causing factors' are inherent in the areas themselves rather than the people living in them, and (2) that 'traditions of delinquency' are transmitted through successive generations. As such, the rapid growth, residential mobility, racial heterogeneity and poverty that characterize the area in transition result in the development of a diverse range of moral values (Shaw and McKay, 1969). Furthermore, the associated **social disorganization** weakens the traditional institutions of control (for example family, school and the church) and provides youths with the freedom to engage in crime and delinquency. Consequently, the high proportion of delinquents in the area in transition is maintained through exposure to, and contact with, similar aged delinquents and older offenders.

Differential association theory

Differential association theory built upon Shaw and McKay's observation that criminal traditions were transmitted from one generation to the next. Its chief proponent, Edwin H. Sutherland, was particularly concerned with addressing the question 'Why do people *disobey* the rules of society?'

According to Sutherland and Cressey (1970), criminal behaviour is learned through social interaction and communication, and includes the techniques of committing crime as well as the associated attitudes, motives and drives. The learning of criminal behaviour involves the same mechanisms as the learning of any other behaviour, while attitudes and motives are learned from 'definitions' that are favourable as opposed to unfavourable to breaking the law. Consequently, a person is more likely to engage in criminal behaviour after exposure to an excess of definitions favourable to breaking the law. However, it was acknowledged that the influence of associations with different groups and definitions will vary according to the frequency, duration and intensity of a person's exposure.

Sutherland and Cressey (1970) also developed Shaw and McKay's notion of social disorganization, and argued that the nature of a person's associations with different groups is determined by the **differential social organization** of the area in which they live. As such, differences in crime rates across areas reflect variations in the degree to which different groups are organized to support or oppose criminal involvement.

Social control theory

Social control theory built upon Shaw and McKay's observation that criminal behaviour is more prevalent in areas characterized by social disorganization. However, unlike differential association theory, it addresses the question 'Why do people *obey* the rules of society?' Consequently, unlike most criminological theories that take conformity for granted, social control theory asserts that nonconformity can be assumed and that conformity needs to be explained (Hirschi, 1969). After all, nonconformity (that is, crime and delinquency) usually represents the quickest and easiest way to achieve goals of success.

According to Travis Hirschi, people vary in their morality and 'delinquent acts result when an individual's bond to society is weak or broken' (Hirschi, 1969, p. 16). An individual's social bond to conventional society consists of the following four interrelated elements:

- *Attachment*. Attachment to others and the extent to which an individual identifies with them and is sensitive to their opinions. The less an individual is attached to others, the more freedom he or she has to deviate (that is, there are fewer moral restraints).
- *Commitment*. Commitment to conventional activities such as gaining an education or developing a career. The more an individual is committed to conventional activities, the more he or she has to risk by deviating.
- *Involvement*. Involvement in conventional activities such as studying or working. The more an individual is involved in conventional activities, the less opportunity he or she has to deviate.
- *Belief*. Belief in conventional values and rules such as the morals and laws of society. The less an individual believes in conventional values and rules, the more likely he or she is to deviate.

As such, people are most likely to obey the rules of society in the presence of effective social controls, and disobey the rules when social bonds are weak or lacking (Gottfredson and Hirschi, 1990).

Thinking scientifically → **The applicability of differential association theory and social control theory**

Research considering the general application of differential association theory reported that people's use of particular drugs is related to the number of close friends they have who use the same drugs (Dull, 1983), and that people's self-reported criminal behaviour is associated with their exposure to definitions favourable to breaking the law (Jackson, Tittle and Burke, 1986). In this study, definitions reflected a combined measure of the intensity, pattern, frequency and duration of known persons' criminal behaviour.

Other research comparing the relative explanatory power of differential association and social control theories found that variables relating to differential association theory are more closely linked to self-reported offending than are variables relating to social control theory (Alarid, Burton and Cullen, 2000). However, research considering the application of social control theory found that attachment to parents, teachers and school and commitment to conventional activities are related to a reduction in reported delinquency (Hindelang, 1973).

When considering the relative explanatory power of the different theoretical perspectives, it is important to acknowledge that research has generally utilized **cross-sectional designs**. Consequently, it is difficult to determine causation (Farrington, 2002). For example, it is uncertain whether the presence of close friends using drugs in Dull's (1983) study caused or was a consequence of people's use of similar drugs. Furthermore, although **longitudinal designs** are frequently employed to establish cause and effect, it still remains difficult to determine causation (Smith, 2002). This difficulty occurs because longitudinal designs actually represent a series of retrospective surveys (often repeated at 12-month intervals) that cover a relatively long period of time given the complexity of people's social interactions.

Labelling theory

Most social theories view crime as an absolute (that is, behaviour is criminal if it violates the law) and seek to identify the environmental causes of crime. In contrast, labelling theory proposed by Howard S. Becker views crime as relative (that is, behaviour is criminal if it is defined as such) and focuses on the causes and consequences of defining certain behaviours and/or people as criminal.

Labelling theories were dominant during the 1960s and 1970s, and were characterized by three basic assumptions (Becker, 1963):

- Crime is a label that is attached to behaviour for certain social, economic, and political reasons (for example to serve the interests of the powerful).
- Reactions by the criminal justice system are governed by the characteristics of the person committing the crime (for example race, age and class) rather than the characteristics of the crime itself.
- The labelling of a person as 'criminal' results in a **self-fulfilling prophecy**.

Becker (1963) proposed that the criminal justice system's treatment of people as 'generally criminal' rather than 'specifically criminal' actually increases the likelihood of future criminal involvement. This increase occurs because people labelled as criminal are treated accordingly by the community. As such, the labelling process restricts their ability to have ordinary lives and makes them more susceptible to further criminal involvement. Lemert (1972) described this process as the transition from primary to secondary deviation:

- *Primary deviation*. Refers to irregular deviant behaviour that arises in a variety of contexts and has little impact on an individual's sense of self. However, this behaviour becomes secondary deviation once detected by the criminal justice system.
- *Secondary deviation*. Refers to a more regular pattern of deviant behaviour that is caused by society's reaction to primary deviation (that is, the labelling of an individual as deviant). It is argued that secondary deviation is used to deal with society's reaction and that over time the individual creates a sense of self that is consistent with the negative label that has been applied.

Summary

Social theories of offending developed as an alternative to the biologically oriented theories of criminal behaviour. Although they differ with regard to the specific causes of crime, social theories agree that criminal behaviour is a social phenomenon. Social theories propose that crime is the result of a lack of access to culturally defined goals of success (strain and subcultural theories), the social disorganization of certain neighbourhoods (social disorganization theory), excessive exposure to definitions favourable to breaking the law (differential association theory) and weak or broken bonds to society (social control theory). Additionally, labelling theory views crime as a relative phenomenon and focuses instead on the causes and consequences of defining certain behaviours as criminal.

Psychological theories of offending

Although psychological theories did not develop as theories of offending per se, some have been applied to criminal behaviour (for example psychodynamic theories and the maternal deprivation hypothesis). Alternatively, certain social theories of offending have incorporated the psychological processes of **classical conditioning**, **operant conditioning** and/or modelling (for example differential reinforcement theory and social learning theory).

Psychodynamic theories

Several theorists have used Sigmund Freud's psychoanalytic theory of personality to 'throw light' on the study of criminology, each considering the relative influence of the id, the ego and the superego (Ewen, 1993; Strachey, 1975):

- *The id.* The id is present at birth, operates according to the pleasure principle and contains unconscious instinctual drives for immediate satisfaction.
- *The ego.* The ego emerges from the id when a child is between six and eight months of age, and operates according to the reality principle. Once fully developed, the ego is able to balance the demands of the id with the demands of the environment.
- *The superego.* The superego emerges from the ego when a child is between three and five years of age. The superego represents the internalization of the rules, morals and values held by the child's parents and society as a whole.

According to psychodynamic theories, most people do not commit crime because the ego is able to manage the competing demands of the id and the superego (Aichhorn, 1965). However, there are instances where the superego fails to develop properly, causing some people to engage in criminal behaviour (Aichhorn, 1965; Ewen, 1993). These are:

- *Overdeveloped superego*. People with an overdeveloped superego experience constant and intense feelings of guilt. As such, a person engages in criminal behaviour in order to gain a sense of relief by being punished.
- *Underdeveloped superego*. People with an underdeveloped superego are driven by the need for immediate gratification. Consequently, a person engages in criminal behaviour because of a lack of conscience (that is, the internalization of the rules, morals and values).
- *Deviant superego*. People with a deviant superego have developed normally, but have been exposed to deviant rules, morals and values (for example from a criminal father). As such, a person engages in criminal behaviour because of a lack of appropriate rules, morals and values.

Maternal deprivation hypothesis

John Bowlby theorized that the quality of care a child receives during the first three years of life is vitally important to future development (Bowlby, 1965). Consequently, it is essential that children experience warm, intimate and continuous relationships with their primary caregivers (for example parents) in order to avoid the negative effects of **maternal deprivation**. In severe cases, disruption to the relationship between children and their primary caregivers can dramatically reduce their capacity to form attachments with other people. Evidence also suggests that delinquents are particularly likely to have experienced disrupted relationships with their primary caregivers during early childhood.

It is hypothesized that children who experience severe maternal deprivation form schematic representations of the world as harsh and/or hostile, and are more likely to react to this world in an antisocial manner as a result (Hollin, Browne and Palmer, 2002). This hypothesis is certainly consistent with Bowlby's (1944) finding that juvenile delinquents were more likely to have experienced prolonged separation (that is, six months or more) from their mothers during the first five years of life. Of the 44 thieves investigated, Bowlby found that a quarter of the sample had experienced a major separation during early childhood. Furthermore, in a subgroup of 14 juvenile affectionless delinquents (that is, delinquents who displayed a lack of affection, shame or sense of responsibility), 12 had experienced maternal deprivation. Despite these findings, research has indicated that separation is not the crucial factor in most varieties of deprivation (Rutter, 1979). Thus, although separation from a primary caregiver may increase the likelihood of criminal behaviour, most children experience little impact from such deprivation.

More recent research has demonstrated a consistent positive relationship between the number of family transitions, delinquency and drug use. For example, Thornberry et al. (1999) found that 90 per cent of youths who endured five or more parental disruptions engaged in criminal behaviour. Similarly, Loeber et al. (2005) followed more than 1500 boys from childhood to 30 years of age, and found that children who experienced two or more disruptions by the age of 10 were almost twice as likely to commit violent crimes as those who did not.

Differential reinforcement theory

According to C. Ray Jeffery's differential reinforcement theory, criminal behaviour is 'operant behaviour' and develops as a consequence of direct reinforcement and punishment (Jeffery, 1965). Thus, Jeffery revised and extended Sutherland's differential association theory by accounting for the way in which crime is learned. In this context, reinforcement refers to any stimuli that increase the frequency of behaviour, while punishment refers to any stimuli that decrease the frequency of behaviour. Therefore, deviant behaviour can be explained by the following four contingencies of reinforcement and punishment:

- *Positive reinforcement*. The presentation of stimuli that increase the frequency of behaviour.
- *Negative reinforcement*. The removal of stimuli that increase the frequency of behaviour.
- *Positive punishment*. The presentation of stimuli that decrease the frequency of behaviour.
- *Negative punishment*. The removal of stimuli that decrease the frequency of behaviour.

Property crimes such as burglary and theft are likely to involve positive reinforcement (that is, the stolen items) while violent crime such as murder and assault are likely involve negative reinforcement (that is, the removal of the person) (Jeffery, 1965). In both types of crime, the risk of being injured, arrested and/or imprisoned acts as potential positive and negative punishment. Therefore, the likelihood of a person engaging in future criminal behaviour depends on their experience of reinforcement and punishment in the past (Jeffery, 1965).

Social learning theory

Social learning theory was proposed during the 1970s when the fields of behaviourism and cognitive psychology converged. Prior to this convergence, behaviourism focused on observable behaviour while cognitive psychology focused on unobservable cognitive processes (Hollin, 1992; McGuire, 2004).

Albert Bandura's social learning theory sought to further develop behavioural theory through the acknowledgement that cognitive processes have an important role to play in the learning of behaviour. Although Bandura (1977) accepted that some behaviour involves 'learning by response consequences' (that is, a consequence of direct reinforcement and punishment), he argued that most behaviour involves 'learning through modelling'. As such, it is possible to learn new behaviours, and the likely outcomes of these behaviours, through the observation of other people. This observation process and the learning of new behaviour are governed by a four-component process:

1. *Attentional processes*. A person observes and attends to the important features of the modelled behaviour.
2. *Retention processes*. A person formulates a symbolic representation of the modelled behaviour in his or her memory.
3. *Motor reproduction processes*. A person converts this symbolic representation into the appropriate behaviour.
4. *Motivational processes*. A person considers the modelled behaviour to result in a rewarding outcome, rather than a punishing one.

Hence, cognitive processes are of central importance in the observation, retention, reproduction and motivational components of learning new behaviour. Due to its adoption of an interactional approach in which learning is a consequence of cognitive, behavioural and environmental determinants, social learning theory has also been referred to as social cognitive theory in the field of psychology (Bandura, 1986).

Social learning theory in criminology

In the field of criminology, several theorists have utilized concepts and principles taken from social learning theory to extend Sutherland's assertion that criminal behaviour is learned. Although differential association theory emphasized that criminal values are learned through association, it offered little explanation as to what the mechanisms of learning are (Akers, 1999). Consequently, social learning theory was used to extend the explanation offered by Jeffery, which relied on direct reinforcement and punishment, to incorporate the process of imitation (that is, modelling) in the learning of criminal behaviour.

Ronald L. Akers established the first notable attempt to develop a social learning theory of crime that integrated elements of differential association theory, differential reinforcement theory and other principles of learning. Although the theory was initially proposed in collaboration with Robert L. Burgess and known as differential association-reinforcement theory, Akers went on to revise and develop it further, at which time it became known as Akers' social learning theory (Akers, 1973, 1999).

The development of social learning theory focused on four major processes involved in the learning of behaviour, including criminal behaviour (Akers, 1999). These are:

- *Differential association.* The groups that people associate with that provide the social context in which behaviour is learned.
- *Definitions.* The attitudes and meanings people attach to behaviours. Definitions can be general (that is, concerning general beliefs) or specific (that is, concerning a particular behaviour), as well as positive (that is, making behaviour morally acceptable), negative (that is, making behaviour morally unacceptable) or neutral (that is, justifying or excusing behaviour).
- *Differential reinforcement.* The balance of anticipated or actual reinforcement and punishment that people experience as a consequence of behaviour.
- *Imitation.* The learning of behaviour through the observation of people performing similar behaviours.

As such, Akers offered a more detailed theory of criminal behaviour through the addition of imitation to the already established processes of differential association, definitions and differential reinforcement (Akers, 1999). Imitation was thought to be particularly important in the learning of new behaviour and less important in the maintenance or cessation of already established behaviour.

Summary

Psychological theories did not develop as specific theories of offending, but some have been applied to criminal behaviour. For example, psychodynamic theories propose that criminal behaviour is a consequence of the relative failure of the superego to develop properly, while the maternal deprivation hypothesis proposes that criminal behaviour is caused by disruptive relationships with primary caregivers during childhood. Furthermore, psychological processes have been incorporated to extend social theories of offending. For example, differential reinforcement theory explains the learning of criminal behaviour through operant conditioning while social learning theory explains the learning of criminal behaviour through differential association, definitions, differential reinforcement and imitation.

Further reading

Curran, D.J. and Renzetti, C.M. (2001) *Theories of Crime* (2nd edn). London: Allyn & Bacon.

Lilly, J.R., Cullen, F.T. and Ball, R.A. (2007) *Criminological Theory: Context and Consequences* (4th edn). London: Sage Publications.

Chapter 4

Biological and cognitive theories

Introduction

Biological explanations of offending focus on variations in functioning as a consequence of heredity, maturation and certain environmental events (for example brain injuries caused by an accident) (Smallbone, 2009). Related sociobiological theories (that is, evolutionary explanations) propose that criminal behaviour is a consequence of natural selection. Finally, cognitive theories propose that criminal behaviour is associated with certain thinking patterns, decision-making processes and cognitive deficits (Raine, 1993; Smallbone, 2009).

Chapter 3 introduced the work of Cesare Lombroso and the importance of cognitive processes in the context of social learning theory. This chapter will provide a more detailed overview of biological and cognitive theories of offending. It will first consider a broad range of biological explanations, including physiological characteristics, heredity, genes and the brain. Sociobiological theories will then be discussed with reference to rape and murder. Finally, cognitive theories will be considered in relation to dysfunctional thinking patterns, rationality, moral reasoning and the attribution of blame.

This chapter will examine:

- Biological explanations of offending
- Sociobiological theories of offending
- Cognitive theories of offending

Biological explanations of offending

Early biological explanations of offending focused on the physiological characteristics of offenders and how they were different to those of non-offenders (for example phrenology, atavism and somatotypes). More recent explanations have recognized that crime is most likely a product of the interaction between biological and social factors (for example heredity, genes, brain structure, brain chemistry, and Eysenck's criminal personality).

Physiological characteristics

A number of the early biological explanations of offending proposed that criminal behaviour could be accounted for by the physiological characteristics of offenders (Lilly, Cullen and Ball, 2007). Physiological characteristics assumed to be related to criminal behaviour included the shape of the brain (that is, phrenology), physical abnormalities (that is, atavism) and body shape (that is, somatotypes).

Phrenology

Franz Joseph theorized that the development and shape of the brain affect personality and social behaviour (Curran and Renzetti, 2001). Two assumptions were central to this theory: (1) that the most important areas of the brain were also the greatest in size, and (2) that the skull formed a perfect cover for the brain. Therefore, it was proposed that any organ (or area of the brain) dominant in an individual would cause protrusions on the skull that could easily be felt by a phrenologist. This method of analysis led to the identification of 26 distinct organs in the body and 3 major regions within the brain. The three regions within the brain related to intellectual, moral and animal faculties. It was believed that these animal faculties (including destructiveness and secretiveness traits) were overdeveloped in offenders and could be used to explain criminal behaviour.

Although a biological basis to criminal behaviour implies that offenders will never stop offending, Joseph argued that animal faculties could be inhibited through the development of intellectual and moral faculties. Implicit in this process was the belief that faculties could be modified, thus enabling an individual to have a productive life in society (Curran and Renzetti, 2001).

Atavism

For Cesare Lombroso, criminal behaviour could be explained through atavism (that is, the reappearance of primitive characteristics), on the grounds that certain instincts and physiological characteristics observed in primates are also observed in offenders (Lombroso, 1911). These physiological characteristics included enormous jaws, high cheekbones, solitary lines on the palms, and handle-shaped ears. Insensibility to pain, acute eyesight, tattooing, excessive idleness and a craving for evil were also recognized as precursors to criminal behaviour. The irresistible craving for evil was expressed as 'the desire not only to extinguish the life in the victim, but to mutilate the corpse, tear its flesh, and drink its blood' (Lombroso, 1911, p. xv).

On this basis, Lombroso proposed that offenders were 'born criminal' and possessed a biological makeup that differed significantly from non-offenders. This proposition was supported by research examining the physiological characteristics of 383 Italian men convicted for various crimes. Findings showed that 21 per cent of the men had just one atavistic trait (for example enormous jaws) while 43 per cent had five or more. Therefore, it was concluded that the presence of five or more atavistic traits indicated criminality (Curran and Renzetti, 2001). This view was very extreme, implying that criminal behaviour was inevitable for certain people. In acknowledgement of this issue, Lombrosso reformulated his ideas and asserted that criminal behaviour is the product of biological, psychological and environmental factors (Hollin, 1992).

Lombroso also observed that women were less likely to commit crime than men, and subsequently argued that women as a group were less evolved than men (Curran and Renzetti, 2001). He proposed that women were naturally vengeful, jealous and insensitive to pain, but that these characteristics were neutralized by 'feminine' traits including passivity, physical weakness, low intelligence and maternal instinct. Consequently, Lombroso described the 'criminal woman' as masculine, a trait that only benefited men and transformed women into 'monsters'.

The validity of Lombroso's research has been criticized on the basis of the samples and methods used (Curran and Renzetti, 2001). Although control or comparison groups were used in his early work, one such group consisted of Italian soldiers who were not representative of the total non-offender population. The eventual downfall of atavism occurred in 1913 when Charles Goring compared 3000 convicts with a large non-convict group and found no differences across the groups (Curran and Renzetti, 2001). After eight years of work, Goring concluded that there were no significant differences between offenders and non-offenders except for stature and body weight (that is, offenders were slightly smaller).

Somatotypes

According to William H. Sheldon, body types can be classified according to three primary components – endomorphy, mesomorphy and ectomorphy – and are associated with certain temperaments (Hartl, Monnelly and Elderkin, 1982; Sheldon, 1971): These are:

- *Endomorphy*. Characterized by a 'roundness in form' (that is, overweight). Endomorphs are relaxed and sociable with a love for physical comfort, food and affection.
- *Mesomorphy*. Characterized by 'bone and muscle' (that is, athletic). Mesomorphs are active, assertive, and have a desire for physical activity.
- *Ectomorphy*. Characterized by a 'stretched out quality' (that is, tall and thin). Ectomorphs are restrained, inhibited and hyper-attentive (that is, very excitable or nervous).

Although this classification system was based on the physiological characteristics of 4000 male college students (Sheldon, 1954), it proved problematic as many people could not be classified into a single component (Andrews and Bonta, 2006). To address this issue, Sheldon (1954, 1971) developed a 'somatotype matrix' whereby each of the three primary components was ascribed a number ranging from one (low) to seven (high). For example, the matrix 7-1-1 represents high endomorphy, low mesomorphy and low ectomorphy. When applying this matrix to juvenile delinquency, Glueck and Glueck (1968, 1970) found that delinquents were more likely to have a mesomorph body type (60%) than a non-mesomorph body type (40%).

Heredity

A more recent explanation for criminal behaviour is that some people inherit a biological predisposition to commit crime (Hollin, 1992). Family, twin and adoption studies have been conducted to investigate the relationship between heredity and criminal behaviour.

Family studies

Family studies provide researchers with an opportunity to compare the behaviour of genetically similar people who live in the same environment (Hollin, 1992). In the context of criminal behaviour, family studies usually examine the arrest or conviction rates of parents and their children (Curran and Renzetti, 2001).

A number of family studies have shown that criminal behaviour often 'runs in the family', and that criminal parents often have criminal children (Curran and Renzetti, 2001; Hollin, 1992). However, these findings need to be interpreted with caution as parents and children are likely to be influenced by similar environmental factors (Fishbein, 1990). Consequently, it is not possible to determine whether criminal behaviour is inherited, is caused by environmental factors, or is a combination of the two (Curran and Renzetti, 2001; Hollin, 1992).

It is also important to acknowledge that family studies have been criticized for lacking appropriate control or comparison groups. Thus, it is difficult to determine whether the arrest and conviction rates of children with criminal parents are genuinely higher compared to those of children with non-criminal parents (Curran and Renzetti, 2001). Furthermore, research has shown that antisocial people are attracted to other antisocial people. Within this context, the influence of environmental factors has to be considered in the interpretation of any similarities in the antisocial behaviour of children and their parents (Andrews and Bonta, 2006).

Twin studies

When discussing twin studies, it is important to understand the difference between maternal monozygotic (MZ) twins and fraternal dizygotic (DZ) twins. MZ twins develop from a single egg fertilized by a single sperm and are therefore genetically identical (Blackburn, 1993; Hollin, 1992). In contrast, DZ twins develop from two different eggs and are fertilized by two different sperm, making them as genetically similar as regular siblings. As MZ twin pairs share 100 per cent of genes, they should demonstrate a greater physical resemblance and concordance (that is, similarity) of behaviour than DZ twins who share 50 per cent of genes.

Twin studies offer researchers the chance to investigate the role of heredity in relation to criminality by comparing the behaviour of MZ and DZ twins. When Raine (1993) reviewed the literature comparing the delinquent behaviour of twins, it was found that the average concordance rate was higher for MZ twins than for DZ twins (52% vs. 21%). Thus, research has provided fairly strong support for the heritability of criminal behaviour.

However, twin studies have been criticized for adopting different measures of criminality, and questions have arisen regarding the methods used to determine zygosity (Curran and Renzetti, 2001). As Fishbein (1990) pointed out, early research often included a disproportionate number of MZ twins because they were easier to identify than DZ twins. Fishbein also highlighted concerns regarding the comparability of MZ and DZ twins on the grounds that MZ twins generally share more similar environments than DZ twins because they look alike. Research has demonstrated that MZ twins are treated more similarly, spend more time together and influence each other to a greater extent than DZ twins (Andrews and Bonta, 2006; Curran and Renzetti, 2001).

Adoption studies

Adoption studies provide researchers with an opportunity to compare the behaviour of genetically similar people who live in different environments. They involve the identification of adopted children so that their criminal behaviour can be compared to the criminal histories of their biological and adoptive parents (Andrews and Bonta, 2006; Hollin, 1992). The underlying assumption is that behavioural similarity with biological parents is attributable to heredity, while behavioural similarity with adoptive parents is attributable to the environment. Overall, adoption studies have demonstrated a moderate relationship between heredity and criminal behaviour, although environmental factors are likely to be of equal (or greater) importance (Blackburn, 1993).

The main criticisms of adoption studies concern the elimination of time variations and the potential for the adoption process to cause a selection bias. Adopted children will have spent varying amounts of time with their biological and adoptive parents, so it is difficult to control for the influence of time in these different environments and its impact on their criminal behaviour (Curran and Renzetti, 2001; Fishbein, 1990). Furthermore, adoption agencies often seek to match biological and adoptive parents on a number of characteristics, so the different environments may actually be relatively similar.

Genes

People are normally born with 46 chromosomes, in 23 pairs, with each chromosome consisting of a string of genes that are made of **DNA** (Anderson, 2007). One pair of chromosomes are the sex chromosomes, responsible for determining whether a child is male or female. People inherit one X chromosome from their mother and an X or Y chromosome from their father so that women have XX chromosomes and men have XY chromosomes (Curran and Renzetti, 2001).

Complications in the development of chromosomes can result in a person having an extra sex chromosome and in a minority of cases men are born with XYY chromosomes. Despite early claims that men with an extra Y chromosome (that is, the chromosome that carries 'male' genes) tend to be more violent, research has found the XYY abnormality to be largely irrelevant in the understanding of criminal behaviour (Halwani and Krupp, 2004; Owen, 1972). Some research has linked the XYY abnormality to aggression through the secretion of testosterone, but this does not change the reality that the vast majority of crime continues to be committed by chromosomally normal XY men (Curran and Renzetti, 2001).

The brain

Research is increasingly focusing on the functioning of the brain in order to better understand the nature of criminal behaviour. Technological advances have been integral in the exploration of brain functioning and the precise links between brain structure, brain chemistry and behaviour (including crime) (Curran and Renzetti, 2001).

Brain structure

There is a general belief that significant head injuries predispose people to engage in criminal and violent behaviour, and Raine (1993) suggested that damage to the brain may indirectly lead to antisocial behaviour by:

- increasing sensitivity to the effects of alcohol
- decreasing cognitive and social skills
- increasing irritability, thus in turn increasing the risk of violence
- increasing anger and hostility.

Research into the structure of the brain has tended to focus on whether damage to a particular part of the brain increases the risk of criminal behaviour (Curran and Renzetti, 2001). Of this research, the majority has focused on the frontal and temporal lobe regions of the brain. The frontal lobe is involved in controlling voluntary movements and inhibiting inappropriate behaviour, while the temporal lobe is involved in processing emotions and responding to environmental stimuli (Anderson, 2007; Curran and Renzetti, 2001).

In order to investigate these regions, researchers have used computed tomography (CT) scans and magnetic resonance imaging (MRI) to view any damage caused by head injuries or disease (Curran and Renzetti, 2001). However, no credible link has been found between damage to different regions of the brain and criminal behaviour. Furthermore, it has been questioned whether any of the associations that have been found can be attributed to the head injuries themselves or whether they are a consequence of a violent upbringing. Research has shown that prisoners often experience physical and/or sexual abuse during childhood. As such, it is possible that the abuse causes changes to the brain structure that in turn increase the risk of criminal behaviour.

Brain chemistry

The nervous system contains specialized cells called neurons that transmit electrical and chemical signals around the body and instruct it how to behave (Anderson, 2007). Three chemical signals, also referred to as neurotransmitters, are of particular interest to the study of criminal behaviour (Curran and Renzetti, 2001):

- *Norepinephrine*. A chemical that helps people react to perceived dangers.
- *Dopamine*. A chemical that produces feelings of pleasure and reward.
- *Serotonin*. A chemical that regulates impulsivity and mood.

Research suggests that excessive levels of norepinephrine increase the likelihood of aggression, violence and other types of antisocial behaviour, and that excessive levels of dopamine increase the likelihood of self-defensive overreactions, hostility and violence (Anderson, 2007; Curran and Renzetti, 2001; Raine, 1993). Meanwhile, reduced levels of serotonin have been linked to impulsive crimes such as arson, murder and suicide.

Findings have been mixed, however, and the relationship between norepinephrine, serotonin and aggression has been found to vary according to individual and social factors (Anderson, 2007; Krakowski, 2003). Furthermore, the majority of research has been conducted with laboratory animals rather than humans, so the precise nature of these relationships remains unclear (Curran and Renzetti, 2001). Irrespective, it appears highly likely that serotonin acts to inhibit impulsive behavioural responses to provocative, emotional events, and therefore plays a role in the regulation of aggressive and violent behaviour (Fishbein, 1990; Hollin, 1992).

Eysenck's criminal personality

According to Eysenck's theory of criminal personality, socialization occurs through the process of classical conditioning. However, it is argued that people vary in their degree of **conditionability** and that this variation is biologically determined (Eysenck, 1964, 1976). As such, genetic factors are extremely important in developing an understanding of criminal behaviour, although their relative impact is mediated by social factors.

Eysenck and Gudjonsson (1989) noted three largely unrelated dimensions to personality that have been used to explain criminal behaviour:

- *Extraversion–introversion*. Extroverts are active, assertive, creative, carefree, dominant, sociable, lively, sensation seeking and venturesome.
- *Psychoticism–superego*. Psychotics are aggressive, antisocial, solitary, cold, creative, egocentric, impersonal, impulsive, tough-minded, cruel and lacking empathy.
- *Neuroticism–stability*. Neurotics are anxious, depressed, emotional, guilt ridden, irrational, sensitive, moody, shy, restless and tense.

Eysenck (1964, 1976) argued that criminal behaviour (and other antisocial behaviour) is caused by a failure in socialization, and that the likelihood of failure is influenced by the three dimensions to personality. For example, people who score low on the extraversion–introversion dimension (that is, introverts) learn quickly through conditioning whereas those high on the extroversion–introversion dimension (that is, extroverts) condition much more slowly. Consequently, a lack of conditioning results in poor socialization and increases the likelihood of criminal behaviour. Psychoticism was thought to relate to criminal behaviour because of the well-documented relationship between crime and psychosis, while neuroticism was thought to increase the strength of the other dimensions of personality (for example increasing the extent to which a person is extroverted).

It is important to acknowledge that Eysenck's theory of criminal personality has been criticized for not specifying the types of crime or offender it relates to (Gudjonsson, 1997). A review of research applying this approach suggests that high neuroticism (but not extroversion) is related to official offending, and that high extroversion (but not neuroticism) is related to self-reported offending. Closer analysis of the individual items suggests that any significant relationships are primarily caused by impulsiveness (Farrington, 2002).

Summary

Early biological explanations of offending looked for physiological characteristics that separated offenders from non-offenders. More recent approaches have investigated the possibility that people inherit a biological predisposition to commit crime, and that criminal behaviour might be caused by genetic abnormalities or brain dysfunction. An alternative explanation concerns the influence of inherent factors that influence conditionability and the likelihood of criminal behaviour.

Sociobiological theories of offending

Sociobiological theories argue that humans have evolved under the influence of natural selection, and therefore have a **genetic propensity** to 'promote fitness' in the family environment (Daly and Wilson, 1997, 1999). As such, evolution represents a process of differential reproductive success and favours attributes that are effective at out-reproducing others. A lack of reproductive success ultimately results in alternative attributes dying out (Daly and Wilson, 1997).

Sociobiological theories focus on sexuality as the prime motivator of criminal behaviour. This focus reflects the evolutionary view that all living things have to reproduce successfully. Although criminal behaviour is recognized as largely maladaptive in today's society, sociobiological theories assert that the mechanisms underlying criminal involvement are evolved adaptations (Walsh and Ellis, 2007). However, Daly and Wilson (1997) acknowledge that sociobiological theories should not be viewed as alternatives to social and psychological theories, but as complementary components to a more complete understanding of behaviour.

In relation to reproductive success, humans follow two strategies to maximize their efforts: (1) **parenting effort** that relates to the proportion of effort placed on the rearing of children, and (2) **mating effort** that relates to the proportion of effort allotted to acquiring sexual partners (Walsh and Ellis, 2007).

Sex differences

Sex constitutes the largest division in reproductive success due to differences in obligatory parental investment. On an evolutionary scale, reproductive success for men is defined by the number of women they have sexual access to. This is a result of the low investment in their relatively unlimited biological resources (that is, sperm). Conversely, women cannot biologically increase their reproductive success by mating multiple male partners. Women have comparatively limited biological resources (that is, eggs) and require greater investment to ensure that they are put to best use. Consequently, men have evolved the propensity to seek multiple partners while women have evolved to obtain resources from each partner in order to increase the probability that their children will live to a reproductive age (Walsh and Ellis, 2007).

These opposing evolutionary traits create an inherent conflict between the reckless, indiscriminate male mating strategy and the careful, discriminate female mating strategy (Walsh and Ellis, 2007). In men, these strategies led to the evolution of traits, such as aggressiveness and low levels of empathy and constraint, to help them overcome both male competitors and female reserve. Although the evolutionary processes underlying these traits were originally selected to promote reproductive success, they can also serve other purposes including criminal behaviour.

Rape

Thornhill and Palmer (2000a, 2000b) considered rape to be motivated by the sexual drives of men who are biologically driven to mate despite being 'disenfranchised' from society (that is, those who do not feel part of society) and lacking sexual access to women. As such, rape is thought to have evolved as a mating strategy that is employed by men who do not possess the physical characteristics, power, resources or social status required to attract a mate. According to Thornhill and Palmer, rapists seek victims with maximum fertility (that is, from mid-teens to late twenties) in order to increase the likelihood of pregnancy and the successful passing on of their genes to the next generation. Evidence from crime statistics certainly appears to support this position as young women are more likely to experience rape than older women, and the age distribution of rape victims parallels the age distribution of women's fertility (Thornhill and Palmer, 2000a).

There are, however, problems with this understanding. For example, a proportion of men who engage in this form of criminal behaviour display some degree of sexual dysfunction (for example impotence) (Bartol, 1991). It also fails to explain the occurrence of rape when there is no chance of reproductive success (that is, anal or oral sex) (Raine, 1993). Finally, sociobiological theories do not account for the significant proportion of rapists who are 'successful' (that is, high social status or married with children). Thus, evolutionary explanations alone are unlikely to provide an adequate account of rape.

Stranger homicide

Although the prevalence of homicide varies considerably over time and between countries, it is apparent that most lethal violence occurs between genetically unrelated people (Daly and Wilson, 1990, 1997). Furthermore, men are far more likely to kill unrelated men than women are to kill unrelated women. Therefore, it follows that there should be an inverse relationship between genetic relatedness and homicide. Research using homicide rates in the US reflects this, showing that victims are killed by relatives in less than a third of cases, the majority of which are non-blood relations (Daly and Wilson, 1988).

A large proportion of these homicides arise from competition for mutually desired resources (for example robbery and 'sexual triangle' homicides) or are the result of more intangible status disputes that act to increase the likelihood of tangible resources in the future (Daly and Wilson, 1997). In addition, the relative lack of lethal violence between genetically related people can be understood as the desire of 'selfish genes' to increase their representation in the next generation's gene pool (Raine, 1993).

Child homicide

The most common form of child homicide is the fatal battering of small children, with step-parents inflicting death much more regularly than biological parents (Daly and Wilson, 2007). Step-parents are also more likely to physically abuse children compared to biological parents. Consequently, the most important risk factor in child homicide appears to be the presence of a step-parent (Daly and Wilson, 1996). Although children are more likely to be abused or killed by step-parents than biological parents, Daly and Wilson (2007) stress that these horrific outcomes are rare. Furthermore, they draw attention to the reality that most step-parents have a positive impact on the lives of children.

One explanation for the aforementioned findings is that step-parents experience a great deal of pressure to 'feel and act' as biological parents would, a pressure that is often resented and sometimes expressed violently (Daly and Wilson, 1994). This interpretation is supported by the reality that stepfathers who kill children are far more likely to do so violently (for example beat them to death) than biological fathers who are more likely to shoot or suffocate them. As such, stepfathers do not only kill children at a higher rate than biological fathers, 'they kill them in different ways, and for different reasons' (Daly and Wilson, 1994, p. 216).

Summary

Sociobiological theories of offending consider criminal behaviour in the context of evolution and natural selection. They argue that although behaviour is now maladaptive, it would have originally served some adaptive purpose. Sociobiological theories have been used to explain sex differences in criminal behaviour, as well as offer causes for specific crimes including rape and homicide. Although evolutionary explanations have been relatively effective in accounting for different patterns of criminal behaviour, they should not be considered in isolation. In combination, sociobiological, social and psychological theories provide a greater understanding of the causes of crime.

Cognitive theories of offending

Cognitive theories of offending propose that criminal behaviour is caused by particular thinking patterns (for example Yochelson and Samenow's criminal personality), decision-making processes (for example rational choice theory), deficits in moral development (for example moral reasoning), and external attributions of blame (for example attribution theory).

Yochelson and Samenow's criminal personality

Yochelson and Samenow's (1998) theory of criminal personality sought to develop an understanding of criminal thinking patterns so that strategies for remedying these could be implemented. Although the theory does not offer an explanation for the origins of the choices that are made, it links non-criminal behaviour with 'responsible thinking and action', and criminal behaviour with 'erroneous thinking patterns'. These erroneous thinking patterns are linked to 40 errors grouped into three types (Blackburn, 1993):

- *Errors that overlap with character traits*. Feelings of fearfulness, worthlessness, and a need for power and control.
- *Automatic errors of thinking*. Failure to assume responsibilities, poor decision making and a lack of trust.
- *Errors associated more directly with criminal acts*. Fantasies of antisocial behaviour and over-optimism.

Yochelson and Samenow (1998) emphasized that irresponsible but non-arrestable people (for example the petty thief) and professional criminals develop similar thinking processes, but to different degrees. Three types of irresponsible person were differentiated:

1. *Non-arrestable criminals* display behaviours including chronic lateness, poor work performance, a lack of dependability, and an inability to fulfil promises or obligations.
2. *Arrestable criminals* display the thinking patterns of the extreme criminal who has recurrent strong desires to violate the law, but are often deterred. They commit minor crimes and rarely get caught.
3. *Extreme criminals* constitute a small fraction of population but pose the greatest problem due to the heavy injuries inflicted.

It was concluded that crime does not go to the potential offender; but that the potential offender goes to the crime (Yochelson and Samenow, 1998). As such, everyone has the capacity to choose their behaviour and offenders make choices and continue to make choices that are consistent with 'being' an offender. It is apparent, therefore, that this approach is consistent to that of rational choice theory.

Rational choice theory

While there is no single model of rational choice theory, collectively they are marked by an interest in the cognitive and situational determinants of the decision to commit a crime. They also converge on the common assumption that most criminal behaviour is mediated by a degree of means-to-end deliberation that may not be rational in an objective sense (Blackburn, 1993).

Cook (1980) argued that potential offenders 'weigh the possible consequences of their actions, both positive and negative, and take advantage of a criminal opportunity only if it is in their self-interest to do so' (pp. 216–17). Cook also acknowledged that potential offenders respond differently to equivalent criminal opportunities because they differ with respect to their willingness to accept risks, their preferences for honesty, their evaluations of the potential gains, and their individual circumstances. Similarly, Cornish and Clarke (1987) contended that offenders decide to engage in criminal behaviour in order to gain some form of benefit for themselves. However, the apparent rationality of these decisions is influenced by the availability of time and information as well as the cognitive abilities of the offender.

Moral reasoning

Kohlberg (1976, 1981) noted that people progress through different stages of moral development across the lifespan. These are:

1. *Preconventional.* People have not yet developed an understanding of the rules or expectations of society and only obey the law because of a fear of punishment. Most children under the age of nine are at this level, as are some adolescents and many offenders.
2. *Conventional.* People have internalized the rules and expectations of society and only obey the law because it is the law. It is common for most adolescents and adults to be at this level.
3. *Postconventional.* People have an understanding of the rules and expectations of society, but accept or reject them on the basis of their underlying moral principles. Consequently, they obey the law if it coincides with higher moral principles irrespective of whether or not it violates the rules and expectations of society. Only a minority of adults reach this level, usually after the age of 20.

Overall, the theory details the progression from viewing rules as fixed and externally imposed (that is, concrete reasoning) to viewing them as flexible and reciprocal (that is, abstract reasoning). However, not everyone reaches the higher stages. When applied to offending, people at different moral stages justify breaking the law in different ways and for different reasons (Hollin, Browne and Palmer, 2002). These include:

1 *Preconventional*. Breaking the law is justified if punishment can be avoided or if the rewards outweigh the costs.
2 *Conventional*. Breaking the law is justified if it helps to maintain relationships or society.
3 *Postconventional*. Breaking the law is justified if it helps to maintain human rights or further social justice.

Crimes are more likely to be committed by people at a lower level of moral development, so offenders are characteristically less mature with regard to their moral reasoning than non-offenders (Hollin et al., 2002).

Attribution theory

Attribution is the process by which an individual attempts to construct causal explanations for his or her behaviour, and the behaviour of others (Gudjonsson and Singh, 1988). Attribution theory recognizes two possible types of cause: internal and external. Therefore, behaviour may be attributed to internal (that is, dispositional) factors or external (that is, situational) factors. It has been found that people generally attribute their own undesirable behaviour to external factors, but attribute the undesirable behaviour of others to internal factors (Gudjonsson, 1984).

Gudjonsson (1984) developed the Blame Attribution Inventory (BAI) to measure the way in which offenders attribute blame for their crimes. The BAI comprises three independent factors:

- *External attribution*. Blaming the crime on social circumstances, the victims or society as a whole.
- *Mental-element attribution*. Blaming the crime on mental illness or a lack of self-control.
- *Guilt-feeling attribution*. Characterized by feelings of regret or remorse for committing the crime.

Gudjonsson and Singh (1988) examined the relationship between blame attributions and different types of offender, and found that sex offenders were likely to experience guilt-feeling attributions (that is, a high degree of regret and remorse) while violent offenders were more likely to use mental-element attributions (that is, blame the crime on mental illness or a lack of self-control). Furthermore, when the relationship between blame attributions and personality characteristics was investigated, Gudjonsson and Singh (1989) found that external attributions of blame correlated positively with psychoticism, hostility and an external locus of control, and correlated negatively with age.

Summary

Cognitive theories of offending look at the decision processes that underlie criminal behaviour. These processes may constitute dysfunctional thinking patterns, rationality or deficits in moral development. This perspective also considers how blame for criminal behaviour is attributed to external sources, although the nature of these attributions varies across different types of crime.

Further reading

Andrews, D.A. and Bonta, J. (2006) *The Psychology of Criminal Conduct* (4th edn). Newark, NJ: LexisNexis.

Curran, D.J. and Renzetti, C.M. (2001) *Theories of Crime* (2nd edn). London: Allyn & Bacon.

Chapter 5

Theory integration and theory application

Introduction

The explanation of criminal behaviour has long been the subject of competing theoretical perspectives. In a bid to increase the explanatory power of traditional theories of offending, attempts have been made to combine elements of several theories to form new integrated theories of criminal behaviour (Farrington, 1996). Other approaches seeking to better explain criminal behaviour have sought to identify different risk factors and developmental processes associated with crime.

Chapters 3 and 4 provided an overview of social, psychological, biological and cognitive theories of offending. This chapter considers the development of integrated theories, the identification of risk factors and the relationship between media violence and violent crime. It will first discuss the value of theory integration as a means of increasing the explanatory power of traditional theories. Different risk factors associated with criminal behaviour will then be considered along with the role of developmental processes in the onset, continuance and cessation of crime. Finally, the possible relationship between media violence and violent crime will be discussed. This discussion is based on Coyne's (2007) informative review article entitled 'Does media violence cause violent crime?'

This chapter will examine:

- Theory integration
- Risk factors
- Developmental processes
- Media violence and violent crime

Theory integration

Traditional theories of offending have not managed to provide powerful predictions or explanations of criminal behaviour, so there has been a move towards combining the more persuasive elements of these theories to form new integrated theories (Bernard and Snipes, 1996; McGuire, 2004). Elliott (1985) argued that the explanatory power of traditional theories of offending has been low because they usually involve 'a single indicator of a single theoretical variable' (p. 126). Therefore, a central assumption of theory integration is that criminal behaviour has multiple causes and that it is necessary to combine different theories of offending in order to fully understand the causes of crime.

Although a number of integrative theories of offending have been developed, several key features are required in order for them to be effective (McGuire, 2004). These include the:

- integration of a large number of potentially contrasting variables
- inclusion of variables from different levels (that is, individual, family, community and society) and the identification of relationships between these variables
- incorporation of both developmental and environmental change
- consideration of both structural (that is, what is happening) and process (that is, why it happens) variables.

Different integrated theories have attempted to combine elements of strain, social control and social learning theories (Elliott, Ageton and Cantor's integrated theory); differential association, social control and social learning theories (Catalano and Hawkin's social development model); and strain, social control, social learning, rational choice and labelling theories (Farrington's integrated cognitive antisocial potential theory). The original theories were discussed in detail in Chapter 3.

Elliott, Ageton and Cantor's integrated theory

Elliott, Ageton and Cantor's (1979) integrated theory combines elements of strain, social control and social learning theories to explain delinquent behaviour. It proposes two dominant paths:

- *Path 1.* Involves the integration of social control theory, which is interested in the strength of socialization to conventional groups, and social learning theory, which is concerned with the context of socialization (that is, deviant vs. conforming). Thus, delinquent behaviour is most likely to occur when social bonds with conventional groups are weak and social bonds with deviant groups are strong. Within this path, individuals are vulnerable to the influence of delinquent peer groups in the absence of conventional restraints.

- *Path 2.* Involves the integration of strain theory, which assumes constant motivation to commit crime and variable bonding to conventional activities, and social learning theory, which assumes variable motivation to commit crime and constant bonding to conventional activities. Consequently, delinquent behaviour is most likely to occur when motivation to commit crime is strong and bonds to conventional activities are weak. Within this path, individuals are motivated to commit crime after failing to achieve the conventional goals of society.

Taken together, delinquent behaviour is most likely to occur when motivation to commit crime is strong (strain theory), social bonds with conventional groups are weak (social control theory) and social bonds with deviant groups are strong (social learning theory) (Bernard and Snipes, 1996).

Catalano and Hawkin's social development model

The social development model integrates differential association, social control and social learning theories, and proposes that separate paths to antisocial and prosocial behaviour exist (Catalano and Hawkins, 1996). As such, the development of antisocial behaviour occurs in three contexts:

- When prosocial socialization breaks down and insufficient social bonds develop with conventional groups (social learning and social control theories).
- When, despite the development of prosocial bonds, the potential reinforcements for delinquent behaviour are perceived to outweigh the potential punishments (social learning theory).
- When social bonds are made to family and friends who have antisocial beliefs or values (differential association theory).

Farrington's integrated cognitive antisocial potential theory

Farrington's (1994) integrated cognitive antisocial potential theory combines elements of strain, social control, social learning, rational choice and labelling theories, and proposes that criminal behaviour involves a four-stage process:

1. *Energizing stage*. Motivations for criminal behaviour include the desire for material possessions and status among friends.
2. *Directing stage*. Motivations for continued criminal behaviour result when satisfaction is regularly obtained in deviant ways.
3. *Inhibiting stage*. Inhibition of criminal behaviour results when there is an appropriate history of reinforcement and punishment.
4. *Decision-making stage*. The decision to engage in criminal behaviour is dependent on perceptions of the associated opportunities, costs and benefits.

Thinking scientifically → **Issues with theory integration**

A fundamental problem associated with the use of integrated theories is that they ignore the different (often contrary) underlying assumptions of traditional theories of offending (Blackburn, 1993). Examples include the contrasting assumptions of social control and social learning theories, and social control and labelling theories.

Social control and social learning theories
Although social control and social learning theories appear compatible, they address fundamentally different questions: 'Why do people *disobey* the rules of society?' as opposed to 'Why do people *obey* the rules of society?' (Lilly, Cullen and Ball, 2007). As such, the notion that criminal behaviour is learned contradicts the assumption people are hedonistic and naturally motivated to break the law.

Subcultural and social control theories
Subcultural theories of offending assume that conformity is the natural order of society, whereas social control theory assumes that people are naturally motivated to break the law (Blackburn, 1993). Consequently, there is a fundamental contradiction between the two theoretical perspectives.

It is important therefore that integrative theories are able to demonstrate how seemingly contradictory assumptions can be reconciled. Although researchers utilizing integrative theories have tended to ignore these contradictory assumptions, treating people as passive receptors, this lack of coherence with regard to the nature of 'man' limited their advancement over traditional theories of offending in the past (Blackburn, 1993).

Summary

Traditional theories of offending have not convincingly explained criminal behaviour. Consequently, several attempts have been made to combine the most persuasive aspects of social theories into new integrated theories. However, the effectiveness of theory integration has been limited because they often ignore the fundamentally different underlying assumptions of the traditional theories.

Risk factors

A number of risk factors have been identified in the development of criminal behaviour. Although described separately, these risk factors are interrelated (for example, family risk factors during childhood are often associated with peer risk factors during adolescence).

Family risk factors

There is evidence to suggest that certain family factors (for example poor parenting skills and the presence of parental conflict, criminal involvement and/or imprisonment) increase the likelihood that children will engage in criminal behaviour, although the relative importance of the different factors remains unclear (Dannerbeck, 2005; Hollin, Browne and Palmer, 2002; Shader, 2003).

Research has shown that youths from disrupted families are more likely to engage in criminal behaviour, irrespective of whether the disruption is caused by parental conflict or imprisonment (Dannerbeck, 2005; Hollin et al., 2002). Potential causes for this relationship include poor parenting skills and a lack of supervision and/or attachment that increase youths' susceptibility to risky behaviours (Andrews and Bonta, 2006; Hollin, 1992; Rankin and Kern, 1994). With respect to parental criminal involvement, social learning theory suggests that youths learn to engage in criminal behaviour through a combination of exposure to definitions favourable to breaking the law, differential reinforcement and imitation (Akers, 1999). However, it is not possible to rule out the possibility that some people inherit a biological predisposition to commit crime (social learning theory was outlined in Chapter 3 and heredity was discussed in Chapter 4).

Peer risk factors

Research has shown that criminal involvement following childhood is heavily influenced by the presence of delinquent peers, although there is some debate regarding the nature of this influence (Blackburn, 1993; Shader, 2003; Sullivan, 2006).

Differential association theory proposes that criminal behaviour is learned through interaction with others and exposure to an excess of definitions favourable to breaking the law (differential association theory was outlined in Chapter 3) (Sutherland and Cressey, 1970). Thus, youths learn to become delinquents as a consequence of interacting with delinquent peers. However, Hollin (1992) argued that it is a mistake to assume that all delinquency and criminal behaviour occurs as a consequence of peer influence. After all, delinquents may simply associate with each other and commit similar crimes. Glueck and Glueck (1950) contend that youths develop antisocial behaviours and attitudes before selectively joining delinquent groups and that the influence of group membership on criminal behaviour is minimal at most.

School risk factors

There is evidence to suggest that criminal involvement in adulthood is related to certain school factors (for example poor academic performance, low academic aspirations, negative attitudes towards schooling and truancy) in childhood (Blackburn, 1993; Loeber et al., 2005).

A possible explanation for the relationship between poor academic performance and criminal involvement relates to the imposition of middle-class values on working-class youths. According to Cohen (1955), working-class youths turn to delinquency as a means of obtaining the status they struggle to obtain, and are often denied, within middle-class schools (strain and subcultural theories of offending were outlined in Chapter 3). As such, school factors heighten the risk of delinquency and criminal involvement when combined with other factors that influence youths from a younger age (for example family and socioeconomic risk factors) (Hollin, 1992).

Socioeconomic risk factors

Research has shown that poverty and living in disadvantaged neighbourhoods are associated with delinquency and criminal involvement, although it is often difficult to separate the risk of socioeconomic factors from other family and peer factors (Hollin et al., 2002; Loeber et al., 2005).

Strain theory asserts that people living in disadvantaged neighbourhoods share the culturally defined goals of success, but often lack the legitimate means for achieving them (Merton, 1938). Consequently, delinquency and criminal behaviour represent the use of illegitimate means to achieve the culturally defined goals of success. Furthermore, subcultural theories propose that delinquent subcultures develop in these circumstances, whereby 'success' is achieved through criminal involvement (strain and subcultural theories were outlined in Chapter 3) (Hollin, 1992).

Summary

Family risk factors include poor parenting skills and the presence of parental conflict, criminal involvement and/or imprisonment. Research has also found delinquency and criminal behaviour to be influenced by the presence of delinquent peers and poor academic performance. However, there is some debate regarding whether delinquent peers are the cause or consequence of criminal involvement. Finally, socioeconomic risk factors include poverty and living in disadvantaged neighbourhoods.

Developmental processes

In order to understand the causes of offending, it is important to consider the role of developmental processes in the onset, continuance and cessation of crime (Farrington, 1994).

Moffitt's life-course-persistent/adolescence-limited theory

Moffitt (1993) claimed that offending is marked by either continuity or change, and distinguished between life-course-persistent and adolescence-limited offenders. **Life-course-persistent offenders** represent a small group who develop antisocial behaviours during childhood and continue through to adolescence and adulthood. In contrast, **adolescence-limited**

offenders represent a much larger group who develop antisocial behaviours during adolescence and then desist in early adulthood.

Moffitt and Harrington (1996) found that adolescence-limited delinquents often have a notable history of antisocial behaviour during childhood, but demonstrate little future potential for such behaviour in adulthood. Common to this behaviour is relatively little continuity or consistency in antisocial behaviour across situations. Conversely, life-course-persistent offenders present high rates of antisocial behaviour across time and diverse situations.

According to Moffitt (1993), the causes of criminal involvement are very different for life-course-persistent offenders and adolescence-limited offenders. Life-course-persistent offending is thought to be a consequence of neurobiological deficits that place children at risk of antisocial behaviour. These deficits are often accompanied by difficult social environments that further increase the risk of criminal behaviour and reduce opportunities for later success. Adolescence-limited offending, by comparison, is thought to be a consequence of adolescent development. Antisocial behaviour is motivated by the desire to appear more mature and therefore subsides when adolescents move into adulthood. Those on the adolescence-limited path, despite being involved in delinquency to the same extent as their counterparts, tend to have backgrounds that are relatively normal and sometimes better than average (Moffitt and Caspi, 2001).

Sampson and Laub's theory of age-graded informal social control

In contrast with Moffitt's life-course-persistent/adolescence-limited theory, Sampson and Laub (1990, 1992) argued against the assertion that continuity and change characterize two distinct sets of offenders. Instead, they viewed the life-course as potentially dynamic and argued that 'trajectories of crime and deviance' are modified by continuity and/or change in social bonds over time.

Sampson and Laub (1990) proposed that childhood antisocial behaviour is linked to a wide variety of troublesome adult behaviour. However, they also acknowledged that social bonds to institutions of informal control (for example work, family and community) during adulthood can influence behaviour over the life-course irrespective of any childhood delinquency and antisocial behaviour. Consequently, changes that strengthen social bonds to society in adulthood decrease criminal involvement, while those that weaken social bonds increase criminal involvement.

Loeber's pathways to crime theory

According to Loeber and Stouthamer-Loeber (1996), a pathway 'is a group of individuals who share a behavioral development that is distinct from the behavioral development of another group of individuals' (p. 19). As such, pathways take account of an individual's history as well as the temporal sequence of his or her problem behaviour on a continuum of increasing seriousness. Loeber (1996) proposed three pathways based on the **Pittsburgh youth study**:

- *Overt pathway*. Represented by escalation from minor aggression (for example annoying others and bullying) to physical fighting and eventually violence (for example robbery and rape).
- *Covert pathway*. Minor covert acts (for example shoplifting and frequent lying) through to property damage (for example fire setting and vandalism) and more serious forms of theft (for example breaking and entering).
- *Authority conflict pathway*. Stubborn behaviour, serious disobedience and deviance. Reflected in authority avoidance before the age of 12, staying out late, truancy, and running away.

It was found that rates of self-reported and official delinquency were lowest for youths who remained on a single pathway, but increased for youths who were simultaneously on two or all three pathways (Loeber, 1996). It was also apparent that boys on the overt pathway were more likely to escalate into the covert pathway than the reverse, thus suggesting that aggressive boys are at greater risk of diversifying and escalating than non-aggressive boys (Loeber et al., 1993). As Kelley, Loeber, Keenan and DeLamatre (1997) pointed out, understanding the nature of these different pathways can help in the identification of problem behaviour and the implementation of effective interventions with 'troubled youths' before they progress to more serious forms of crime.

Thinking scientifically → **Risk factors over the life-course**

Research has shown that a number of factors influence the risk of criminal behaviour during the life-course. For example, separate analyses utilizing data from the **Dunedin multidisciplinary health and**

safety study and the **Cambridge study in delinquent development** revealed that having an undercontrolled temperament at three years of age is related to later criminal convictions (Caspi, 2000; Farrington, 2002). Research has also found that family disruption (for example parental criminality, poor parenting and parental absence) is a strong predictor of criminal behaviour (Eklund and Klinteberg, 2006; Farrington et al., 2006; Murray and Farrington, 2005). Parental absence appears to be related to future criminal behaviour regardless of whether it is the result of imprisonment or an increase in exposure to ineffective parenting (Murray and Farrington, 2005; Phillips et al., 2006).

According to the **Peterborough adolescent development study**, part of the **Social Contexts of Pathways in Crime (SCoPiC)** consortium, the influence of family disruption can be understood through its impact on morality and self-control (SCoPiC, n.d.a). This belief is based on the finding that weak morality and low self-control are important factors in the development of criminal behaviour, and that family risk factors significantly influence children's levels of morality and self-control.

Laub, Nagin and Sampson (1998) argued that childhood and adolescent characteristics are insufficient to determine the future offending of adolescents alone. Research has shown that a number of protective factors may lead to the desistence of criminal behaviour during the life-course, including involvement in intimate relationships. However, the protective nature of these relationships appears to relate to their quality and the level of personal investment involved rather than their existence per se (Laub et al., 1998; Meeus, Branje and Overbeek, 2004; West, 1982).

Analyses utilizing data from the **Sheffield pathways out of crime study**, also part of the SCoPiC consortium, suggests that there are six robust obstacles to the desistence of criminal behaviour. These are an offender's need for excitement, lack of money, lack of employment and drug addiction, along with the area in which they live and that criminal behaviour provides an opportunity to make 'easy money' (SCoPiC, n.d.b). Consequently, it is important that interventions target these obstacles in order to encourage offenders to desist from criminal behaviour and adopt non-criminal lifestyles.

Summary

According to life-course-persistent/adolescence-limited theory, there are two distinct types of offending, those limited to adolescence and those that continue into adulthood. In contrast, the theory of age-graded informal social control argues that a dynamic system is more appropriate as it allows for the explanation of both continuity and change over time according to changes in the strength of social bonds to conventional activities. An alternative view is that three pathways to offending exist, and that these can be used to determine the likelihood that a person will become a chronic offender or engage in criminal behaviour for a short period of time and then desist.

Media violence and violent crime

Research into aggression has often been used to support the claim that there is a relationship between media violence and violent crime (Howitt, 2006). However, this research has been criticized for lacking criminological relevance (that is, violent behaviour that includes the intent to harm). For example, the imitation of modelled play aggression against a Bobo-doll that cannot be knocked over without bouncing up again is not criminologically relevant (Felson, 1996). Consequently, there is still a lack of consensus regarding the nature of this relationship. Methodologies used to investigate the relationship between media violence and violent crime include anecdotal evidence, crime statistics, quasi-experimental studies and longitudinal studies.

Anecdotal evidence

A great deal of anecdotal evidence suggests that there is a relationship between media violence and violent crime. For example, Allan Menzies beat and stabbed his friend to death in 2002 because of an insulting comment he made about Akasha, the heroine of the film *Queen of the Damned* (Robertson, 2003). According to Menzies, he had watched the film over 100 times and Akasha had repeatedly instructed him to kill in order to gain immortality.

Although this case supports the view that violent films can cause violent crime, Menzies was found to be emotionally unstable and to have a **psychopathic personality** disorder (Robertson, 2003). Furthermore, he did not mention the fantasies when first questioned by the police, and it is possible that he manufactured the fantasy afterwards in order to avoid a conviction for murder and/or to help him to cope with the situation. Irrespective, anecdotal evidence suggests violent films can promote new forms of violence that would not be considered otherwise.

Crime statistics

The gradual manner in which television was introduced across and within different countries provided researchers with a unique opportunity to investigate the relationship between media violence and violent crime. This methodology is based on the assumption that if television is related to crime, the introduction of television will be related to an increase in crime (Coyne, 2007). However, research has been unable to demonstrate a clear causal link between exposure to violent television and violent crime.

Hennigan et al. (1982) compared US crime rates in cities where television had been introduced to cities where it had not, and found that there was no consistent effect for the introduction of television on violent crime, burglary or auto theft. Although there was an increase in larceny theft (that is, thefts of bicycles, auto accessories, shoplifting and pickpocketing), Hennigan et al. tentatively attributed this effect to the frustration experienced by some people in response to the 'unobtainable' possessions and lifestyles portrayed on television.

Centerwall (1993) compared changes in homicide rates over the period in which television was introduced in Canada and the US to homicide rates in South Africa where television had not yet been introduced. It was found that while the number of homicides increased dramatically in Canada and the US 10 to 15 years after the introduction of television, the number of homicides reduced in South Africa during the same time period. Centerwall argued that the increase in homicides reflected the introduction of violent television in Canada and the US, and accounted for the time lag with reference to the fact that television primarily influences children while homicides are primarily committed by adults. As such, 'this lag represents the time needed for the "television generation" to come of age' (p. 63).

Although Centerwall (1993) controlled for other factors including differences in economic growth and civil unrest, Coyne (2007) argued that it is difficult to determine causation due to differences between the countries involved. Furthermore, earlier research by Messner (1986) examined the relationship between exposure to television violence and violent crime in the US, and found that high levels of television violence were actually related to comparatively low rates of violent crime (that is, murder, rape, robbery and assault).

Quasi-experimental studies

Quasi-experimental designs have been used to compare the television and film preferences of offenders and non-offenders. Browne and Pennell (1998) showed violent offenders, non-violent offenders and non-offenders a violent film and then interviewed them about it immediately, 4 months later and 10 months later. Most differences were found between the offenders and the non-offenders (that is, the violent offenders and the non-violent offenders combined). For example, offenders were more likely to prefer violent films, to identify with violent characters and to become excited by the portrayal of violence compared to non-offenders.

However, offenders had often experienced a poorer social upbringing than non-offenders, with most suffering parental violence either directly or indirectly through the witnessing of inter-parental conflict (Browne and Pennell, 1998). Furthermore, the relationship between offending and preferences for violent films and characters was not significant in the absence of parental violence. Taken together, these findings suggest that experiencing a poor social upbringing increases people's susceptibility to the influence of media violence. It also supports the view that suffering parental violence increases the likelihood that a person will engage in criminal behaviour in the future.

Longitudinal studies

Longitudinal designs have been used to develop a better understanding of the relationship between violent media and violent crime by monitoring the television preferences and aggressive behaviour of young children. A body of research has shown that exposure to violent television at 6 to 10 years of age increases levels of aggression 10 to 15 years later, even when the influence of other factors (for example ethnicity, socioeconomic status, intelligence and a number of parenting factors) are controlled for (Eron, Huesmann, Lefkowitz and Walder, 1972; Huesmann, Moise-Titus, Podolski and Eron, 2003). The research has also found the relationship to be bidirectional. Consequently, Eron et al. (1972), and later Eron (1982), argued that the relationship between media violence and violent crime involves a circular process whereby violent television increases children's aggression and aggressive children watch increasingly violent television.

It is important to acknowledge that this research has been criticized for using aggression measures that incorporate non-aggressive antisocial behaviours, and for relying on parental reports of children's exposure to violent television (Felson, 1996). Furthermore, other research has found that aggressive behaviour peaks between two and four years of age, and then gradually declines as children get older (Côté et al., 2006; Tremblay, 2000, 2007). Thus, the age-related increases in aggression reported previously were not apparent when the aggressive behaviour of younger children was considered. According to Tremblay (2000, 2007), most children learn to control their aggressive behaviour before they reach 'maximum size', and aggression in older children represents a failure in learning to suppress it.

These findings are particularly important as research suggests that children who display aggressive behaviour at a very young age are more likely to engage in criminal behaviour later in life (Coyne, 2007). Furthermore, it is unlikely that this aggression is caused by exposure to media violence as television aimed at very young children is usually prosocial and non-violent.

The relationship between violent media and violent crime

Overall, media violence appears to have a small yet significant effect on aggression, although its effect on violent crime is less certain. It is generally accepted that the influence of media violence occurs through the modelling of aggressive solutions to problems. In the short term it may increase levels of arousal and aggressive responses, while in the long term it may weaken inhibitions against the use of aggression (Blackburn, 1993; Howitt, 2006).

It is imperative that research continues to examine criminologically relevant aggressive behaviour in order to further understand the relationship between media violence and violent crime. It is also important to acknowledge that media are produced within a social context and that the relationship between media violence and violent crime should not be considered in isolation (Blackburn, 1993; Howitt, 2006).

Summary

Although aggression research has been used to support the claim that there is a relationship between media violence and violent crime, it has often lacked criminological relevance. Methodologies used to investigate this relationship include anecdotal evidence, crime statistics, quasi-experimental studies and longitudinal studies. Overall, it appears that there may be a weak relationship between the two, although it is likely to have a greater impact on some people than others.

Further reading

Blackburn, R. (1993) *The Psychology of Criminal Conduct: Theory, Research and Practice*. Chichester: John Wiley & Sons.

Coyne, S.M. (2007) Does media violence cause violent crime? *European Journal on Criminal Policy*, 13, 205–11.

Howitt, D. (2009) *Introduction to Forensic and Criminal Psychology* (3rd edn). Harlow: Pearson Education Limited.

Section Two

Psychology and the Investigative Process

Chapter 6

Offender profiling

Introduction

An increasing array of books, television shows and feature films portray offender profiling as a 'magical skill' that can be used to solve crimes and catch serial killers (Muller, 2000). In reality, offender profiling can do neither of these things in isolation. Instead, it serves as an additional investigative tool that can be used in conjunction with standard police procedures to focus an investigation and reduce the pool of potential suspects (Kocsis and Palermo, 2007).

This chapter will describe and evaluate offender profiling in terms of its current and future use in police investigations. It will first outline the underlying assumptions of profiling before considering three prominent approaches: crime scene analysis, investigative psychology and geographic profiling. The utility of typologies of serial murder and rape will then be discussed along with issues concerning the effectiveness of offender profiling.

This chapter will examine:

- Assumptions of profiling
- Approaches to profiling
- Typologies of serial murder and rape
- The effectiveness of profiling

Assumptions of profiling

Offender profiling uses information that is available at a crime scene or scenes to generate a profile of the unknown perpetrator. To achieve this aim, the following three questions must be considered (Jackson and Bekerian, 1997):

1 What happened at the crime scene or crime scenes?
2 What type of person would have committed the crime or series of crimes?
3 What personality characteristics would such a person have?

The overarching assumption of offender profiling is that behaviours are exhibited during the commission of a crime and are reflected in the crime scene evidence that is left behind. It is therefore assumed that examination of the crime scene allows inferences to be made about the likely offender (Jackson and Bekerian, 1997). Specifically, it is believed that the crime scene reflects the offender's personality, that the **method of operation (MO)** remains similar, that the signature will stay the same and that the offender's personality will not change (Holmes and Holmes, 2002; Turvey, 2008a, 2008b):

- *The crime scene reflects the offender's personality.* It is assumed that careful examination of the crime scene should help to focus a police investigation because it will provide information about the personality of the offender (that is, the **homology assumption**). Information regarding the manner in which the crime was committed is particularly important along with the presence or absence of physical and/or non-physical evidence.
- *The method of operation remains similar.* The term MO is an abbreviation of the Latin term *modus operandi* which means 'method of operation'. It refers to the choices and behaviours that assist the offender during the completion of the crime. The MO may include the use of a mask, the use of restraints and the way the offender leaves a crime scene. It is assumed that although a series of crimes will be committed in a similar manner, the exact MO may change over time due to experience and learning.
- *The signature will stay the same.* The crime scene also contains behavioural clues that may be identified as the **signature** of the crime. The signature consists of distinctive behaviours that are unnecessary for the completion of the crime, but serve to fulfil the psychological and/or emotional needs of the offender. The signature remains the same over time and can be used to link an offender's crimes.

- *The offender's personality will not change*. Finally, it is assumed that the core of the offender's personality will not change over time, and that this inability to change will result in the perpetration of similar crimes (that is, the **behavioural consistency hypothesis**). While it is accepted that offenders may change aspects of their personality, it is considered extremely unlikely that they will be able to change core elements of their personality in a dramatic way over a relatively short period of time.

Summary

Offender profiling examines what happened at a crime scene in order to determine the type of person who could have committed the crime. It is based on the assumption that behaviours exhibited at the crime scene reflect the offender's personality and that the offender's personality will not change over a relatively short period of time.

Approaches to profiling

There is no universal approach to offender profiling. In fact, the term is used to encompass a range of different scientific and psychological approaches that attempt to focus police investigations by reducing the number of potential suspects (Alison, McLean and Almond, 2007). Diagnostic evaluations were the precursor to what is now referred to as criminal personality profiling, and involved individual psychiatrists and psychologists producing profiles of offenders as and when they were needed. Evaluations were generally based on clinical practice and involved the diagnosis of the likely personality type of the offender (Wilson, Lincoln and Kocsis, 1997). Since this time, the practice of offender profiling has developed considerably and there are currently three prominent approaches: crime scene analysis, investigative psychology and geographic profiling.

Crime scene analysis

Crime scene analysis was developed by the Federal Bureau of Investigation (FBI) during the 1970s in response to an apparent increase in serial murder in the US (Howitt, 2006). It was intended to assist the police in solving the most bizarre and extreme crimes by reducing the number of potential suspects or providing alternative avenues of inquiry (Alison et al., 2007). Crime scene analysis offers a **top-down approach** to offender profiling that utilizes the experience and intuition of the profiler to interpret evidence from the crime scene and develop a profile of the likely offender (Woodworth and Porter, 1999). The process of generating a profile includes six main stages: profiling inputs, decision process models, crime assessment, criminal profile, investigation and apprehension (Ressler, Burgess and Douglas, 1988).

Profiling inputs

The first stage involves the collection of all information that might be pertinent to solving the case. It is acknowledged that information may originally appear trivial, but turn out to be crucial. Inputs include photographs of the crime scene, the preliminary police report, information about the victim, and forensic evidence (Ressler et al., 1988). It is important that the profiler is not provided with details of possible suspects, as this information may unconsciously bias the production of the profile. Taken together, this information helps the profiler determine the risk status of the victim, the level of control exhibited at the crime scene, the offender's emotional state, and the offender's level of criminal sophistication.

Decision process models

During the second stage, information is organized into meaningful patterns with reference to seven decision process models (Ressler et al., 1988):

1. *Murder type*. Whether the murder represents a **mass murder**, a **spree murder** or a **serial murder.**
2. *Primary intent*. Whether murder was the primary intent of the offender, or secondary to another crime.
3. *Victim risk*. Whether the victim was a high, medium or low risk target on the basis of age, occupation and lifestyle characteristics.
4. *Offender risk*. Whether the offender was taking high or low risks during the commission of the crime.
5. *Escalation*. Whether the seriousness of crimes will escalate and be repeated in a 'serial fashion'.
6. *Time factors*. Whether the crimes take a long or short time to commit and whether the crimes are committed during the day or at night.
7. *Location factors*. Whether the death and crime scenes are the same or different.

Crime assessment

The third stage involves the profiler reconstructing the sequence of events along with the behaviour of the offender and the victim (Ressler et al., 1988). Based on decisions made during the previous stage, the classification of how events occurred and how people behaved during events is used to inform the development of the profile. It is during this stage that crimes are classified as being committed by an **organized offender** or a **disorganized offender** (Ressler et al., 1988):

- *Organized offender*. Organized crime scenes are generally planned and the victim is targeted. The offender personalizes the victim, controls the conversation and demands that the victim is submissive. Aggressive acts are performed prior to death, the weapon is absent, and the body is often transported and hidden from view. Organized offenders are generally of high intelligence, socially and sexually competent, and work in a skilled occupation. They have a high birth order (for example the eldest child) and experienced inconsistent discipline in childhood. They usually live with a partner, have a car that is in good working order and follow their crimes in the media.
- *Disorganized offender*. Disorganized crime scenes are generally unplanned and the victim is selected at random. The offender depersonalizes the victim, avoids conversation, and engages in sudden violence towards the victim. Sexual acts are performed after death, the weapon is often present, and the body is left in view at the death scene. Disorganized offenders are generally of average intelligence, socially immature, sexually incompetent with a poor work history. They have a low birth order (for example the youngest child) and experienced harsh discipline in childhood. They usually live alone, live or work close to the crime scene and take little interest in media coverage of their crimes.

Criminal profile

During the fourth stage, the available information is used to construct the profile. It is essential that the profile is consistent with the aforementioned decision process models and reconstruction of the sequence of events (Ressler et al., 1988). The profile includes hypotheses regarding the likely demographic and physiological characteristics, behavioural habits and personality dynamics of the offender. The profile may also include recommendations regarding appropriate strategies for the identification, apprehension and interviewing of the offender.

The investigation

The fifth stage is where the written report is provided to the investigating agency. The recommendations generated by the profiler during the preceding stage are applied to the investigation and suspects matching the profile are evaluated (Ressler et al., 1988). If a suspect is apprehended and a confession is obtained, then the profile is judged to be successful. If additional information is generated within the investigation, separate to the profile, the new information is incorporated and the profile is revised.

The apprehension

The sixth stage involves the evaluation of the profile and the profiling process. The evaluation involves assessing the value of the profile in assisting the police to successfully apprehend the suspect (assuming that the apprehended suspect is found to be the offender) (Ressler et al., 1988).

Thinking scientifically → **Arthur Shawcross: The Genesee river killer**

A number of prostitutes were murdered in the state of New York between 1988 and 1989 (Owen, 2004). The murderer took the victims to a secluded area for sex and then killed them either by strangulation or by a 'heavy blow'. The bodies were then dumped by the Genesee river. On several occasions the genital area of the victims had been removed.

The profile

Greg McCrary, a profiler from the FBI, was called in to help with the police investigation. His profile included the following predictions about the likely offender (Owen, 2004):

- The offender is a man in his late 20s or early 30s.
- The offender has a nondescript car.
- The offender is in a relationship.
- The offender returns to the victims' bodies to mutilate them further.

These assumptions were based on the age of the victims, the fact that the bodies of the victims were transported from one place to another, the fact that prostitutes trusted him as a potential client, and evidence of post-mortem mutilation.

On the basis of McCrary's profile, the police planned to catch the offender when he returned to the victims' bodies to further mutilate them (Owen, 2004). As they were patrolling the area by helicopter, police officers on the search for another victim spotted a woman's body by the river and a man on a nearby bridge getting into his car and driving away. The man was followed, arrested and identified as Arthur Shawcross. Shawcross was married and had a girlfriend at the time of his arrest, and had returned to the woman's body to mutilate it further. Upon his arrest, it was discovered that Shawcross had spent 15 years in prison for the murder of two young children 17 years earlier. Although Shawcross was initially released due to a lack of evidence, he finally confessed to the murders when the police found an earring that belonged to one of the victims in his girlfriend's car. Shawcross was found guilty on 11 counts of murder and received 10 life sentences without the chance of parole.

Inconsistencies

Shawcross was 45 when he was arrested and did not own a car (Owen, 2004). According to McCrary, the age difference could be accounted for by the 15 years he spent in prison, as it would have delayed his criminal development. With regard to the car, Shawcross did not need one of his own as he had regular access to his girlfriend's car.

Investigative psychology

Investigative psychology originated in the UK during the mid-1980s in parallel to crime scene analysis, which originated in the US (Wilson et al., 1997). Investigative psychology is largely attributed to the work of David Canter, a psychologist who proposed an approach to profiling based on research (Petherick and Turvey, 2008). In contrast to crime scene analysis, investigative psychology offers a **bottom-up approach** to offender profiling that utilizes psychological theory and research to interpret evidence from the crime scene and develop a profile of the likely offender (Woodworth and Porter, 1999). It is still founded on the assumption that analysis of the crime scene allows inferences to be made about the likely offender, but the profile generation process relies on statistical techniques rather than the experiences and intuition of the profiler (Howitt, 2006; Muller, 2000). Investigative psychology has also been applied to a wider range of crimes, including tax evasion, burglary and arson.

Egger (1999) summarized the five assumptions of investigative psychology that deal with different aspects of the 'criminal transaction' between the offender and the victim. These are:

- *Interpersonal coherence*. The way offenders commit crimes will reflect the way they behave in everyday life. For example, offenders' interactions with victims will be similar to their interactions with people generally.
- *Time and place*. The locations offenders use to commit crimes will provide information about their area of residence. For example, offenders are more likely to commit crimes in areas that they are familiar with.
- *Criminal characteristics*. The criminal characteristics of offenders can be used to classify them into categories that may be helpful to the police.
- *Criminal career*. The fact that offenders tend to commit crimes in a similar way can be used to identify their probable criminal careers.
- *Forensic awareness*. Offenders who demonstrate knowledge of the evidence-gathering procedures of the police are likely to have had previous contact with the criminal justice system.

Smallest space analysis

Smallest space analysis is a statistical technique that produces a spatial representation of the co-occurrence of different variables (Salfati and Canter, 1999). In the context of investigative psychology, it has been used to plot the co-occurrence of different crime scene and offender characteristics from a number of crimes. The most common crime scene and offender characteristics are displayed in the centre of the plot while the least common characteristics are displayed at the edge of the plot. The co-occurrence of different crime scene and offender characteristics is represented by their proximity (that is, the more they co-occur, the closer the characteristics are).

House (1997) used smallest space analysis to examine the co-occurrence of 39 behaviour variables with a sample of 60 North American rape cases. The analysis revealed that while some behaviours were common to all rapes (for example vaginal penetration, an element of surprise and the removal of clothing) other behaviours were less common and could be classified into four underlying themes:

- *Aggression*. Refers to the offender's use of aggressive actions including physical and verbal violence.
- *Criminality*. Refers to the offender's level of organization and criminality, including the use of a disguise and weapon.

- *Intimacy*. Refers to the offender's distorted attempts to establish a relationship, including compliments of the victim and the need for the victim to 'participate'.
- *Sadism*. Refers to the offender's use of sadistic actions including behaviour that humiliates or tortures the victim.

Of the 60 rapes cases, 10 had insufficient information regarding the 39 behaviour variables for classification (House, 1997). Of the remaining 50 rape cases, 29 were classified within the intimacy theme, 26 within the aggression theme, 18 within the criminality theme and 9 within the sadism theme. Variations were also apparent when offenders' previous criminal activity was compared across the four themes. For example, offenders in the sadism theme were less likely to have previous arrests or convictions compared to offenders in the aggression, criminality and intimacy themes. However, they were more likely to have committed deceptive crimes in the past compared to offenders in the aggression and criminality themes.

Other research has used smallest space analysis to investigate the co-occurrence of 48 crime scene and offender variables with a sample of 82 UK-based solved stranger murder cases (Salfati and Canter, 1999). The analysis revealed three underlying crime scene and offender themes:

- *Instrumental opportunistic*. The crime scenes were characterized by frenzied attacks in which multiple wounds were inflicted on the victim's body, particularly around the face region. Offender variables linked to this theme included violent, sexual, drug and traffic offences, and offences of public disorder and property damage. Offenders were married at the time of the murder and/or had been married previously. Offenders were also likely to be female.
- *Instrumental cognitive*. The crime scenes were characterized by the theft of property in which injuries were inflicted by hand. Injuries tended to be located around the neck area and the face was often hidden. Offender variables linked to this theme included previous offences for theft, vehicle theft and burglary. Offenders had come to the attention of the police previously, were unemployed, familiar with the area, and knew the victim prior to the murder.
- *Expressive impulsive*. The crime scenes were characterized by attempts to hide the crime. The victim's body was often transported and hidden from view, and attempts were made to remove forensic

evidence from the crime scene. Offender variables linked to this theme included serving in the armed forces and serving a prison sentence.

Of the 82 stranger murder cases, 29 could not be classified. Of the remaining 53 crime scenes, 21 were classified within the instrumental cognitive theme, 16 within the instrumental opportunistic theme, and 16 within the expressive impulsive theme (Salfati and Canter, 1999).

Thinking scientifically → **John Duffy: The railway rapist**

During the 1980s there were a series of rapes that escalated into murders in the Greater London area (Owen, 2004). The rape victims were approached and the murder victims were dumped close to the railway lines. The murder victims were raped and then strangled.

The profile

David Canter from the University of Surrey was asked by the police to help with the investigation. His profile included the following predictions about the likely offender (Owen, 2004):

- The offender is male, approximately 5′ 9″ tall, fair-haired and between 25 and 30 years of age.
- The offender lives in North West London.
- The offender lives with his wife or girlfriend.
- The offender has been arrested or imprisoned for some unrelated crime.

These assumptions were based on the descriptions of the offender, the locations of the first three rapes, the fact that he was able to ask his victims for directions without alarming them, and the break in crimes between 1982 and 1984.

On the basis of the profile the police re-examined the 2000 potential suspects and noticed that the 1505th potential suspect matched many aspects of the profile (Owen, 2004). John Duffy was 28 when he was arrested, lived in North West London, and had been arrested previously for raping his ex-wife. When the police arrested Duffy they found fibres on his clothing that matched those of the victims as well as an unusual type of string in his home that matched the type used to restrain the victims. The surviving victims were also able to identify him from a lineup. It was later revealed that Duffy escalated from rape to murder after seeing one of his victims when he attended court for the rape of his ex-wife. Duffy was found guilty on four counts of rape and two counts of murder, and received a life sentence without the chance for parole. Duffy later admitted to a further 17 rapes and 1 murder when he also implicated David Mulcahy, his accomplice during the early rapes.

Inconsistencies
Duffy was considerably shorter than the profile predicted. This overestimation of height is a well-documented occurrence in the context of threatening situations (Owen, 2004). Furthermore, the presence of Mulcahy during the early rapes may have confused victim descriptions of the offender.

Geographic profiling

Similar to investigative psychology, geographic profiling developed during the mid-1980s when it was realized that examining the geographical locations of a series of crimes could be used to estimate the offender's probable area of residence (Canter and Youngs, 2008). Geographic profiling is situated within the general framework of investigative psychology and is based on the following principles:

- *Locatedness*. All crimes have a distinct location. In the context of murder, locations may include where the offender encountered the victim, attacked the victim, murdered the victim and disposed of the victim's body. All are relevant and may offer information about the offender's area of residence.
- *Systematic crime location choice*. The locations where crimes occur are not random. They vary as a function of opportunity and factors internal to the offender (for example familiarity and personal preferences).
- *Centrality* (commuters and marauders). Crimes are most likely to occur in locations where the offender is familiar. Commuters travel to commit their crimes, while marauders commit crimes near their area of residence.
- *Comparative case analysis* (linking crimes). The more crimes that can be linked to a single offender, the more powerful the application of geographic profiling will be.

Overall, geographic profiling focuses on the locations of crime scenes, the spatial relationships between them, and how they relate to the offender's area of residence (Rossmo, 1997). This information can then be used by the police to develop investigative strategies that maximize the effectiveness of limited resources:

- *Suspect prioritization*. Geoprofiles can be used to prioritize suspects, leads and 'tips' to help avoid information overload.
- *Patrol saturation and static stakeholders*. Geoprofiles can be used to direct the use of police patrols and stakeouts. This strategy is most useful when the crimes occur during specific time periods.
- *Neighbourhood canvassing*. Geoprofiles can be used to direct the door-to-door canvassing of particular areas.
- *Postal code prioritization*. Geoprofiles can be used to prioritize postal code areas in order to optimize searches and rankings of address databases.
- *Bloodings*. Geoprofiles can be used to direct the DNA testing of potential suspects in postal code areas that have already been prioritized.

Evaluation

Crime scene analysis has been criticized on the grounds that it lacks a clear theoretical foundation, that it relies on the experience and intuition of profilers, and that the technique was originally based on the analysis of 37 imprisoned serial murderers (Wilson et al., 1997; Woodworth and Porter, 1999). As Godwin (2002) pointed out, the murderers who volunteered to participate in the original research did so for a variety of reasons (for example restitution to victims, attention and/or legal benefits) and therefore are unlikely to provide a representative sample of serial murderers (Godwin, 2002; Salfati and Canter, 1999). Furthermore, the organized–disorganized typology has been criticized on the grounds that it has a weak evidence base and that the classifications are not mutually exclusive (Godwin, 2002; Canter, Alison, Alison and Wentink, 2004). Salfati and Canter (1999) also acknowledged that this criticism applied to their crime scene and offender theme typology.

In contrast to crime scene analysis, investigative psychology and geographic profiling are considered to be more scientific. They are also limited, however, by issues relating to the nature of the samples used and the quality of the data obtained in the development and testing of the approach (Canter and Youngs, 2008). Criminal activities are not usually open to public scrutiny and official records are not produced for the purpose of detailed analysis. Consequently, the samples are often restricted to offenders who have been apprehended and the data may be incomplete or inaccurately recorded. Given that the approaches of investigative psychology and geographic profiling are based on data from offenders who have been apprehended, it is problematic to generalize these approaches to those who have not yet been apprehended as their offending behaviour is likely to be different from those who have.

Summary

There are three main approaches to offender profiling: crime scene analysis, investigative psychology and geographic profiling. Crime scene analysis was developed in the US by the FBI and utilizes the experiences and intuition of the profiler to solve bizarre and extreme crimes. Investigative psychology has developed in the UK and utilizes psychological theory and research to solve a wider range of crimes. Finally, geographic profiling is situated within the general framework of investigative psychology and examines the geographical locations of crimes to estimate the offender's probable area of residence.

Typologies of serial murder and rape

Although offenders of particular types of crime, such as rape or murder, share similarities in the way they commit crimes, differences also exist between individual offenders. In order to explain the behaviour of various categories of offenders, typologies have been developed for different types of crime including serial murder and rape. The organized–disorganized typology associated with crime scene analysis and the crime scene and offender theme typology associated with investigative psychology were summarized with their respective approaches to profiling.

It is assumed that the development of typologies represents a fundamental stage in the creation of an adequate knowledge base regarding offending behaviour. It is further assumed that typologies provide important information to the police regarding the factors associated with different types of crime that may assist in narrowing the pool of possible suspects (Holmes and DeBurger, 1988).

Serial murderers

Holmes and DeBurger (1988) developed the following typology of male serial murderers on the basis of interviews with and case studies of 110 serial murderers who were serving prison sentences in the US:

- *Visionary*. The murderer acts on the basis of voices or visions that demand the killing of certain types of people.
- *Mission-oriented*. The murderer has made the conscious decision to kill a certain group of people who are considered to be unworthy of life.
- *Hedonistic*. The murderer gains pleasure from the killing of another person. Hedonistic lust murderers experience elevated sexual arousal, while hedonistic thrill murderers experience a sense of excitement.
- *Power/control-oriented*. The murderer gains pleasure from the total control and domination of another person.

It is apparent that there is variation in the motives, victims, methods and locations of these different types of male serial murderers (Holmes and DeBurger, 1988):

- *Motives*. Visionary and mission-oriented murderers are motivated by the act of killing while hedonistic and power/control-oriented murderers are motivated by the process itself.
- *Victims*. Mission-oriented and power/control-oriented murderers target their victims while visionary, lust and thrill murderers select their victims at random.
- *Methods*. Mission-oriented, lust and power/control-oriented murderers are organized and plan the killings while visionary and thrill murderers are disorganized and the killings are unplanned.
- *Locations*. Visionary, mission-oriented and lust murderers are geographically stable (that is, kill in concentrated locations) while visionary and thrill murderers are geographically mobile (that is, kill in dispersed locations).

Although serial murderers are predominantly male, Holmes, Hickey and Holmes (1991) developed a typology to help the police understand and apprehend female serial murderers:

- *Visionary*. Similar to male serial murderers. Motivated to kill by voices or visions that demand the killing of certain types of people.
- *Comfort*. Motivated to kill for material gain (for example insurance benefits and inheritance). The comfort serial murderer usually kills someone they know and often live with.
- *Hedonistic*. Similar to male serial murderers. Motivated to kill by the elevated sexual arousal and/or sense of excitement they experience.

- *Power seeker*. Similar to male power/control-oriented murderers. Motivated to kill by the total control and domination of another person. Power seekers may suffer from a severe form of **Munchausen syndrome by proxy**, which is characterized by repeatedly poisoning a person and then nursing them back to health. Once they are dead, the murderer moves on to another person.
- *Disciple*. Motivated to kill with another person by mutually shared sexual and violent fantasies. Disciple murderers would generally not kill without the involvement of the other person.

With regard to the motives, victims, methods and locations of comfort and disciple murderers, comfort murderers are geographically mobile and motivated by the act of killing, while disciple murderers are geographically mobile and motivated by the process itself (Holmes et al., 1991). Both comfort and disciple murderers are organized and plan the killings of targeted victims.

Rapists

Knight and Prentkey (1987) realized that rapists represent a markedly heterogeneous group and so developed the following typology on the basis of 108 men who were convicted of rape (that is, sexual offences committed by adult men against adult women) in the US:

- *Power-reassurance (aka compensatory)*. The rapes represent an expression of sexual fantasies and act as a compensatory defence against low self-esteem and feelings of inadequacy. The offender is highly sexually aroused and the rape hinges on the acting out of a distorted relationship with the victim. The offender is often concerned over the victim's welfare and 'enjoyment' during the rape.
- *Anger-retaliation (aka displaced anger)*. The rapes represent a means of physically harming and degrading the victim. The offender uses sexual action as a means of aggression. The anger-retaliation type is dependent on four factors: (1) excessive non-sexualized aggression and violence towards the victim, (2) verbal and physical behaviour that demeans and dehumanizes the victim, (3) no evidence of sexual gratification from injuring the victim, and (4) injuries that are not focused on the sexual organs of the victim.
- *Power-assertive (aka exploitative)*. The rapes represent a means of dominating the victim. The offender has little interest in arousing

the victim who essentially acts as a 'masturbatory object'. The power-assertive type is dependent on two factors: (1) no more force than is necessary to control the victim, and (2) indifference towards the welfare or comfort of the victim.

- *Anger-excitement (aka sadistic)*. The rapes represent an expression of sexually aggressive fantasies. Increases in sexual arousal are related to increases in aggression and violence, and vice versa. The anger-excitement type is dependent on two factors: (1) excessive aggression and violence that exceeds the amount necessary to control the victim, and (2) clear evidence of sexual gratification from injuring the victim.

Thinking scientifically →

Strategies for the interviewing of suspects

The development of typologies has provided a number of strategies that can be used during interviews to encourage the cooperation of suspects during this crucial stage of the investigation (Egger, 1999). For example, Knight and Prentkey's (1987) typology of rapists has been used to provide the police with different interview strategies dependent on the classification of the suspect (Holmes and Holmes, 2002):

- *Power-reassurance*. The rape served as an expression of sexual fantasy: the offender had no real intent to harm the victim and was compensating for low self-esteem and feelings of inadequacy. A possible interview strategy therefore is for the interviewer to appeal to a suspect's sense of masculinity. The interviewer could point out that he or she knows the suspect did not mean to hurt the victim and that the victim did not experience excessive trauma. The use of this sympathetic approach should encourage the suspect to cooperate.
- *Anger-retaliation*. The rape served as a means of physically harming and degrading the victim: the offender was expressing his hatred for women and intended to demean and dehumanize the victim. A possible interview strategy therefore is to start the interview with a male and a female interviewer. The male interviewer should adopt a professional manner and ask the female interviewer to leave the room as and when the suspect responds negatively towards her. This approach makes the male interviewer appear more experienced and powerful than the female interviewer, and should encourage the suspect to cooperate. A controversial alternative approach is for the male

interviewer to talk about the female interviewer in a derogatory manner once she has left the interview.

- *Power-assertive and anger-excitement.* The rape served as a means of dominating the victim (power-assertive) or as an expression of sexually aggressive fantasies (anger-excitement). There is no simple interview strategy that will increase the cooperation of these types of suspects. However, they will be resistant if the interview is poorly organized and based on assumptions or speculation. It is important therefore that the interviewer is certain of the suspect's involvement in the rape and has verified the details of the case prior to the interview. The interviewer should then conduct the interview in a professional business-like manner.

It is important to note that thorough preparation and planning should form a central role in all interviews. Issues concerning the interviewing of suspects are discussed in more detail in Chapter 8.

Evaluation

The use of typologies for the classification of offenders has been criticized on the following grounds (Gresswell and Hollin, 1994):

- The types are often not mutually exclusive.
- The types are generally not exhaustive.
- The types are not sensitive to interactions between the offender, the victim and/or the environment.

Typologies have also been critiqued for not considering the underlying causes of criminal behaviour, and for relying on offenders' self-reports which are susceptible to intentional and/or unintentional deception (Godwin, 2002). Holmes and DeBurger's (1988) typology of male serial murderers has been criticized on the grounds that it lacks depth with regard to offender and crime scene characteristics, and as such may be of little use in police investigations (Keppel and Walter, 1999). Concerns have also been raised about the lack of methodological details and empirical support for the development of the classification system (Canter and Wentink, 2004).

When Canter and Wentink (2004) tested the application of Holmes and DeBurger's (1988) typology they found little direct support for the four types of serial murderer. The research used 100 US cases of serial murder, each committed by a different offender. Content analysis was first performed on the available information to identify the presence or absence of 37 offender and crime scene variables taken from the classification system. Smallest space analysis was then performed to examine the co-occurrence of the 37 variables across the 100 cases. The analysis revealed that several offender and crime scene variables intended for the control/power-oriented type were also present in the visionary, hedonistic and power-oriented types. Furthermore, it was difficult to relate identifiable crime scene variables to the mission-oriented type. Overall, Canter and Wentink argued that the typology lacked sufficient depth or empirical support to be useful in police investigations without modification.

Summary

A number of typologies have been developed for different types of crime on the assumption that they represent a fundamental stage in the creation of an adequate knowledge base that may be useful in police investigations. For example, a typology of rapists has been used to provide a number of interviewing strategies to encourage the cooperation of suspects. However, typologies have been criticized on the grounds that they lack depth and fail to provide mutually exclusive or exhaustive classifications of offenders.

The effectiveness of profiling

Offender profiling is increasingly regarded as a useful investigative tool, with the number of cases that have been profiled increasing substantially (Snook et al., 2008). Profiles have been found to be most useful in bizarre and extreme cases or in serial cases where there are multiple crime scenes for the extraction and comparison of information (Wilson et al., 1997). Profiles have not been found to be as useful in the context of property or drug crimes.

Despite the increasing acceptance of the behavioural consistency hypothesis, there has been little evidence to support the homology assumption (Turvey, 2008b; Woodhams and Toye, 2007). As Turvey (2008b) pointed out, many offenders commit crimes under the influence of drugs and/or alcohol. Consequently, information obtained from the crime scene may not provide an accurate representation of the offender when they are no longer 'under the influence' (Turvey, 2008b).

Offender profiling has been criticized on the grounds that it is reductive (that is, narrows the field of suspects) rather than productive (that is, identifies the offender), and that a large number of people in a given geographical area will share the characteristics of the profiled offender (Woodworth and Porter, 1999). Concerns have also been raised in relation to the potential for inaccurate profiles to mislead investigations and the fact that the utility of profiles in the apprehension of offenders is still unknown (Snooks et al., 2008; Woodworth and Porter, 1999). As Kocsis and Palermo (2007) pointed out, the usefulness of a profile may not present itself in an identifiable manner as it is often difficult to separate the value of a profile from the broader context of the investigation.

Alison, Smith and Morgan (2003) investigated perceptions of the accuracy of a genuine profile in a real case involving the brutal murder and mutilation of a young woman. Police officers received the profile along with one of two versions of the offender's characteristics. One version presented the characteristics of the genuine offender while the other version presented the characteristics of a fabricated offender. The characteristics of the fabricated offender contrasted with those of the genuine offender in a number of ways including the age of the offender (37 vs. 19), and whether the offender knew the victim (no, yes), was employed (no, yes), had any previous convictions (no, yes), and whether the offender admitted to committing the crime (no, yes). Despite these fundamental differences in the offender's characteristics, over 75 per cent of police officers rated the profiles as somewhat accurate and over 50 per cent rated them as generally or very accurate. Furthermore, police officers' mean confidence ratings for the profiles did not differ according to whether they received the characteristics of the genuine or fabricated offender. Thus, it appears that police officers tend to selectively attend to the aspects of the profile that are consistent with the offender while ignoring those that are inconsistent.

Challenges

Bekerian and Jackson (1997) highlighted a number of challenges that offender profiling has to overcome if it is to become an integral part of police investigations, and they are still relevant today:

- *Increased understanding*. There needs to be a greater understanding between profilers and the police. For example, profilers need to understand the requirements and the needs of the police who in turn need to understand the nature and use of profiles.

- *Appropriate framework*. There needs to be some agreement regarding the appropriate framework for offender profiling. At present there is no agreed approach, and although the use of 'hybrid' profiles (that is, one that integrates features of the different approaches) may be useful, it is also likely to be expensive and difficult to implement.
- *Explanatory theory*. There needs to be an explanatory theory that accounts for the relationships between different types of offender and different types of crime. It is not enough to simply identify these relationships without some form of theoretical explanation. Otherwise, recommendations may reflect inaccurate assumptions and, as a result, mislead investigations.

Ethical concerns

Finally, Bekerian and Jackson (1997) pointed out that offender profiling operates in a sensitive area and that offenders can increase their forensic awareness by reading academic books and articles. Consequently, 'one question that faces all professionals is how to balance the need for open communication with the possible consequence of educating the offender' (Bekerian and Jackson, 1997, p. 220).

Summary

The increasing acceptance of the value of offender profiling has been accompanied by a rise in the number of cases profiled. However, there is little evidence to support the homology assumption, and offender profiling has been criticized on the grounds that such profiles are reductive and have the potential to mislead investigations if inaccurate. Questions have also been raised about how to determine the accuracy and usefulness of profiles. It has been argued that if offender profiling is to become an integral part of police investigations there needs to be (1) a better understanding between profilers and the police, (2) some agreement regarding an appropriate framework, and (3) an explanatory theory that accounts for the relationships between different offender and crime characteristics.

Further reading

Holmes, R.M. and Holmes, S.T. (2002) *Profiling Violent Crimes: An Investigative Tool* (3rd edn). London: Sage Publications.

Jackson, J.L. and Bekerian, D.A. (eds) (1997) *Offender Profiling: Theory, Research and Practice*. Chichester: John Wiley & Sons.

Kocsis, R.N. (ed.) (2007) *Criminal Profiling: International Theory, Research, and Practice*. Totwa, NJ: Humana Press Inc.

Turvey, B.E. (2008) *Criminal Profiling: An Introduction to Behavioral Evidence Analysis* (3rd edn). London: Elsevier Inc.

Chapter 7

Eyewitness testimony

Introduction

Eyewitness testimony remains one of the most persuasive forms of evidence to be presented during a trial despite research to suggest that it can be a highly unreliable source of information (Howitt, 2006). The fallibility of eyewitness testimony is particularly worrying because misidentifications represent a double failure of the criminal justice system. Not only is an innocent person convicted, but a guilty person also remains free to commit further crimes. Consequently, it is important that sound empirical research informs the practices of the criminal justice system in order to enhance the reliability of eyewitness testimony (Wells, 1978).

This chapter will consider the fallibility of eyewitness testimony and issues associated with false and recovered memories. It will first outline some of the factors that contribute to the fallibility of eyewitness testimony. Police interview and lineup procedures that have been implicated in unreliable eyewitness testimony will then be discussed together with ways to improve the accuracy of this descriptive and identification evidence. Finally, consideration will be given to false and recovered memories, including issues relating to the **false memory debate**.

This chapter will examine:

- The fallibility of eyewitness testimony
- Descriptive evidence
- Identification evidence
- False and recovered memories

The fallibility of eyewitness testimony

It is often assumed that memory is like a video recording whereby details of people and events are simply 'replayed' in the person's mind, exactly as they originally occurred (Ainsworth, 1998). Unfortunately, people tend to focus attention selectively on certain aspects of people and events. Then, when asked to recall information, the **reconstructive nature of memory** leads people to fill the 'gaps' in their memories with information about what they think happened rather than what actually happened.

Attributional biases, schemas and stereotypes

Attributional biases influence the way people perceive, interpret and remember other people and events (Ainsworth, 1998). For example, Gudjonsson (1984) describes how people often attribute their own undesirable behaviour to external (that is, situational) factors, but attribute the undesirable behaviour of others to internal (that is, dispositional) factors (attribution theory was discussed in relation to offenders' attributions of blame in Chapter 4). Given the reconstructive nature of memory, attributional biases can lead witnesses to interpret the same crime differently according to their expectations. As Ainsworth (1998) pointed out, people tend to see what they expect to see and ignore what they do not expect to see.

The influence of attributional biases can be demonstrated by the impact schemas and stereotypes have on the accuracy of people's recall. **Schemas** are cognitive systems that help organize and make sense of information while **stereotypes** are widely shared generalizations about members of social groups that are often prejudicial. Schemas and stereotypes reflect people's knowledge and understanding of the world and may lead to attributional biases that direct attention and influence memories for people and events (Davis and Loftus, 2007).

The influence of schemas on memory was demonstrated in 1932 by Frederic C. Bartlett. Bartlett presented English participants with a variety of materials from other cultures including the American Indian folktale 'The War of the Ghosts' (Ainsworth, 1998). Bartlett found that participants recalled certain aspects of the folktale accurately, while other aspects were reinterpreted to reflect their own culture. As such, participants' memories of the story were distorted by their expectations and frames of reference (that is, schemas) as they tried to make sense of the story.

The prejudicial impact of stereotypes was illustrated by Gordon W. Allport and Leo J. Postman in 1947, when they briefly showed participants a drawing of several people on a subway train (Ainsworth, 1998). The drawing portrayed two men standing in the foreground facing each other: a black man and a white man who was holding a razor. Descriptions of the picture were then passed from one participant to the next until six or seven participants had relayed the details. Allport and Postman found that in more than 50 per cent of cases the final description of the picture had changed so that the black man was described as holding the razor rather than the white man. This research, conducted in the US in the late 1940s, demonstrated how the stereotypes held by participants (that is, that a black man was more likely to carry a knife than a white man) biased their memory of the original picture.

Estimator and system variables

Although there are many factors that affect the accuracy of eyewitness testimony, Wells (1978) identified two types of variables that are particularly relevant to research:

- **Estimator variables** are factors that influence the accuracy of eyewitness testimony, but *are not* under the control of the criminal justice system.
- **System variables** are factors that influence the accuracy of eyewitness testimony and *are* under the control of the criminal justice system.

Estimator variables occur at the time of the event and so affect the encoding stage of memory. These variables can be further categorized into witness characteristics (for example age, sex, race and personality) and event characteristics (for example time of day, duration of the incident and seriousness of the incident) (Kapardis, 2003; Wells, 1978). In contrast, system variables impact on the retrieval stage of memory and include the capacity of investigatory procedures used by the criminal justice system to gather accurate descriptive and identification evidence (for example police interview techniques and lineup procedures).

Emotion and memory

Research investigating the influence of estimator variables on the accuracy of eyewitness testimony has considered the impact of emotion on memory, identifying two significant occurrences: **flashbulb memories** and the **weapon focus effect**.

According to Brown and Kulik (1977), flashbulb memories are highly detailed and accurate memories that are created during significant and unexpected events (for example the death of Princess Diana and the terrorist attacks of 9/11). They require two elements, a high level of surprise and a high level of emotional arousal, otherwise no flashbulb memory will be created. Although flashbulb memories are thought to be correct, it is often difficult to determine the accuracy of these retrospective accounts.

In the context of eyewitness testimony, research has often shown that higher levels of emotional arousal are associated with poorer accuracy. For example, Clifford and Scott (1978) showed participants videos of a violent or non-violent incident and found that the presence of violence (that is, an emotional element) significantly reduced the accuracy and completeness of accounts. However, this type of research has been criticized for not creating the high levels of emotional arousal and surprise that are necessary to create flashbulb memories. Furthermore, research using archival and field approaches to investigate the accuracy of eyewitness testimony in response to real crimes (Woolnough and MacLeod, 2001; Yuille and Cutshall, 1986) has demonstrated that memories for violent events can be highly accurate (see 'thinking scientifically' boxes for further details).

Thinking scientifically → **Watching the birdie watching you: Eyewitness memory for actions using CCTV recordings of actual crimes (Woolnough and MacLeod, 2001)**

The research examined the accuracy of information contained in police statements given by witnesses in response to eight real crimes. The research employed an archival approach.

Eight crimes of assault comprising 9 victims and 10 witnesses were used for the research. All cases included more than one witness statement and a CCTV recording of the crime in which all witnesses were clearly visible. Information obtained from the witness statements was coded according to whether it provided action, object, perpetrator or verbal details. Each coded detail was then compared to the information contained in the CCTV recordings.

Victims and witnesses were found to have very accurate memories for the details of the crimes (mostly action details), with both receiving an accuracy score of 96 per cent. While victims reported slightly more details than witnesses this difference was non-significant. There was no evidence to suggest that emotional arousal has a detrimental impact on memory. On the contrary, the number of action details reported by witnesses increased with the level of emotional arousal experienced. Furthermore, this increase did not reduce accuracy.

Evaluation

This research represents the first attempt to use CCTV footage to assess the accuracy of eyewitness memory. However, the ability to generalize these findings is limited by the use of a small number of cases. CCTV recordings also have a number of technical constraints that limit their use. For example, there are occasions when the crime moves out of shot, it is not possible to verify verbal details, and poor filming conditions may make it difficult to verify certain object and/or perpetrator details. As such, it is not clear whether the accurate memories of the victims and witnesses in the current research would extend to memories for other details or other types of crime.

The weapon focus effect refers to the attention witnesses give to a perpetrator's weapon during the commission of a crime (Kapardis, 2003). This attention is associated with a reduction in their ability to identify other aspects of the crime including the perpetrator. Loftus, Loftus and Messo (1987) conducted one of the first studies to examine this effect in which participants were presented with a series of slides depicting a queue of people in a restaurant. In one of the slides a person in the queue was either shown to hand the cashier a cheque (**control condition**) or shown to pull out a gun (weapon condition). In both instances, the cashier handed the person some money.

Participants were found to fixate on the object in the person's hand more and for a longer period of time in the weapon condition in comparison to the control condition (Loftus et al., 1987). They were also found to be less accurate in their descriptions of the person (56% vs. 67% accuracy) and in their identifications of him from a lineup (15% vs. 35%) in the weapon condition. In the context of real crimes, this effect may be accounted for by the presence of a weapon increasing already high levels of stress; however, it is unlikely that participants in this study found the series of slides particularly stressful. Consequently, Loftus et al. speculated whether the weapon focus effect could simply reflect a tendency to fixate on unusual objects.

Hope and Wright (2007) investigated this possibility using a similar methodology to Loftus et al.'s (1987). Participants were presented with a series of slides depicting a man entering a grocery store and withdrawing a wallet (control condition), a feather duster (unusual condition) or a gun (weapon condition). Although participants in the weapon condition were able to provide a more accurate and detailed description of the object (that is, the gun) than participants in the control condition, they were less accurate at describing other details of the events. For example, when asked to describe the appearance of the man, those in the weapon condition recalled details with 59 per cent accuracy, compared to 70 per cent accuracy in the unusual condition, and 80 per cent accuracy in the control condition. Participants in the weapon condition were also less confident in their descriptions of the man compared to participants in the control and unusual conditions. Consequently, the weapon focus effect cannot be fully explained by people's tendency to fixate on unusual objects.

Summary

A number of factors can influence the accuracy of eyewitness testimony. These include factors that are not under the control of the criminal justice system (for example various witness and event characteristics) as well as those that are under the control of the criminal justice system (for example police interview techniques and lineup procedures). Emotional arousal is one variable that has been found to increase the accuracy of memory during significant and unexpected events, and decrease the accuracy of memory when high levels of stress are accompanied by the presence of a weapon.

Descriptive evidence

The interviewing of witnesses provides the police with an opportunity to gather important information (that is, descriptive evidence) about an event that may help to solve a crime (Kapardis, 2003). However, research has demonstrated that it is possible to contaminate witnesses' memories during police interviews through the use of leading questions and/or the introduction of misleading information. A body of research by Elizabeth F. Loftus has been particularly influential in demonstrating that under certain circumstances it is possible to alter people's memories for events.

Loftus and Palmer (1974) conducted research in which participants watched a film of a car accident and then answered a series of questions about the accident. Participants were asked one of five versions of the following critical question 'About how fast were the cars going when they smashed into each other?' Other versions of the question replaced the word smashed with collided, bumped, hit or contacted. Estimates of speed were found to differ according to the wording of this critical question. For example, participants' average estimates of speed were 40.5mph when the word 'smashed' was used compared to 31.8mph when the word 'contacted' was used. Participants were also asked a separate series of questions the following week when the critical question was 'Did you see any broken glass?' Although there was no broken glass following the accident 16 per cent of participants who heard the word smashed answered yes compared to 7 per cent who heard the word hit.

In a later study Loftus (1975) demonstrated that it is also possible to introduce a non-existent object into memory. The study investigated the accuracy of verbal memory in response to leading questions and misinformation. Again, participants viewed a brief film of a car accident and then answered questions about the event. The critical question concerned a speeding white car. Half the participants were asked 'How fast was the white sports car going when it passed the barn while travelling along the country road?' (misinformation condition) and half were asked 'How fast was the white sports car going while travelling along the country road?' (control condition). Although there was no barn, 17 per cent answered yes to seeing a barn in the misinformation condition compared to 3 per cent in the control condition.

Loftus, Miller and Burns (1978) extended this research to examine the accuracy of visual memory under similar conditions. Participants were shown a series of slides depicting an accident between a car and a pedestrian in which a red Datsun approached a road intersection with either a stop sign or a yield sign. The car turned right and collided with a pedestrian who was crossing the road. Participants were then asked a series of questions including one of two versions of the critical question 'Did another car pass the red Datsun while it was stopped at the stop sign?' The other version of the question replaced 'stop sign' with 'yield sign'. The manipulation of the questions and slides meant that the critical question presented either consistent information (that is, stop-stop and yield-yield) or inconsistent information (that is, stop-yield and yield-stop) in relation to the slides that participants had seen. Participants were later shown two slides, one of which depicted the Datsun stopped at a stop sign while the other depicted a Datson stopped at a yield sign. Participants were then asked to select which of the pair they had seen before. Seventy-five per cent of participants were able to correctly identify the critical slide they had seen previously when they had received consistent information compared to 41 per cent when they had received inconsistent information.

Although these studies have been criticized for focusing on peripheral details of an event (that is, those that are not specific or central to the event itself), more recent research has demonstrated that it is possible to induce entirely false memories of an event (Loftus, 2003). For example, experimental manipulations have led participants to believe that they have been lost in a shopping centre for an extended period of time, have been rescued by a lifeguard and have survived a vicious animal attack. The use of fake photographs is one of the most effective methods of implanting these implausible memories. In a study conducted by Loftus, participants were shown fake photographs of a hot air balloon ride in which they and members of their family were present. Participants were then asked on three separate occasions to recall everything they could remember about the event irrespective of how trivial it seemed. The use of this procedure resulted in 50 per cent of participants in the study recalling partial or clear memories of the fictional balloon ride (Loftus, 2003).

Taken together, this body of research demonstrates that people can be influenced by leading questions and develop false memories for events that did not happen on the basis of misleading information (Loftus, 2003). However, only a proportion of participants were affected by the experimental manipulations in the studies described. It is therefore apparent that individual factors also play an important role in determining how susceptible people are to suggestion (otherwise all participants would have been equally affected).

Thinking scientifically → **A case study of eyewitness memory of a crime** (Yuille and Cutshall, 1986)

The research investigated the accuracy of witness accounts in response to a real violent crime. The research employed a field approach.

The crime involved a shooting in which one person was killed and another was seriously injured. Twenty-one witnesses were interviewed by the police at the time of the shooting and 13 agreed to be interviewed for this research four or five months later. Witnesses were initially asked to recall what happened in their own words. Follow-up questions were then used to clarify certain details and introduce two items of misleading information. One item of misleading information concerned a broken headlight and the other concerned a yellow panel on a nearby car (there was no broken headlight and the panel was blue).

Most witnesses were highly accurate in their accounts at the time of the crime (82% accuracy) and continued to be so four or five months later (81% accuracy). Furthermore, accounts were not influenced by inaccuracies in media reports of the crime or the introduction of misleading information during the interviews. The sustained accuracy of witness accounts was thought to be caused by the high levels of surprise and emotional arousal associated with the crime (that is, the creation of flashbulb memories).

Evaluation

This research was the first to use witnesses of a real crime to investigate the accuracy of eyewitness memory and the findings suggest that the largely negative view presented by previous research may be unwarranted. However, the ability to generalize from the findings is limited by the use of a single crime and a small number of witnesses. Furthermore, the ineffectiveness of the misleading information manipulation may have been caused by the timing of the interviews (four or five months later), as the effect of leading questions is greatest immediately after the witnessing of an event.

Although it is now widely accepted that the use of leading questions and/or the introduction of misleading information can alter people's memories for events, there is ongoing controversy regarding what happens to the original memories (Kapardis, 2003). There are currently a number of theories that attempt to explain this, including the alteration hypothesis, coexistence theory and source misattribution (Ainsworth, 1998):

- *Alteration hypothesis*. Argues that the original memory no longer exists because it has been altered or transformed into a new memory.
- *Coexistence theory*. Suggests that the original and the altered memories coexist and that both can potentially be recalled.
- *Source misattribution theory*. Argues that **source monitoring errors** lead to misleading information being incorrectly attributed to the original memory.

In terms of the practical implications of these theories, the alteration hypothesis suggests that there is little the police can do to counter the effects of any leading questions and/or misleading information that a witness has been exposed to before, or during, an interview (Ainsworth, 1998). The hypothesis implies that no amount of questioning or probing of a witness will assist in the recall of the original information because the original memory no longer exists. The coexistence and source misattribution theories, however, suggest that witnesses may still be able to access their original memories by reinstating the context of the event during the interview or focusing on the source of their memories.

Improving the accuracy of descriptive evidence

Given the importance of interviews with witnesses, it is essential that they are conducted in a manner that maximizes the amount of information and minimizes the risk of contamination (Kapardis, 2003). The **cognitive interview** was developed by Ronald P. Fisher and R. Edward Geiselman in order to reduce the use of leading questions or the introduction of misleading information during police interviews with witnesses (the use of the cognitive interview technique with suspects is discussed in Chapter 8). In contrast to many traditional forms of police interview, the cognitive interview is interviewee- rather than interviewer-led, and normally comprises the following five stages (Fisher and Schreiber, 2007):

1. *Introduction*. The interviewer develops a rapport with the witness while conveying the need for detailed and accurate information. It is important that the interviewer understands that some witnesses will find it difficult or embarrassing to provide certain information.
2. *Open-ended narration*. The interviewer asks the witness to provide his or her account of events. The interviewer should not interrupt the witness and any questions should be open-ended to encourage more expansive answers.
3. *Probing*. The interviewer asks the witness follow-up questions to make sure that he or she has provided an exhaustive account of events.
4. *Review*. The interviewer reviews the information provided by the witness to check that it is accurate. The witness is given the opportunity to correct errors or provide additional information.

5 *Close*. The interviewer collects any necessary details regarding the witness and ends the interview. The witness is given the opportunity to get in touch if he or she remembers anything else about the event.

The cognitive interview relies on four main techniques (Ainsworth, 1998):

- *Recreating the context*. This technique is based on the assumption that an individual's memory for an event is affected by the context that existed at the time of the event. Therefore, encouraging a witness to recreate the context of the event in their mind during the interview will aid their ability to recall information from their memory.
- *Focused attention*. This technique is based on the assumption that people have general and highly detailed memories. Therefore, telling a witness that all the information is stored and that they need to focus their attention when recalling information should improve their memory for details.
- *Multiple retrieval attempts*. This technique is based on the assumption that people's memory retrieval is like a search process. It is often beneficial therefore to ask a witness to recall the event again even if they are reluctant to do so. The use of this technique may lead to the recall of additional information, but it only works if the witness has the 'original memory' to access.
- *Varied retrieval*. This technique is based on the assumption that people naturally recall events in chronological order and from their own perspective. It is often beneficial therefore to ask a witness to recall the event from a different perspective or in reverse order. However, care is required to make sure that witnesses do not guess what another person would probably have seen.

A review of the literature suggests that the cognitive interview can produce more accurate information compared to traditional interviews without increasing the error rate (Geiselman, 1999). Furthermore, the cognitive interview is easy to implement, as it can be taught in a few hours, requires little theoretical knowledge and is easy to administer (Fisher, Geiselman, and Amador, 1989). With regard to limitations, its effectiveness is restricted to cooperative witnesses and there is some evidence to suggest that certain techniques (for example recall from a different perspective or in reverse order) can cause witnesses difficulty and confusion. The cognitive interview also takes longer to administer than traditional interviews, so the police may decide that the extra time is not warranted given the ever increasing demands placed on them (Ainsworth, 1998).

With these limitations in mind, Davis, McMahon and Greenwood (2005) developed a modified version of the cognitive interview in which additional recall attempts replace the use of varied retrieval techniques. This approach not only has the potential to overcome the difficulties associated with varied retrieval, but also to reduce the length of time the interview takes to administer. An evaluation of the effectiveness of the modified cognitive interview suggests that it is comparable to the original cognitive interview (that is, produces more accurate information than traditional interviews), while also taking less time to administer.

Child witnesses

The criminal justice system has long been sceptical about the ability of children to provide accurate eyewitness testimony. This scepticism is based on assertions that children's cognitive abilities are not well developed, that they are not always able to differentiate between truth and fantasy, and that they are highly suggestible (Ainsworth, 1998). Melnyk, Crossman and Scullin (2007) identified a number of procedures that can affect the suggestibility of child witnesses during police interviews:

- *Open-ended and direct questions*. Open-ended questions tend to lead to accurate but incomplete accounts, while direct questions increase the completeness but decrease the accuracy of children's accounts.
- *Repeated questions*. Repeated questions may cause children to change their answers because they believe that their first answer must have been incorrect.
- *Repeated interviewing*. Repeated interviewing may increase the accuracy of children's accounts if the interviewer remains neutral, but there is a risk that biases will inadvertently result in the use of leading questions.
- *Stereotypes*. Stereotypes (for example the description of a particular person as a 'bad man') introduced during the interview may be incorporated into children's accounts.

- *Nonverbal techniques*. Nonverbal techniques (for example the use of anatomically detailed dolls) may reduce the accuracy of children's accounts.
- *Atmosphere*. An 'accusatory atmosphere' (for example telling the child witness 'you'll feel better once you've told') may cause children to provide inaccurate accounts.

Overall, research shows that while certain interviewing procedures (such as those detailed above) can lead child witnesses to make false reports of physical or sexual abuse, it also shows that few child witnesses make false reports in response to one or two leading questions (Ceci and Bruck, 1995). Consequently, it is unlikely that the accidental use of a suggestive procedure by a neutral interviewer will affect the accuracy of children's accounts. Instead, the accuracy of child witnesses is most at risk when suggestive procedures are employed repeatedly or over a prolonged period of time by a biased interviewer.

Improving the accuracy of descriptive evidence

It is now accepted that children are capable of producing detailed and accurate information providing they are interviewed in an appropriate manner (Ainsworth, 1998). Melnyk et al. (2007) make the following recommendations in order to improve and maintain the quality of police interviews with child witnesses:

- *Structured interview*. The interviewer should use a structured interview for guidance.
- *Supportive atmosphere*. The interviewer should provide a supportive atmosphere for the child.
- *Purpose of interview*. The interviewer should make sure that the child fully understands the purpose of the interview.
- *Build rapport*. The interviewer should build rapport with the child to make the interview as relaxed and comfortable as possible.
- *Open-ended questions*. The interviewer should use open-ended questions to avoid influencing the child's account. Anatomically detailed dolls and other props may also be used.
- *Probing questions*. The interviewer should use open-ended probing questions when the child appears to have missed out crucial details.
- *Interview closure*. The interviewer should make sure that the child is in a positive frame of mind at the end of the interview.

The use of anatomically detailed dolls with child witnesses as a communicative or memory aid is a contentious issue. Although the use of anatomically detailed dolls can be effective with older children (that is, over five years of age), they are much less effective with younger children (Koocher et al., 1995). This comparative ineffectiveness is largely caused by younger children finding it difficult to understand that the dolls represent their own bodies (Melnyk et al., 2007). Overall, research comparing the amount of correct and incorrect information produced by the use of anatomically detailed dolls suggests that the gains outweigh the risks (Memon, Wark, Bull and Koehnken, 1997). However, external confirmation of reported details should be obtained whenever possible.

Summary

Although police interviews provide an opportunity to gather important information, the accuracy of this information may be contaminated by the use of leading questions and/or the introduction of misleading information. It is essential therefore that police interviews are conducted in a manner that maximizes the amount of information and minimizes this risk of contamination. Children are considered to be particularly suggestible, but it is now accepted that they can offer accurate information providing the interviews are conducted appropriately.

Identification evidence

The identification of a suspect from a lineup (that is, identification evidence) is critical in establishing whether or not a suspect is the perpetrator of a crime (Thomson, 1995b). However, the criminal justice system now acknowledges that mistaken identifications occur and that they are more likely when lineup procedures are suggestive and/or unfair (Cutler and Penrod, 1995). Suggestive procedures increase the likelihood of eyewitnesses making an identification regardless of whether they truly believe the perpetrator is present or not, while unfair procedures increase the likelihood of eyewitnesses identifying the suspect rather than other members of the lineup (that is, **foils**).

Identification procedures vary from country to country but typically involve eyewitnesses viewing a lineup containing the suspect and a number of foils, and deciding whether or not the perpetrator of the crime is in the lineup (Dupuis and Lindsay, 2007). Although eyewitnesses should only make an identification if they are certain that a member of the lineup is the perpetrator, they may feel pressured to make an identification even if they are uncertain (Cutler and Penrod, 1995). For example, being asked to attend a lineup suggests that the police have located the perpetrator of the crime. Therefore, eyewitnesses may feel pressure to make an identification, as they will be letting the police down if they are unable to identify the perpetrator from the lineup. Cutler and Penrod outline a further five factors that may result in suggestive and unfair lineup procedures:

- *Lineup instruction bias* occurs when instructions lead eyewitnesses to assume that the perpetrator is in the lineup.
- *Foil bias* occurs when the suspect 'stands out' from the lineup because there are an insufficient number of foils and/or they do not match the witness's description of the perpetrator.
- *Clothing bias* occurs when the suspect is wearing clothing that is the same or similar to that worn by the perpetrator during the crime.
- *Presentation bias* occurs when all members of the lineup are presented simultaneously.
- *Investigator bias* occurs when the police officer conducting the identification procedure unintentionally (or intentionally) lets the eyewitness know which member of the lineup is the suspect.

Instruction and presentation biases involve the use of suggestive procedures and increase the likelihood of eyewitnesses making an identification (Cutler and Penrod, 1995). In contrast, foil, clothing and investigator biases involve the use of unfair procedures and increase the likelihood of the eyewitness identifying the suspect.

An extreme example of foil bias occurred in Minneapolis where a black murder suspect was placed in a lineup with five white men (Ellison and Buckhout, 1981). The police justified the use of this procedure on the grounds that they wanted the lineup to be representative of the predominantly white town's population. They also used the excuse that there were no other black people in the building.

With regard to presentation bias, simultaneous lineups are thought to increase the use of relative rather than absolute judgement (Wells, 1984). Relative judgement occurs when eyewitnesses consider which member of the lineup looks most similar to the perpetrator of the crime in relation to the other foils present in the lineup. Thomson (1995b) likened this process to a multiple-choice exam whereby the eyewitness discounts each member of the lineup until only one member remains. This member is then identified as the perpetrator even though the eyewitness may not be certain of their identification. Absolute judgement on the other hand, refers to a process whereby the eyewitness compares each foil to their own memory of the perpetrator.

Although research has consistently demonstrated that suggestive and/or unfair lineup procedures increase the risk of false identifications, critics have argued that the use of experimental designs has limited the **ecological validity** of many studies. Criticisms often focus on the use of low-impact situations and the fact that there are no repercussions associated with any false identifications (Wells, 1993). However, studies using more realistic field approaches have not contradicted the findings of research using experimental designs. Furthermore, post-trial DNA testing has demonstrated that people have been wrongly convicted on the basis of mistaken identifications (see the 'thinking scientifically' box for further details) (Connors, Lundregan, Miller and McEwen, 1996). Currently, more than 200 convictions have been overturned in the US on the basis of DNA testing, three-quarters of which involved inaccurate eyewitness testimony (Spinney, 2008).

Thinking scientifically → **Convicted by juries, exonerated by science: Case studies in the use of DNA evidence to establish innocence after trial (Connors et al., 1996)**

The research identified and reviewed cases in the US in which convicted defendants had been released from prison as a consequence of post-trial DNA testing.

Cases were identified via a combination of legal and newspaper databases, and interviews with legal and DNA experts. Twenty-eight cases were identified in which a defendant had been convicted of a crime or series of crimes and had arranged to have their DNA compared to DNA evidence from the case. DNA evidence from the cases included blood or blood related evidence left by the perpetrator and found on the victim's body, as well as traces of semen found on the victim's clothing or nearby items.

All cases involved some form of sexual assault and six involved murder. The 28 defendants had served a total of 197 years in prison before being released. The length of time served in prison by the defendants ranged from 9 months to 11 years. In the majority of cases eyewitness testimony was the most compelling form of evidence presented at trial. All the cases (except for the murder cases) involved identifications of the defendant by the victim before and during the trial. Many cases also involved identifications of the defendant by other witnesses who placed the defendant with the victim or nearby. In one case, five witnesses wrongfully identified the defendant. Many defendants had alibis that were corroborated by family and friends, but these were insufficient to counter the strength of the eyewitness evidence.

Improving the accuracy of identification evidence

Research has shown that certain lineup procedures are likely to increase the risk of mistaken identifications (Wells et al., 1998). Consequently, the American Psychology-Law Society appointed a subcommittee chaired by Gary L. Wells to develop a set of good-practice guidelines for the improvement of lineup procedures. The subcommittee produced the following 'four simple rules' to prevent lineup procedures from being suggestive and/or unfair (Wells et al., 1998):

- *Who conducts the lineup*. The person conducting the lineup should not know which member of the lineup is the suspect. Otherwise the person conducting the identification procedure may behave in a manner that draws attention to the suspect.
- *Instructions on viewing*. Eyewitnesses should be told that the perpetrator may or may not be present in the lineup and that they should not feel pressure to make an identification. Eyewitnesses should also be told that the person conducting the identification procedure does not know which member of the lineup is the suspect. Otherwise eyewitnesses are more likely to make an identification and/or look to the person conducting the lineup for help in selecting the 'right person'.
- *Structure of the lineup*. The suspect should not stand out from the lineup on the basis of eyewitnesses' descriptions of the perpetrator or any other aspect that draws attention to the suspect. Otherwise there is a risk that the suspect will appear more similar to the perpetrator in comparison to the foils. Exceptions include instances when the suspect's appearance is dramatically different from eyewitnesses' descriptions or the suspect has some unique feature that the eyewitnesses did not mention.

- *Obtaining confidence statements*. Eyewitnesses should be asked to provide confidence statements regarding their identifications prior to any feedback on whether or not they identified the suspect. Otherwise it is not possible to determine whether eyewitnesses' confidence statements obtained during the trial reflect the 'goodness of memory' or events that occurred after the identification.

According to Wells et al. (1998), the different guidelines can be implemented independently of one another and still be effective at reducing the risk of mistaken identifications. Consequently, the improvement of lineup procedures is not dependent on the implementation of all four rules (although the more rules that are implemented the better).

Confidence, time and memory

Jurors generally believe that confidence statements can be used to assess the accuracy of identification evidence despite widespread agreement that the confidence–accuracy relationship is weak at best (Leippe and Eisenstadt, 2007). In a **meta-analysis** of 30 studies, Sporer, Penrod, Read and Cutler (1995) found that confidence ratings were reliably higher for accurate identifications than false identifications, but Leippe and Eisenstadt (2007) pointed out that the weak nature of this relationship means that the finding is of limited practical use.

Other research has shown that there is a negative relationship between the time eyewitnesses take to identify a suspect and the accuracy of the identification. For example, Dunning and Perretta (2002) found that 90 per cent of identifications made within 10 to 12 seconds of viewing the lineup were accurate compared to 50 per cent of identifications that took longer. However, Weber et al. (2004) found that this time–accuracy relationship varied when identifications were repeated with the same (or different) lineup procedures, and when eyewitnesses of different ages made identifications. Furthermore, the proportion of accurate identifications was still small irrespective of the time it took eyewitnesses to identify a member of the lineup.

Blank and sequential lineups

Two additional procedural variations that may reduce the risk of mistaken identifications are the use of blank and sequential lineups. Blank lineups screen out eyewitnesses who are most susceptible to making relative judgements through the initial presentation of a lineup in which the suspect is absent (Lindsay and Wells, 1985). Research has shown that eyewitnesses who make an identification from the blank lineup are more likely to make false identifications in the subsequent lineup irrespective of whether the perpetrator is present or absent (Wells, 1984). Although blank lineups appear to provide an effective screening tool, they are more expensive and require more foils than traditional lineups. They are also reliant on eyewitnesses remaining ignorant to the fact that the first lineup is 'blank' (Lindsay and Wells, 1985).

Sequential lineups are those in which foils are presented one at a time. According to Lindsay and Wells (1985), they reduce the risk of mistaken identifications providing they adhere to the following guidelines:

- The person conducting the identification procedure does not know which member of the lineup is the suspect.
- Eyewitnesses do not know how many members are going to be presented during the lineup.
- Members of the lineup are presented individually and once only.
- Eyewitnesses are required to make clear decisions regarding each member of the lineup as they are presented and these decisions cannot be changed afterwards.

The underlying logic of these guidelines is that eyewitnesses are unable to compare the different members of the lineup to one another (that is, make a relative judgement) and therefore are forced to compare each member of the lineup to their memory of the perpetrator (that is, make an absolute judgement) (Dupuis and Lindsay, 2007).

A meta-analysis of 23 studies clearly indicated that sequential lineups are superior to simultaneous lineups (Steblay, Dysart, Fulero and Lindsay, 2001). The overall pattern of findings revealed that simultaneous lineups increase the number of accurate identifications when the perpetrator is present compared to sequential lineups, but also increase the number of false identifications when the perpetrator is absent. Furthermore, the difference in the number of accurate identifications was found to decrease when the two lineup procedures were compared under real world conditions while the difference in false identifications was maintained.

In comparison to blank lineups, sequential lineups are beneficial because they are relatively inexpensive to run, they do not require more foils, and they are not reliant on eyewitnesses being ignorant as to the procedure used (Cutler and Penrod, 1988). However, the effectiveness of sequential lineups in real police investigations has been limited by the use of modified versions of the procedure. As Lindsay and Bellinger (1999) pointed out, sequential lineups are very sensitive and any changes are likely to seriously reduce their superiority over simultaneous lineups. Modified versions of sequential lineups used by the police include allowing the person conducting the identification procedure to know which member of the lineup is the suspect, allowing eyewitnesses to know how many members are going to be presented during the lineup, and allowing eyewitnesses to make their decision after all members of the lineup have been presented (Dupuis and Lindsay, 2007; Lindsay and Bellinger, 1999).

Face recognition

It is important to acknowledge that face recognition is often taken for granted, but represents a cognitively demanding process that can influence the accuracy of identification evidence. As Ainsworth (1998) pointed out, the recognition of a face involves three stages:

1. Is the face familiar?
2. How is the face familiar?
3. What is the name of the person?

Mistakes can occur at any stage and may involve a person failing to recognize a familiar face or conversely incorrectly recognizing an unfamiliar face as familiar. Mistakes may also involve a person recognizing a familiar face but not knowing how or where they know the person from, or recognizing a familiar face but not being able to recall the person's name (Ainsworth, 1998).

Mistakes are more likely to occur the less familiar the face is because of a lack of mental images of the face that are stored in memory for subsequent comparisons (Bruce, Burton and Hancock, 2007). For example, the recognition of a familiar face is facilitated by the accumulation of numerous different images from a variety of angles. In contrast, the recognition of a less familiar face may be reliant on a limited number of images from one or two angles. Consequently, the recognition of unfamiliar faces is more likely to be influenced by various estimator and system variables, including viewing angle, lighting, exposure time and the introduction of misleading information (Ainsworth, 1998).

Composite faces

Victims and witnesses of crimes are often asked to provide detailed descriptions of the unknown perpetrator (Ainsworth, 1998). Composite faces provide impressions of the facial appearance of the perpetrator on the basis of these descriptions. Although they do not usually allow for the identification of the perpetrator, they help the police to reduce the number of potential suspects according to whether their general appearance is consistent with the facial composite (Ainsworth, 1998). Consequently, only a small proportion of composite faces are released to the media (about 10 per cent in the UK) and the majority are used internally to guide police investigations (Davies and Valentine, 2007).

Although police sketch artists would traditionally create an impression of the perpetrator, a number of techniques have been developed to help with the production of facial composites (Ainsworth, 1998; Davies and Valentine, 2007):

- *Identikit system.* The identikit system was introduced in the UK in 1959 and used drawings of different facial features (for example separate drawings of the eye region and the nose region) to create a facial composite.
- *Photofit system.* The photofit system was introduced in the UK in 1970 and replaced the drawings of the identikit system with photographs of different facial features. It was argued that the use of photographs would enhance the realism of the facial composites.
- *Software systems.* Various software systems (for example E-Fit and Identikit III) have since been introduced to further enhance the realism of the facial composites. They enable greater control over the manipulation and configuration of facial features, and enable the blending of these features to create a 'complete' face.

Despite the development of these techniques, they all ultimately rely on the accuracy of the descriptions provided by victims and witnesses, and none has been found to equal or outperform the impressions created by police sketch artists (Davies and Valentine, 2007).

Morphing composite faces

Composite faces of unknown perpetrators often provide a poor likeness of the actual perpetrator when they are based on the descriptions of individual victims or witnesses (Hasel and Wells, 2007). However, there is the opportunity to morph several facial composites in situations where there are multiple victims and/or witnesses. Research suggests that morphed composites produce a better likeness of the perpetrator compared to the use of individual facial composites (Bruce et al., 2002). Furthermore, while it is recognized that some facial composites are better than others, morphed composites have been found to be comparable to highly accurate individual facial composites.

Morphed composites are thought to provide a better likeness of the perpetrator because more weight is placed on accurate over inaccurate details (assuming that inaccurate details vary across victim and witness descriptions) (Bruce et al., 2002). Thus, the morphing of several facial composites in situations where there is more than one victim or witness offers a potentially useful approach that is relatively simple and inexpensive to implement (Hasel and Wells, 2007). Nevertheless, it is important to acknowledge that some of the benefits of morphed composites are illusory. The morphing of several facial composites produces a 'prototype effect' in which the facial features become more generic and therefore less distinctive to the perpetrator.

Summary

Police lineups are often critical in establishing whether or not a suspect is the perpetrator of a crime, but research and post-trial DNA testing have demonstrated that mistaken identifications do occur. It is essential therefore that lineup procedures are conducted in a non-suggestive and fair manner. Although sequential lineups have been shown to reduce the risk of mistaken identifications, the police often use modified versions of the procedure that reduce its effectiveness. While a number of techniques have been developed to help with the production of facial composites, they all rely on the accuracy of the descriptions provided by victims and witnesses and none has equalled or outperformed the impressions provided by police sketch artists.

False and recovered memories

The 1990s saw a dramatic increase in the number of allegations of childhood sexual abuse (and other forms of abuse) that were not reported until adulthood (Kapardis, 2003; Thomson, 1995a). Some of these previously unreported allegations represent the recovery of previously inaccessible memories (that is, recovered memories), while others represent unconscious or conscious fabrications (that is, false memories). Explanations for recovered and false memories include (Thomson, 1995a):

- *Repression*. A psychodynamic concept that refers to the 'removal' of memories for painful events from consciousness to prevent a person from becoming overwhelmed by pain and fear.
- *Suppression*. In contrast to repression the person is always conscious of the painful events. They have just decided not to report them for some reason.
- *Normal forgetting*. Over time a person may genuinely forget past events. The likelihood of a person forgetting an event increases the longer the period of time between the event and the attempted recall.
- *Unconscious fabrication*. A person may confuse separate or fabricated events with memories for genuine events.
- *Conscious fabrication*. A person may purposefully fabricate events that never occurred.

Thomson (1995a) argued that forgetting and unconscious fabrication are the two most likely causes of recovered and false memories.

Although there is no doubt that many children are abused and that this is a tragedy, it is often not possible to determine whether an allegation represents a recovered or a false memory without further information (Lindsay and Read, 1994; Thomson, 1995a). Consequently, the false memory debate centres on whether the extensive use of **memory recovery techniques** increases the risk of fabricated allegations of childhood abuse among people who were not abused (Lindsay and Read, 1994).

According to Lindsay and Read (1994) there is a general agreement that some adults do not remember experiences of childhood abuse and that it is possible to recover these memories during careful non-leading, non-suggestive therapy. However, there is also considerable evidence from psychological research on the reconstructive nature of memory that suggests that the extensive use of memory recovery techniques can lead to **false memory syndrome**. Examples of memory recovery techniques frequently employed with clients during therapy include the following (Lindsay and Read, 1994):

- *Hypnosis*. Although hypnosis can increase the amount of information clients report about past events, there is evidence to suggest that this increase is greater for inaccurate details than for accurate details.
- *Guided imagery*. Involves clients closing their eyes, relaxing and letting their imaginations 'play out' scenarios suggested to them by therapists. It does not induce a hypnotic state, but may still increase the reporting of inaccurate details.
- *Journalling*. Involves clients attempting to recover memories by repeatedly writing them down and reading them aloud. Evidence suggests that this is a dangerous exercise that may result in inaccurate recall.
- *Dream interpretation*. There is no evidence to support the view that clients' dreams can be reliably interpreted as accurate recall of information from memory. There is a distinct danger that therapists' personal biases may influence their interpretations of clients' dreams.

Overall, the risk of false memories is much lower when therapists approach treatment in an open-minded unbiased manner without the use of memory recovery techniques (Lindsay and Read, 1994). Consequently, issues associated with childhood abuse should be treated as one of a number of potential factors that can be explored during therapy. Furthermore, Lindsay and Read argued that therapists should be aware of the harmful effects of exploring memories for childhood abuse, irrespective of whether the allegations represent recovered or false memories.

Summary

There has been a dramatic increase in the number of allegations of childhood sexual abuse that was not reported until adulthood. Some represent the recovery of previously inaccessible memories (that is, recovered memories) and others represent fabrications (that is, false memories). Forgetting is the most likely cause of recovered memories while unconscious fabrication is the most likely cause of false memories. It has been argued that the extensive use of memory recovery techniques can lead to false memories so it is important that therapists approach treatment in an open-minded unbiased manner.

Further reading

Ainsworth, P.B. (1998) *Psychology, Law and Eyewitness Testimony*. Chichester: John Wiley & Sons.

Lindsay, R.C.L., Ross, D.F., Read, J.D. and Toglia, M.P. (eds) (2007) *The Handbook of Eyewitness Psychology: Volume II Memory for People*. London: Lawrence Erlbaum Associates.

Memon, A., Vrij, A. and Bull, R. (2003) *Psychology and Law: Truthfulness, Accuracy and Credibility* (2nd edn). Chichester: John Wiley & Sons.

Toglia, M.P., Read, J.D., Ross, D.F. and Lindsay, R.C.L. (eds) (2007) *The Handbook of Eyewitness Psychology: Volume I Memory for Events*. London: Lawrence Erlbaum Associates.

Chapter 8

Investigative interviewing

Introduction

Interviewing practices in the UK and many countries around the world have changed dramatically over the last few decades in response to a number of highly publicized **miscarriages of justice** that were primarily caused by the use of trickery and deception during police interviews (Shawyer, Milne and Bull, 2009). The principles of investigative interviewing were introduced during the 1990s in a bid to change the police culture from seeking a confession to the search for accurate information (Bull and Milne, 2004).

This chapter will consider recent advances in the investigative interviewing of suspects to determine how the use of effective interviewing techniques might help in the prevention of further miscarriages of justice (issues concerning the interviewing of witnesses were included in Chapter 7). It will first outline some of the causes of **false confessions** before considering the US approach to interviewing and interrogation. Efforts to improve police interviewing methods in the UK will then be discussed along with recent developments in detecting deception (that is, lies).

This chapter will examine:
- Confessions and false confessions
- Interviewing and interrogation in the US
- Interviewing in the UK
- Detecting deception

Confessions and false confessions

A confession in which a suspect admits guilt for a crime is one of the strongest forms of evidence that can be presented in a trial, drastically increasing the chance that a suspect will be formally charged and convicted (Kapardis, 2003). However, the reliability of confession evidence is undermined by the occurrence of false confessions in which an innocent suspect admits guilt for a crime that he or she did not commit.

Between 49 and 61 per cent of suspects confess in England and Wales, compared to between 50 and 65 per cent of suspects in the US (Memon, Vrij and Bull, 2003). The proportion of confessions that are false is unknown because it is impossible to determine the proportion (that is, the base rate) of suspects who are genuinely guilty of the crimes with which they are accused. As such, the risk of false confessions is low if the proportion of guilty suspects is high and the risk is high if the proportion of guilty suspects is low (Gudjonsson, 2003). While it is not possible to accurately estimate the occurrence of false confessions, anecdotal evidence and publicized miscarriages of justice show that they do occur. Gudjonsson identified that of 22 landmark British Court of Appeal cases, the majority involved disputed confession evidence. Furthermore, Innocence Projects in the US that investigate claims of wrongful conviction have documented over 300 wrongful convictions involving false confessions (Davis and Leo, 2006).

Causes of false confessions

There are a number of factors that contribute to a false confession, including the use of trickery and deception by the police during the interviewing of suspects (Kassin, 1997). Other factors associated with false confessions include the age and intellectual functioning of the suspect, the length and intensity of the interview, and the use of threats and/or promises during the interview (Buckley, 2006). Particular caution is necessary when interviewing young or intellectually impaired suspects.

Kassin and Wrightsman (1985) propose three psychologically distinct types of false confession:

- **Voluntary false confessions** are provided by innocent suspects in the absence of any external pressure from the police.

- **Coerced-compliant false confessions** occur when innocent suspects know that their confessions are untrue, but confess in order to avoid the aversive conditions of the interview or gain a more favourable outcome.
- **Coerced-internalized false confessions** are given when innocent suspects come to believe that they committed the crime they are accused of despite having no memory of it.

Voluntary false confessions are thought to occur for a variety of reasons, including the inability to separate reality from fantasy, the unconscious need for self-punishment, and the morbid desire for notoriety. For example, over 200 people provided false confessions for the Lindbergh kidnapping in which a toddler was abducted and murdered close to the family home in the US (Gudjonsson, 2003). The protection of a friend or family member and the concealment of some other non-criminal activities (for example a love affair) have also been raised as possible causes of voluntary false confessions. However, these causes are more likely to occur in the context of minor crimes. The details of the crime that are provided by the individual when giving a false confession of this type are usually derived from information presented in the media (for example newspapers and television).

Coerced-compliant false confessions result from the use of manipulative and suggestive methods of interviewing. Two factors work together in facilitating this type of confession: (1) compliance to authority and (2) persuasion. Suspects give in to the demands and pressures placed on them by the interviewer in order to escape from the intolerable interview or to gain a more favourable outcome (for example a shorter sentence). In these circumstances, suspects perceive the guaranteed immediate gains of providing a confession (that is, the end of the interview) to outweigh the uncertain long-term consequences of maintaining their innocence (that is, a criminal conviction). Suspects who provide false confessions of this type may believe that the truth will become known at a later stage of the investigation (Gudjonsson, 2003).

Coerced-internalized false confessions are also thought to result from the use of manipulative and suggestive methods of interviewing. However, with this type of false confession suspects actually begin to question their own memories and believe in their own guilt. Gudjonsson (2003) distinguishes between two situations: (1) where the suspect has no memory of what he or she was doing at the time of the crime and comes to believe they must have committed the act, and (2) where the suspect has a clear recollection of not committing the crime, but gradually comes to doubt his or her own memory. The process by which a suspect comes to distrust his or her own memory, relying instead on external sources for information, is known as **memory distrust syndrome**, and can be likened to false memory syndrome which was discussed in Chapter 7 (Milne and Bull, 1999).

Vulnerable suspects, such as those with impaired intellectual or physical functioning, are particularly susceptible to the use of manipulative interviewing methods. Research utilizing the Gudjonsson Suggestibility Scales and the Gudjonsson Compliance Scales has demonstrated that some suspects are more suggestible or compliant than others. Suggestible suspects are at a higher risk of accepting and internalizing accusations of guilt, while compliant suspects are at a higher risk of agreeing with, but not internalizing, accusations of guilt for some immediate gain (Gudjonsson, 2003). Although the scales are useful tools, they are unable to provide an indication of whether the level of suggestibility or compliance is likely to result in a false confession (Trowbridge, 2003).

Thinking scientifically → **The Birmingham Six**

The case of the Birmingham Six has been described as one of the worst miscarriages of justice in recent UK history. The case dates back to 1975 when six men were convicted and sentenced to life imprisonment for the IRA bombings of two public houses in Birmingham, which killed 21 people. The evidence against the six men consisted of forensic evidence, written confessions from four of the men, and circumstantial evidence about their associations with known members of the IRA (Gudjonsson and MacKeith, 2003).

During the 1980s, it transpired that the forensic evidence that two of the men had traces of nitroglycerine on their hands (a substance associated with the handling of explosives) could have originated from contact with playing cards. Five of the men had been playing cards shortly before they were arrested. It was also alleged that the written confessions were provided involuntarily due to coercion during the interrogations, and that the police had fabricated additional evidence against the six men (Gudjonsson and MacKeith, 2003). It was not until 1991 that the Court of Appeal finally quashed the men's convictions and they were released from prison.

So why did four of the six men provide false confessions? In 1987 Gudjonsson and MacKeith (2003) were given the opportunity to administer the Gudjonsson Suggestibility Scales and the Gudjonsson Compliance Scales to the six men. The most striking finding was that the scores reflected whether false confessions were provided, with the two men who did not provide written confessions receiving the lowest scores on the suggestibility and compliance scales. It is therefore probable that the personality characteristics of the six men influenced how they responded to the police interrogations. However, the men's scores on the suggestibility and compliance scales were measured many years after the interrogation and it is impossible to determine whether the men's scores were the same prior to being interrogated by the police. It is possible therefore that the process of being interrogated and/or the time spent in prison influenced the men's levels of suggestibility and compliance, which were then reflected in their subsequent personality scores (Gudjonsson and MacKeith, 2003).

Although the classification of false confessions into three psychologically distinct types has been central in developing an understanding of the nature of false confessions, some have argued that the classification is overly simplistic. For example, compliant and internalized false confessions are not necessarily coerced by police officers, and may occur because of the uncertainty and anxiety associated with the interview process (Gudjonsson, 2003). Also, a false confession made by a suspect who is unable to separate reality from fantasy is very different from a false confession made by a suspect who is protecting a friend or family member (Davison and Forshaw, 1993). Several authors have developed similar or modified typologies in an attempt to address these limitations. For example, Ofshe and Leo (1997) describe five types of false confession that distinguish between stress-compliant and coerced-compliant false confessions, and between non-coerced-persuaded and coerced-persuaded false confessions. The term 'persuaded' is used instead of 'internalized' to reflect the reality that suspects are only temporarily persuaded that they are guilty of a crime.

Summary

False confessions occur when an innocent suspect admits guilt for a crime he or she did not commit. The three main types of false confession are voluntary, coerced-compliant and coerced-internalized. A major cause of coerced-compliant and coerced-internalized false confessions is the police's use of trickery and deception during the interviewing of suspects, particularly vulnerable suspects such as those with impaired intellectual or physical functioning.

Interviewing and interrogation in the US

Police officers in the US are permitted and encouraged to use trickery and deception during interviews with suspects in order to obtain a confession (Sear and Williamson, 1999). However, this approach is problematic because it does not discriminate between innocent and guilty suspects when seeking a confession. As such, the use of trickery and deception is likely to increase the number of confessions irrespective of whether the suspect is innocent or guilty (Gudjonsson, 2003).

The most influential training manual in the US is that of Inbau, Reid and Buckley (1986), entitled *Criminal Interrogation and Confessions*, in which a distinction is made between the 'interview' and the 'interrogation'. The interview is a non-accusatory information-gathering process whereby the police officer attempts to assess the suspect's innocence or guilt. The interrogation, by comparison, is a confrontational, accusatory process and is only conducted when a police officer has 'reasonable' grounds to believe the suspect is guilty.

The nine-step procedure

The interrogation employs a nine-step procedure, often referred to as the Reid technique, which uses maximization and minimization techniques to break down a reluctant suspect's resistance and increase the likelihood of a confession (Kassin, 1997). Maximization techniques may include the use of false or exaggerated claims about the crime and/or available evidence while minimization techniques include the underplaying of the seriousness of the crime. Police officers trained in the nine-step procedure are taught to account for the suspect's emotional state and to modify their interrogation style according to whether he or she is emotional or non-emotional (Inbau et al., 1986). A sympathetic approach and minimization techniques are recommended for emotional suspects because they feel guilt and remorse for the crime; while a factual approach and maximization techniques are considered to be more appropriate for non-emotional suspects because they do not experience feelings of guilt or remorse. Although ordered, it is not always necessary to use all nine steps or to use them in the order described. The nine steps are (Inbau et al., 1986):

1. *Direct, positive confrontation*. A suspect is presented with a statement that he or she is presumed to have committed the crime. The interrogator then monitors the suspect's verbal and nonverbal reactions before repeating the accusation.
2. *Theme development*. Step 2 varies according to whether the interrogator judges the suspect to be emotional or non-emotional. An emotional suspect is presented with moral excuses that allow him or her to accept responsibility for the crime while relieving the emotional guilt. A non-emotional suspect is persuaded that it is futile to resist telling the truth because there is already sufficient evidence to establish his or her guilt.
3. *Handling denials*. If a suspect attempts to make subsequent denials of guilt, the interrogator stops him or her from doing so. The interrogator then returns to the theme development of Step 2.
4. *Overcoming objections*. If a suspect changes tact and tries to explain why the accusation is false, the interrogator allows him or her to do so. The interrogator then offers an expression of understanding before overcoming the objection by incorporating it into the developing theme.
5. *Procurement and retention of suspect's attention*. If a suspect becomes preoccupied, the interrogator gains his or her attention by moving closer and maintaining eye contact.
6. *Handling suspect's passive mood*. When a suspect is preoccupied, the interrogator offers possible motives for the crime while maintaining a sympathetic and understanding persona.
7. *Presenting an alternative question*. When a suspect stops objecting to the accusation, the interrogator presents an alternative question in which the suspect is given a choice between two explanations for the crime. One presents an inexcusable motivation while the other presents a more acceptable motivation. If the suspect does not respond, the interrogator makes a supporting statement that reinforces the belief that the more acceptable motivation is the correct choice.
8. *Having suspect orally relate various details of the offence*. When a suspect accepts one of the two explanations offered in the

alternative question, he or she has made an initial admission of guilt. The interrogator then develops the admission into a legally acceptable confession that describes the details of the crime.

9 *Converting an oral confession into a written confession*. Once a suspect has confessed, the interrogator puts the confession in writing which is given to the suspect to sign as soon as possible. Otherwise the suspect may reflect on the legal consequences of his or her confession and withdraw it.

According to the nine-step procedure, certain verbal and nonverbal responses are indicative of deception (Inbau et al., 1986). For example, it is believed that an innocent suspect will express immediate denial when presented with a statement that he or she is presumed to have committed the crime, while a guilty suspect is more likely to ask questions about the accusation. It is also assumed that a guilty suspect is more likely to change tack from denial to objection, and to make multiple objections, than an innocent suspect.

Collectively, theoretical models suggest that guilty suspects are more likely to confess to crimes that they committed when (1) the perceived evidence against them is strong, (2) they need to relieve feelings of guilt, (3) they have difficulties dealing with custodial pressure, and/or (4) they focus on the immediate consequences of their actions (Gudjonsson, 2006). Unfortunately, there are occasions when the police make judgements in the absence of evidence and innocent suspects are targeted for interrogation on the basis of a hunch (Buckley, 2006). These situations are particularly worrying given that there are a number of inherent dangers in the use of the nine-step procedure with innocent suspects. The dangers include the presumption of guilt, the presentation of false evidence, and reliance on nonverbal behaviour as indicators of deception (Gudjonsson, 2007; Kassin, 2006).

Research has shown that the presumption of guilt engages a strong **confirmation bias** in which interrogators look for behaviour and information that supports their beliefs of guilt, even with innocent suspects (Davis and Leo, 2006; Kassin, Goldstein and Savitsky, 2003). For example, Vrij, Mann, Kristen and Fisher (2007) found that accusatory styles of interviewing, based on presumptions of guilt, resulted in a greater number of truth tellers being falsely accused of lying than when non-presumptive information-gathering approaches were used.

Thinking scientifically → **Behavioral confirmation in the interrogation room: On the dangers of presuming guilt (Kassin et al., 2003)**

The research examined whether presumptions of innocence and guilt influence the behaviour of interrogators and suspects. The research used a 2 × 2 (interrogator expectation × suspect status) experimental design. There was an even number of participants in each experimental condition.

One-hundred and four students acted as interrogators or suspects. Interrogators were given information either that 80 per cent of suspects were guilty (guilty expectation) or that 20 per cent of suspects were guilty (innocent expectation). Suspects were either guilty of a crime (having been instructed to steal $100 from a locker) or not guilty of a crime (having participated in a related but innocent task). Seventy-eight psychology students also acted as neutral observers by listening to recordings of the interrogators only, the suspects only, or both the interrogators and the suspects. Interrogators were first asked to secure a confession and then to make an accurate determination of innocence or guilt. Observers judged whether the interrogators had guilty or innocent expectations, and whether these expectations influenced their behaviour and/or the behaviour of the suspect.

Interrogators with guilty expectations were more likely to judge suspects to be guilty compared to interrogators with innocent expectations. They also asked more guilt presumptive questions, used more interrogation techniques (including the presentation of false evidence and promises of leniency), and exerted more pressure on the suspect to confess. The actual guilt or innocence of suspects had a contradictory effect in which interrogators placed the greatest pressure on innocent suspects. Observers were able to differentiate between interrogators with guilty as opposed to innocent expectations on the basis of their behaviour. It was also noted that suspects were more defensive when interrogators had guilty expectations. Thus, expectations of guilt resulted in a confirmation bias whereby interrogators applied more pressure, suspects became more defensive, and guilty judgements were more likely.

Evaluation

The real-life applicability (that is, the ecological validity) of this research may be questioned on the grounds that the participants were all students and were fully aware that the crime was simulated. Also, the incentives for interrogators to be thorough and for suspects to be convincing were small in comparison to genuine criminal investigations.

Studies using Kassin and Kiechel's (1996) computer paradigm have also demonstrated that some people are willing to falsely confess to crashing a computer, and internalize responsibility for the act, when presented with false incriminating evidence (Blair, 2007; Forrest, Wadkins and Larson, 2006). Finally, despite popular beliefs, psychological research has failed to support the claim that nonverbal behaviour can be used to accurately detect deception and many studies have shown that people are poor at distinguishing between truthful and deceptive behaviour regardless of their profession and 'expertise' (Davis and Leo, 2006; Kassin et al., 2007; Kassin and Gudjonsson, 2004).

Thinking scientifically → **The social psychology of false confessions: Compliance, internalization, and confabulation (Kassin and Kiechel, 1996)**

The research investigated whether the presentation of false information can lead people (who are in a heightened state of uncertainty) to confess and internalize responsibility for an act they did not commit. The research used a 2 × 2 (high or low vulnerability × presence or absence of a false incriminating witness) experimental design.

Seventy-nine students took part in a staged reaction time task on a computer. The task involved **confederates** reading aloud a list of letters which participants then typed into the computer. Prior to the task, participants were warned not to press the ALT key because it would cause the computer to crash. Sixty seconds into the task, the computer apparently crashed and a distressed experimenter accused participants of pressing the ALT key. The experimenter then confirmed that the data had been lost and asked participants if they had hit the ALT key. The vulnerability of participants was manipulated by changing the pace of the task (fast or slow). The presence or absence of a false incriminating witness was manipulated by changing whether or not the confederate falsely 'admitted' to seeing the participant hit the ALT key.

Participants were least likely to falsely confess to hitting the ALT key in the slow-pace/no-witness condition (35%) and most likely to falsely confess in the fast-pace/witness condition (100%). Furthermore, no participants in the slow-pace/no-witness condition internalized the belief that they hit the ALT key or made up details to support this belief compared to 65 per cent and 35 per cent of participants in the fast-pace/witness condition.

Evaluation
This research has been criticized on the grounds that the situation was artificial, the confessions had no immediate or explicit negative consequences, and there was the possibility that participants had accidentally pressed the ALT key (Horselenberg, Merckelbach and Josephs, 2003).

Summary

In the US, a distinction is made between the non-accusatory interview and the confrontational accusatory interrogation. During the interrogation, police officers use a nine-step procedure in order to increase the likelihood of obtaining a confession. However, research suggests that the use of trickery and deception, inherent in the nine-step procedure, heightens the risk of false confessions, particularly with vulnerable suspects.

Interviewing in the UK

Police officers in the UK have traditionally used US approaches to interviewing and interrogation, including the nine-step procedure outlined by Inbau et al. (1986). However, concern over a growing number of miscarriages of justice led to several legal changes that aimed to rule out the use of trickery and deception in interviews with suspects (Williamson, 2004).

The Police and Criminal Evidence Act

The **Police and Criminal Evidence (PACE) Act** (1984) was introduced to regulate interviewing procedures in the UK and represented the first shift away from the US style of interviewing and interrogation. Requirements of the Act included the cautioning of all suspected individuals, the provision of adequate rest for individuals detained for any 24-hour period, special requirements for vulnerable individuals, and the tape recording of all interviews (Home Office, 2005b, 2006b). A new ethical framework for police interviewing was also introduced, stating that interviewers should search for the truth and approach investigations with an open mind (Sear and Williamson, 1999).

The PACE Act aimed to reduce the use of procedures that are associated with the occurrence of false confessions. For example, physical custody and isolation have been shown to increase the risk of false confessions, particularly when accompanied by coercive interrogation techniques and strong assertions of guilt (Kassin and Gudjonsson, 2004). Furthermore, some people are more vulnerable to the use of trickery and deception than others, particularly people with impaired intellectual and physical functioning, and are more prone to exhibit suggestibility and compliance (Davis and Leo, 2006). The capabilities of vulnerable individuals often reduce their ability to encode information and accurately recall past experiences (Gordon and Fleisher, 2006). Consequently, there is a heightened risk that suggestive interviewing procedures will influence the accuracy of statements provided by vulnerable individuals (Milne and Bull, 1999).

Although the introduction of the PACE Act was important, the role of the police investigation continued to be one of persuading suspects to confess rather than a search for accurate information (Williamson, 2004). In an evaluation of audio and video recordings of interviews with suspects, Baldwin (1992, 1993) was surprised by the 'feebleness' of many interviews. In particular he found that police officers often lacked confidence, assumed guilt, anticipated a confession, and demonstrated poor interviewing techniques. These, and similar concerns, prompted the development of a basic five-day training course in the interviewing of suspects and witnesses for all police officers (McGurk, Carr and McGurk, 1993). The Home Office also produced the principles of investigative interviewing and circulated these to all police forces. The principles focused on the acquisition of accurate and reliable information, and emphasized that police officers should approach interviews with an open mind, test information against what is already known, and give special consideration to vulnerable suspects (Gudjonsson, 2007; Williamson, 2006). However, there is no agreed procedure for the identification of vulnerable suspects so there is no guarantee that these individuals receive the additional safeguards they are entitled to (Redlich, 2004; Sear and Williamson, 1999).

PEACE

The mnemonic **PEACE** was used to describe the five stages that comprise investigative interviewing: *P*reparation and planning, *E*ngage and explain,

*A*ccount, *C*losure and *E*valuation. The PEACE interview model recognizes that information gathering should not be confined to the interview, but should also form a central role in the planning and preparation stages (Bull and Milne, 2004). As Gudjonsson (2007) pointed out, the risk of false confessions is increased when evidence against the suspect is weak or flawed. The importance of engaging with the suspect as well as attempts to reduce their feelings of anxiety are also emphasized along with the realization that the effective interviewing of suspects has major similarities with the effective interviewing of witnesses (Milne and Bull, 1999). With regard to the closure and evaluation stages of the PEACE model, suspects are provided with a summary of the interview and given the opportunity to correct or add information. Then, once the interview is concluded, evaluations of both the information obtained and the performance of the interviewers are recommended (Gudjonsson, 2003).

The similarities that exist between the effective interviewing of witnesses and suspects are not surprising given that suspects are generally polite and cooperative (to a certain extent). For example, Pearse and Gudjonsson (1996) conducted 161 interviews with suspects before they were interviewed by the police and found that 97 per cent of their reactions were polite. Furthermore, it is unlikely that suspects will be polite or cooperative if police officers assume guilt, fire accusations, and/or use coercive techniques (Bull and Milne, 2004). Exploratory research on murderers' and sexual offenders' experiences of Swedish police interviews has shown that interviews characterized by impatience, aggression and blame reduce the likelihood of a confession (Holmberg and Christianson, 2002). Causality could not be determined because the study utilized a correlational design. Therefore, 'offenders could be more likely to confess because officers responded positively to them, or alternatively, officers could have responded more positively to the offenders because they were confessing' (Kebbell and Hurren, 2006, pp. 111–12).

Police officers trained in the PEACE model are taught to use cognitive interview (originally designed for the interviewing of witnesses) and **conversation management** techniques during the account stage of the interview (Gudjonsson, 2007). The cognitive interview comprises four separate techniques (recreating the context, focused attention, multiple retrieval attempts and varied retrieval) that can be implemented individually or in combination to improve the recall of cooperative interviewees. In contrast, conversation management is considered an effective and reliable technique for dealing with uncooperative interviewees, whereby the interviewer is required to 'manage' varying degrees of interviewee resistance (Schollum, 2005). Emphasis is placed on establishing rapport, stating the aims and objectives of the interview, eliciting information through the use of appropriate interviewing strategies, and directing the overall flow of the interview (Milne and Bull, 1999). The last aspect of the technique is where conversation management is markedly different from the cognitive interview. While control over the direction of the interview is governed by the interviewer in conversation management, it is governed by the interviewee in the cognitive interview (Milne and Bull, 1999). The cognitive interview was discussed in detail in Chapter 7.

In an evaluation of the PEACE five-day training course, McGurk et al. (1993) reported significant and sustained improvements in the knowledge and interviewing skills of police officers following the course. Unfortunately, there were no established mechanisms for the supervision or monitoring of police officers' interviewing skills following the training, as the implementation of quality control was considered to be a low priority (Stockdale, 1993). In contrast to McGurk et al.'s findings, Clarke and Milne (2001) found little difference in the performance of PEACE trained and non-PEACE trained police officers. It was noted, however, that even the non-PEACE trained officers would have had some exposure to the PEACE model, and that many officers would have observed their PEACE trained colleagues conduct interviews. A more recent evaluation of 80 police interviews largely revealed 'ethical' interviewing tactics (Soukara, Bull, Turner and Cherryman, 2009). Minimization, maximization and intimidation were almost never used, while techniques emphasized by the PEACE model were common. Such techniques included the use of open and repetitive questioning, emphasizing contradictions in suspects' accounts, and the challenging of suspects' accounts through the presentation of contrasting evidence.

The 5-Tier interview training strategy

The PEACE model has now been surpassed by a 5-Tier interview training strategy. This strategy is designed to provide police officers with interview training specific to their requirements, and to develop previously neglected aspects of investigative interviewing (for example the interviewing of vulnerable suspects and the supervision and monitoring of interviews). The 5-Tier training strategy focuses on the following areas (Griffiths and Milne, 2006):

- *Tier 1* provides an introduction to interviewing.
- *Tier 2* is similar to the original PEACE training course and focuses on everyday crimes.
- *Tier 3* offers separate courses for the interviewing of witnesses, suspects and vulnerable witnesses, and focuses on complex and serious crime.
- *Tier 4* concerns the monitoring and supervision of interviews.
- *Tier 5* introduces the role of the interview coordinator.

Tier 3 has received the most consideration and represents an advanced three-week training course. Police officers have to pass an access test before gaining entry to the course and are formally assessed at the end of the three weeks. The start of the course is largely theory driven, becoming more practically oriented towards the end (Griffiths and Milne, 2006). Preliminary findings suggest not only improvements in interviewing skills following the attendance of Tier 3 training, but also the transfer of these skills to the workplace. However, there is a marked decline in some of the more complex skills over time, suggesting the need for refresher training in complex areas (Griffiths and Milne, 2006; Gudjonsson, 2007).

Interviewing around the world

Although discussion has focused on interviewing practices in the UK, there is a growing interest in investigative interviewing in many countries around the world. While countries have developed their own unique training programmes, there is evidence of a transfer of knowledge between countries (Williamson et al., 2009). Many training programmes have common features that attempt to prevent the occurrence of **tunnel vision** and overcome the overreliance on confession evidence. As such, there has been a shift away from the traditional interviewing and interrogation paradigm to the more recent investigative interviewing paradigm where emphasis is placed on a search for the truth and the collection of accurate information (Williamson, Milne and Savage, 2009).

Summary

In the UK, there has been a shift away from the US style of interviewing and interrogation. The PACE Act (1984) was introduced to regulate interviewing procedures, while the PEACE interview model and the 5-Tier interview training strategy were implemented to provide police officers with appropriate practical knowledge and interviewing skills. The current ethos is that the interviewing process represents a search for the truth and should be approached with an open mind.

Detecting deception

Overall, research suggests people are poor at detecting deception, with accuracy levels approximating those expected by chance. According to Vrij (2007) there are three main reasons why people are unable to detect deception accurately and lies go unnoticed: (1) a lack of motivation to detect lies, (2) the difficulty of detecting lies, and (3) common errors in detecting lies. A lack of motivation reflects the fact that in certain situations people may prefer to live in ignorance than know the truth.

With regard to the difficulty of the task, there are no uniform verbal or nonverbal cues that differentiate liars from truth tellers. This does not mean that cues do not exist, only that they vary from person to person and across situations. The detection of deception is further complicated because lies are often embedded in the truth, so a person may recall a truthful situation and simply change a few vital details. Also, some people are very good at lying. They do not find lying to be cognitively demanding, nor do they experience the fear, guilt or delight often associated with 'duping' another person (Vrij, 2008).

Common errors in the detection of deception include the use of inaccurate cues, and the neglect of interpersonal and intrapersonal differences (Vrij, 2008). For example, the assumption that nervousness is a cue to deceit is inaccurate as truth tellers are often nervous, especially when communicating with police officers. It is also incorrect to assume that simple cues, such as looking away or making repeated grooming gestures, are necessarily signs of deception. Cues to deception vary between people and within the same person across different situations. Consequently, the examination of suspects' verbal and nonverbal behaviour during the introductory stage of police interviews is of little use in the detection of deception. The introductory stage of the interview represents a 'low stake' situation and suspects are likely to behave differently when the stakes increase irrespective of whether they are lying or telling the truth (Vrij, 2008).

Good practice

In order to overcome the difficulties associated with lie detection Vrij (2008) offers a number of suggestions for improving the detection of deception. These include the use of flexible decision frameworks, the consideration of **cognitive load** and comparative truth, and the use of indirect lie detection techniques.

Flexible decision frameworks, which guide decision making as to whether or not a person is lying, are preferable to rigid decision frameworks because certain cues, or combinations of cues, may be useful with a particular person or situation but not others. The simultaneous consideration of verbal and nonverbal cues has also been shown to improve accuracy in the detection of deception (Vrij, 2008). Cognitive load and comparative truth are important in combination because research suggests that liars are more likely to exhibit verbal and nonverbal cues to deception when they experience increased cognitive load. However, these cues are only informative when related to honest reactions in similar situations (that is, comparative truth). This latter point is essential as it allows the interviewer to establish a base rate that accounts for intrapersonal differences. It may also be beneficial to use indirect techniques to detect deception (Vrij, 2008). For example, it is often more effective to ask the question 'is a person having to think hard?' rather than 'is a person lying?' Finally, it is imperative to keep an open mind and to consider alternative explanations for apparent cues to deception, as cues do not exclusively demonstrate lying. After all, truth tellers may also worry that an interviewer does not believe them and so may present cues indicative of deception.

Cognitive load is particularly important in the context of police interviews and has been central in the development of the non-presumptive information-gathering approach to interviewing. The traditional accusatory approach often encouraged short responses and resulted in liars and truth tellers exhibiting similar behavioural responses to accusations (Vrij and Granhag, 2007). Cognitive load relies on the assumption that liars prepare fabricated alibis prior to the interview. Consequently, open and specific follow-up questions are used to force liars to elaborate on their alibis and potentially offer details that were not previously prepared. This makes it harder for liars to follow their pre-prepared alibi and increases the likelihood that inconsistencies will become evident in their story. However, further research is necessary to develop an understanding of what causes an increase in the cognitive load experienced by liars. Three possibilities include: (1) the formulation of the lie itself, (2) the energy required to control natural behavioural responses, and (3) the monitoring of interviewer responses to determine whether they are believed or not (Vrij and Granhag, 2007).

Post-admission narratives

A full confession contains an admission of guilt as well as a **post-admission narrative** whereby the suspect recounts details of the event (Kassin, 2006). Consequently, police officers can use recordings of interviews to assess the accuracy of suspects' accounts by verifying their statements with other sources of information, such as witness statements. The expectation is that post-admission narratives will fit the crime scene details and case facts for true confessions, but not false confessions (Davis and Leo, 2006). The evaluation of post-admission narratives can be used to assess the conditions in which the confession was made, consider whether the statement details match the verifiable facts of the crime, and identify the source of the details provided (Kassin, 2006). It is also essential that the investigating officer keeps an open mind to the possibility of eliciting false confessions, otherwise confirmation biases may prevent them from recognizing inconsistencies in the suspect's account (Davis and Leo, 2006).

It is apparent that Kassin's (2006) procedure could be a useful tool in the identification of the various types of false confession, as police officers would be able to establish whether coercive techniques were used during the interview. Unfortunately, the careful examination of interview recordings to assess the accuracy of suspects' accounts places significant demands upon time and resources. Its effectiveness may also be limited by the fact that interviewing officers often inadvertently provide suspects with the facts of the crime (Davis and Leo, 2006).

The strategic use of evidence

Research concerning people's abilities to distinguish truthful from deceptive behaviour has neglected an important characteristic of police investigations: that there is often evidence against the suspect in question (Hartwig, Granhag, Strömwall and Vrij, 2005). Consequently, there is now a growing emphasis on the use of evidence in the detection of deception. In a laboratory study, Hartwig et al. (2005) tested the notion that, when handled correctly, case evidence could be effective in the detection of deception. The findings revealed that the late disclosure of evidence improved lie-detection accuracy with regard to a mock theft compared to the early disclosure of evidence. Thus, Hartwig, Granhag, Strömwall and Kronkvist (2006) argued that the late disclosure of evidence provides a more accurate basis for the judgement of honesty than the early disclosure of evidence, particularly if suspects are uncertain of the evidence against them. This discovery led to the development of the **strategic use of evidence (SUE)** technique.

The SUE technique requires the identification of potentially incriminating evidence before the interview and the late disclosure of this evidence during the interview (Granhag, Strömwall and Hartwig, 2007). Police officers should initially seek a free account from the suspect prior to the disclosure of potentially incriminating evidence. After the statement has been secured, officers are in the position to ask suspects to explain any inconsistencies or contradictions between their account and the available evidence (Bull and Milne, 2004). Similar to the analysis of post-admission narratives, an innocent suspect's account should be consistent with the officer's knowledge of the case, while a guilty suspect's account should contradict what the officer knows (Granhag et al., 2007).

Initial research concerning the effectiveness of the SUE technique has been encouraging. Hartwig et al. (2006) found that SUE trained police officers were significantly better at detecting deception than non-SUE trained police officers. In addition, SUE trained officers refrained from disclosing potentially incriminating evidence at the start of the interview, and then proceeded to ask suspects for free recall, to address any incriminating information, and to explain any inconsistencies between their initial statement and the available evidence. It was noted that guilty suspects avoided mentioning incriminating evidence during free recall and often 'escaped' from addressing any incriminating information. Innocent suspects, by comparison, showed less avoidance and escape.

Further research is now required to determine the effectiveness of the SUE technique as a function of the suspect's certainty regarding the evidence against him or her, the complexity of the offence, and the time delay between the commission of the offence and the interview (Vrij and Granhag, 2007). Nevertheless, Hartwig et al.'s (2006) research suggests that the SUE technique could be a powerful tool in the process of detecting deception, and ultimately preventing false confessions.

GRIMACE

Bull (2007, 2009) pointed out that there is a growing emphasis in a number of countries to train police officers in the **GRIMACE** approach which comprises the *G*athering of *R*eliable *I*nformation, *M*otivating a free recall *A*ccount, and *C*hallenging *E*ffectively. In accordance with the GRIMACE approach, the suspect is not interviewed until reliable information has been gathered. Only then is it possible to challenge statement–evidence inconsistencies effectively. This stage is particularly important as current research suggests that highly demanding interviews place substantial cognitive load on interviewees and may reveal verbal and/or nonverbal cues to deception (Vrij et al., 2007). Furthermore, deception research, including experimental studies and the analysis of police interviews with real suspects, suggests that the information-gathering style of interviewing is more cognitively demanding and allows interviewers to be better able to differentiate truth tellers from liars (Vrij, Fisher, Mann and Leal, 2009).

Summary

People are generally poor at detecting deception because there are no simple cues that differentiate liars from truth tellers. However, cues to deception are more apparent when liars experience an increased cognitive load. Within the context of police interviews, the late disclosure of evidence can be used to increase the cognitive load experienced by suspects to reveal cues to deception.

Further reading

Gudjonsson, G.H. (2003) *The Psychology of Interrogations and Confessions: A Handbook*. Chichester: John Wiley & Sons.

Memon, A., Vrij, A. and Bull, R. (2003) *Psychology and Law: Truthfulness, Accuracy and Credibility* (2nd edn). Chichester: John Wiley & Sons.

Vrij, A. (2008) *Detecting Lies and Deceit: Pitfalls and Opportunities* (2nd edn). Chichester: John Wiley & Sons.

Williamson, T., Milne, B. and Savage, S.P. (eds) (2009) *International Developments in Investigative Interviewing*. Cullompton: Willan Publishing.

Section Three

Psychology and the Courtroom

Chapter 9

Jury decision making

Introduction

Trial by jury is regarded as a central component of the judicial system in many countries and has been for many years. The underlying assumption is that jurors are able to provide their undivided attention for the duration of the trial, to discard any information not formally admitted into evidence, and to carefully evaluate a mass of information in order to arrive at an unbiased verdict (Devine et al., 2001; Memon, Vrij and Bull, 2003).

This chapter will consider the dominant models of jury decision making and the role of **majority influence** and **minority influence** in the context of the jury. It will first outline the different methods used for jury research. Models of jury decision making will then be discussed with specific reference to the **story model**, **predecisional distortion** and source monitoring errors. Finally, the role of majority and minority influence will be considered.

This chapter will examine:
- Methods of jury research
- Models of jury decision making
- Majority and minority influence

Methods of jury research

There are a number of methods used for jury research, each with respective strengths and weaknesses (Kapardis, 2003; Memon et al., 2003). These include:

- *Case studies* involve collecting data concerning past verdict decisions from real trials. Case studies are high in ecological validity, but analysis is conducted post-hoc and it is not possible to control for **confounding variables**. Consequently, it is difficult to infer causal relationships.
- *Mock jury studies* involve presenting often simplified written or videotaped trials to mock jurors who provide verdicts on the basis of the presented evidence. Mock jury studies enable the manipulation of particular variables while controlling for others, but lack the realism afforded by other methods.
- *Shadow jury studies* involve collecting data concerning jury decision making through the use of shadow juries that sit in on real trials but are not responsible for providing legally binding verdict decisions. Although shadow jury studies are more realistic than mock jury studies, they are difficult to arrange and do not allow for the manipulation or control of variables.
- *Post-deliberation studies* involve asking jurors about their decision making and verdict decisions during particular trials. Post-deliberation studies enable the investigation of real verdict decisions, but rely on the accurate recollections of jurors. Furthermore, it is illegal to interview jurors in many countries, including the UK, Canada and Australia.

To a large extent, the relative strengths and weaknesses of the different methods of jury research are complementary (Devine et al., 2001). For example, mock jury studies are criticized for lacking realism but offer a high degree of control, while case studies, shadow jury studies, and post-deliberation studies are more realistic but offer no control over confounding variables. Consequently, the ideal situation is for a combination of methods to be used to investigate any given area of jury decision making.

Thinking scientifically → **Mock jury research**

Although a variety of methods are available to researchers interested in jury decision making, the prohibition of jury observation has often led researchers to rely on the analysis of mock jury studies (Memon et al., 2003). As such, the ecological validity of these studies is limited due to the use of artificial settings, simple stimulus materials and a lack of consequentiality with respect to verdict decisions (Bornstein, 1999; Studebaker et al., 2002). The use of simple stimulus materials is potentially problematic because experimental manipulations are more 'visible' and have a much stronger influence than they would have in actual trials (Kramer and Kerr, 1989).

However, a comprehensive review of jury research reveals few differences in the behaviours of student samples compared to more representative population samples, or between simulations using simple stimuli (for example short transcripts) and simulations utilizing more realistic stimuli (for example live trial presentations) (Bornstein, 1999). Furthermore, although the use of simple stimuli can exaggerate the influence of experimental manipulations on jury decision making, they often produce similar effects when compared to the use of more realistic stimuli (Kramer and Kerr, 1989).

Summary

There are a number of methods used for jury research, including case studies, mock jury studies, shadow jury studies and post-deliberation studies. Although mock jury studies are the most common, they are often criticized for their overreliance on student samples and use of simple stimulus materials. Ideally a combination of methods will be used to investigate any given area of jury decision making to overcome the respective strengths and weaknesses of the different methods.

Models of decision making

There are two main decision-making frameworks: mathematical and explanation models (Hastie, 1993). Mathematical models suggest that jurors make a series of mental calculations to formulate verdict decisions. Explanation models propose that jurors formulate plausible stories of the offence and make verdict decisions that are consistent with these stories.

Story model

Pennington and Hastie's (1986, 1992) story model is arguably the most influential approach to jury decision making. The story model asserts that jurors incorporate trial information into 'one or more plausible accounts or stories describing "what happened" during events testified to at the trial' (Pennington and Hastie, 1992, pp. 189–90). These accounts are not based solely on the evidence presented during a trial, but also reflect jurors' attitudes and experiences. The story model describes three stages of decision making: story construction, verdict representation and story classification (Pennington and Hastie, 1992).

Story construction

During the story construction stage, jurors actively make sense of trial information and attempt to incorporate it into one or more coherent accounts. Such accounts are based on combinations of information obtained from the trial, knowledge about similar events, and expectations concerning what 'makes a complete story' (for example actions are usually motivated by goals). When several stories are constructed, one is usually considered to be more acceptable on the basis of three certainty principles (Pennington and Hastie, 1992):

- *Coverage*. The degree to which a story accounts for the trial information.
- *Coherence*. The degree to which a story is consistent, both internally and in relation to outside knowledge.
- *Completeness*. The degree to which a story 'has all its parts'.

Verdict representation

The verdict representation stage occurs when jurors are presented with alternative verdict decisions. These usually derive from the judge's instructions on the law, but may also be influenced by jurors' prior knowledge (Pennington and Hastie, 1992). The alternative verdict decisions are defined according to a list of features including the identity, actions and mental state of the defendant as well as the circumstances of the crime. The combination of features then influences the acceptance or rejection of the alternative verdict decisions.

Story classification

During the story classification stage, jurors consider a judge's procedural instructions regarding the presumption of guilt and the requirement of proof while determining the 'best match' between the accepted story and the alternative verdict decisions. The fourth and final certainty principle is applied during this process (Pennington and Hastie, 1992):

- *Goodness of fit*. The degree to which a story matches the alternative verdict decisions of guilty and not guilty. If the match to alternative verdict decisions is insufficient, the default verdict is not guilty.

Consistent with the story model, Pennington and Hastie (1988) found that the coherence of evidence influenced perceptions of evidence strength. Furthermore, research has demonstrated that mock jurors who choose opposing verdicts differ in their evaluations of the same evidence (Huntley and Costanzo, 2003).

Thinking scientifically → **Explanation-based decision making: Effects of memory structure on judgment**
(Pennington and Hastie, 1988)

The research investigated whether the order of testimony (that is, prosecution and defence evidence) influences verdict decisions, confidence ratings and perceptions of evidence strength. The research used a 2 × 2 (order of prosecution evidence × order of defence evidence) experimental design.

One-hundred and thirty students listened to evidence from an actual murder trial. Students were then required to provide a verdict decision (guilty or not guilty), confidence ratings (five-point Likert scales from 1 = pure guess to 5 = very certain) and perceptions of prosecution and defence evidence strength (five-point Likert scales from 1 = very weak to 5 = very strong). The prosecution and defence evidence was presented in story or witness order to produce four experimental conditions: prosecution and defence in story order, prosecution in story order and defence in witness order, prosecution in witness order and defence in story order, and prosecution and defence in witness order. Story order involved the evidence items being presented chronologically, while witness order involved the evidence items being presented non-chronologically. The witness order was more comparable to the actual trial where the testimony of witnesses did not necessarily correspond to the order of events testified to during the trial.

The defendant was most likely to be found guilty of murder when the prosecution evidence was presented in story order and the defence evidence was presented in witness order (78%). The defendant was least likely to be found guilty when the prosecution evidence was presented in witness order and the defence evidence was presented in story order (31%). Perceptions of prosecution and defence evidence strength were greatest when the evidence was presented in story order and the opposition's evidence was presented in witness order. Finally, the highest confidence ratings for guilty and not guilty verdicts were obtained when both prosecution and defence evidence was presented in story order. The lowest confidence ratings were obtained when both prosecution and defence evidence was presented in witness order. These findings suggest that developing a clear understanding of the competing evidence is important in securing confident verdict decisions.

Predecisional distortion

In contrast to the story model's assumption of multiple stories, predecisional distortion asserts that jurors hold a single dominant story that best accounts for the trial information (Carlson and Russo, 2001). This dominant story leads to the biased interpretation and evaluation of new evidence to support the current leading verdict or dominant story (that is, guilty or not guilty). Biased interpretations and evaluations are driven by the *coherence* certainty principle and although it is possible for the dominant story to radically alter as a result of new evidence, predecisional distortion makes it difficult for jurors to change to an opposing verdict (that is, change from a guilty verdict to a not guilty verdict or vice versa) (Carlson and Russo, 2001).

In accordance with the concept of predecisional distortion, Carlson and Russo (2001) found that mock jurors tended to distort their evaluations of new evidence in line with pre-existing preferences rather than by objectively assessing new information. Similarly, Hope, Memon and McGeorge (2004) found that jurors who received negative pretrial publicity about the defendant evaluated the majority of testimonies in line with a built-in pro-prosecution bias which resulted in an increase in guilty verdicts.

Source monitoring errors

Source monitoring refers to the decision processes associated with determining the origins of information (Johnson, Hashtroudi, and Lindsay, 1993). The central claim is that the origin (that is, source) of information is not directly retrieved with the corresponding memory, but attributed through certain decision processes at the point of remembering. As such, source monitoring errors involve the misattribution of certain information to a different source. The likelihood of these errors occurring will be influenced by the uniqueness of the source characteristics associated with a particular memory. Consequently, it will be more difficult to specify the correct source when two or more memories have similar characteristics. Johnson et al. (1993) identified three types of source monitoring errors:

- *External.* Errors in the attribution of external sources (for example a person incorrectly attributing a statement made by one person to a different person).
- *Internal.* Errors in the attribution of internal sources (for example a person incorrectly attributing memories for what they thought to memories for what they said).
- *Internal-external.* Errors in the attribution of internal sources as external sources or vice versa (for example a person incorrectly attributing memories for thoughts to memories for events).

In the context of jury decision making, these errors may occur if jurors mistakenly identify information that has not been formally admitted into evidence as being derived from the trial. Research has shown that jurors exposed to negative pretrial publicity sometimes misattribute this information to both the trial and the press (Ruva, McEvoy and Bryant, 2007). Rather than forgetting that they read the information in the press, jurors mistakenly believe it was also presented at the trial, thus making it influential in their verdict decisions.

Summary

The story model asserts that jurors incorporate trial information into one or more plausible accounts and select the verdict decision that represents the best match to the accepted story. In contrast, predecisional distortion suggests that jurors hold a single dominant story that leads to the biased interpretation and evaluation of new evidence. Although it is possible for the dominant story to change, it is difficult for jurors to change to an opposing verdict. Source monitoring errors involve the misattribution of information to a different source and may lead jurors to construct stories that incorporate information not formally admitted into evidence.

Majority and minority influence

The processes of majority and minority influence are often associated with the classic studies of Solomon E. Asch and Serge Moscovici. Asch's studies employed a discrimination task in which groups of seven to nine students were shown two cards (Asch, 1952). One card displayed a standard line while the other displayed three comparison lines. The students' task was to call out which of the comparison lines matched the standard line in length. Students were presented with 12 sets of cards in total. Although there were between seven and nine students in each group, only one student was a genuine participant (who always completed the task second to last). The others were confederates who were instructed to provide the same wrong answer in 7 of the 12 trials.

Asch (1952) found that participants provided answers that were correct and independent of the unanimous majority in 67 per cent of trials. However, this 33 per cent error rate was much higher than the 7 per cent error rate obtained when a separate group of participants completed the task individually. When participants were asked why they conformed to the majority three reasons were given:

- *Distortion of perception*. Participants thought they saw the lines as the majority claimed they did (extremely rare).
- *Distortion of judgement*. Participants knew they saw the lines differently, but thought they were wrong.
- *Distortion of action*. Participants knew they saw the lines differently, but went along with the majority so that they did not stand out.

It is important to note that the error rate was reduced to 13 per cent in a variation of the study in which one of the confederates was instructed to provide correct answers in all 12 trials (Asch, 1952).

Moscovici's studies also used a discrimination task in which groups of students were asked to judge the colour of a series of slides. All slides were in fact the same colour, just shown at varying light intensities (Moscovici and Lage, 1976). After a series of trials designed to reinforce perceptions of the slides as blue, 36 critical slides were presented in three sets of 12. Similar to Asch's studies, students in each group comprised a combination of genuine participants and confederates, the proportions of which varied across three minority and two majority influence conditions:

- *Consistent minority*. Groups comprised two confederates and four participants. Confederates completed the task first and fourth, and consistently judged the slides to be green.

- *Consistent individual*. Groups comprised one confederate and three participants. The confederate completed the task first and consistently judged the slides to be green.
- *Inconsistent minority*. Groups comprised two confederates and four participants. Confederates completed the task first and fourth, and judged the first 24 slides to be green and the last 12 slides to be blue.
- *Unanimous majority*. Groups comprised three confederates and one participant. Confederates completed the task first, second and third, and consistently judged the slides to be green.
- *Non-unanimous majority*. Groups comprised four confederates and two participants. The order in which confederates completed the task varied. Although they consistently judged the slides to be green, the majority was broken up by the inclusion of two participants.

Moscovici and Lage (1976) found that 10 per cent of participants judged the slides to be green in the consistent minority condition compared to just over 1 per cent in the consistent individual condition and just under 1 per cent in the inconsistent minority condition. In the majority influence conditions, 40 per cent of participants judged the slides to be green when the majority was unanimous compared to 12 per cent when the majority was non-unanimous. These judgements contrasted with the finding that almost all students who completed the task individually (that is, in a control condition) judged the slides to be blue.

Overall, research suggests that majority influence predominates and that minority influence is most likely to occur in small groups of six or fewer with a minority of two (Tanford and Penrod, 1984). Although both majority and minority influence have been found to occur, the processes by which they operate are somewhat different (Nemeth, 1986). For example, majority judgements are likely to be considered from the start as a source of knowledge (that is, informational social influence) or due to the need for acceptance (that is, normative social influence) (Deutsch and Gerard, 1955). Consideration of minority judgements, by comparison, is largely dependent on the consistency and confidence with which the judgements are made (Nemeth, 1986). Furthermore, majority influence is more likely to induce **compliance behaviour** while minority influence is more likely to induce **conversion behaviour** (Moscovici, 1985). Compliance behaviour involves a public but not a private change in opinion, while conversion behaviour involves both a public and a private change in opinion.

In the context of jury decision making, majority influence has been found to have a much stronger impact on verdict decisions than minority influence. For example, Kalven and Zeisel (1966) found that the majority view (that is, guilty or not guilty) held by jurors at the start of the deliberation process was the same as the final verdict in approximately 90 per cent of the 225 jury trials studied. Similarly, Sandys and Dillehay (1995) reported a 93 per cent agreement rate in a study of 43 jury trials. However, the **decision rule** has been shown to moderate the relative impact of majority influence over minority influence (issues concerning the decision rule are also discussed in Chapter 10). For example, Nemeth (1987) found majority influence to prevail more quickly when a non-unanimous decision rule was employed rather than a unanimous decision rule.

Summary

Majority influence occurs when a minority changes its views to conform to those of a larger group while minority influence occurs when a majority changes its views to conform to those of a smaller group. Research suggests that majority influence predominates and that minority influence is most likely to occur in smaller groups. In the context of jury decision making, majority influence has been found to have a much stronger impact on verdict decisions than minority influence.

Further reading

Kapardis, A. (2010) *Psychology and Law: A Critical Introduction* (3rd edn). Cambridge: Cambridge University Press.

Memon, A., Vrij, A. and Bull, R. (2003) *Psychology and Law: Truthfulness, Accuracy and Credibility* (2nd edn). Chichester: John Wiley & Sons.

Chapter 10

Influencing the jury

Introduction

During the course of a trial each juror is expected to reach a verdict based solely on the information formally admitted into evidence (Fein, McCloskey and Tomlinson, 1997). Although trials are carefully coordinated, jurors are often exposed to biased non-evidentiary information and methods of countering these biases are relatively ineffective (Kassin and Sommers, 1997). Consequently, there is a genuine danger that information not formally admitted into evidence will bias jurors' verdict decisions.

Chapter 9 discussed methods of jury research, models of jury decision making, and majority and minority influence. This chapter will consider factors that bias jury decision making and the effectiveness of methods of countering these biases. It will first outline the main procedural, case and participant factors that may bias jury decision making. The utility of **voir dire**, **judicial admonitions** and **jury deliberations** will then be discussed along with some promising alternative methods of countering biases. The discussion of procedural, case and participant factors is based on sections of Devine et al.'s comprehensive review article entitled 'Jury decision making: 45 years of empirical research on deliberating groups'.

This chapter will examine:

- Procedural and case factors
- Participant factors
- Countering biases within jury decision making

Procedural and case factors

There are a number of procedural and case factors that may influence jury decision making, including jury size, the decision rule, strength of evidence, inadmissible evidence, pretrial publicity and expert testimony.

Jury size and the decision rule

Juries comprise 12 members of the public in England and Wales, while in Scotland they comprise 15 (Memon, Vrij and Bull, 2003). In the US, juries have traditionally consisted of 12 members, but some states now use juries with as few as 6 (Greene, Heilbrun, Fortune and Nietzel, 2007). There are also variations in the level of agreement required (that is, the decision rule) for guilty and not guilty verdicts. A majority of 10 to 2 is accepted in England and Wales if the jury is unable to reach a unanimous verdict after two hours (otherwise it is a **hung jury**). A much smaller majority of 8 to 7 is required in Scotland, although jurors have a choice of three verdict decisions: guilty, not proven and not guilty. Not proven verdicts are used when the judge or jury has reasonable doubt as to the guilt of the defendant but there is insufficient evidence to secure a conviction. In the US, a unanimous verdict is usually required although smaller majorities of three-quarters are sometimes accepted (Greene et al., 2007).

Research has shown that deliberation times are longer with both large juries and unanimous verdict requirements, while hung juries are less likely in large juries but more likely with unanimous verdict requirements (Devine et al., 2001; Nemeth, 1987). Disregarding the proportion of hung juries, neither jury size nor the decision rule has been shown to influence verdict decisions (that is, the proportion of guilty and not guilty verdicts) although jurors report being more satisfied and confident when they reach a unanimous verdict.

Strength of evidence

Strength of evidence encompasses the quality and quantity of the information presented for the prosecution and the defence during a trial (Devine et al., 2001). In mock jury studies, strength of evidence has been examined directly through the manipulation of various factors including the presence or absence of corroborating witnesses and additional evidence (for example science or confession evidence), and the proportion of incriminating versus acquitting facts included in the trial (Devine et al., 2001; Memon et al., 2003). In field studies, strength of evidence has been examined indirectly through the use of naturally occurring factors, including the nature of the crime and the number of witnesses who testified during the trial. Overall, research suggests that strength of evidence is the most important determinant of jury verdict decisions, although its importance relative to other biasing factors is unclear.

Inadmissible evidence and pretrial publicity

Inadmissible evidence refers to information not formally admitted into evidence that is deemed to be unreliable and potentially biasing. Examples include hearsay evidence and evidence obtained via illegal methods. Pretrial publicity is a particular type of inadmissible evidence that may influence prospective jurors long before the trial begins (Devine et al., 2001). Pretrial publicity is often detrimental to the defence because stories tend to focus on details relating to the alleged crime and the arrest of the defendant (Ogloff and Vidmar, 1994). Studies generally suggest that jurors are influenced by inadmissible evidence and exposure to pretrial publicity, but in different ways (Bornstein, Whisenhunt, Nemeth and Dunaway, 2002; Devine et al., 2001). Inadmissible evidence has been found to have a greater influence when it favours the defence, while pretrial publicity has been shown to be severely prejudicial when it favours the prosecution.

Thinking scientifically → **Understanding pretrial publicity: Predecisional distortion of evidence by mock jurors** (Hope, Memon and McGeorge, 2004)

The research examined whether exposure to negative pretrial publicity biases evaluations of trial evidence and influences verdict decisions. The research used an experimental design.

One-hundred and sixteen students were randomly assigned to one of two conditions. In Condition 1 they read a short news article that portrayed the defendant in a negative light. In Condition 2 they read a similar length article that was unrelated to the trial. Participants then completed unrelated filler tasks before reading the transcript of a murder trial which contained the testimonies of six witnesses and the defendant. Participants rated each testimony to determine whether it favoured the defence or the prosecution, identified the current leader in the trial (defence or prosecution), and provided verdict decisions at the end of the trial (guilty or not guilty).

Participants exposed to negative pretrial publicity were more likely to identify the prosecution as leader during the trial and to find the defendant guilty at the end of the trial compared to those who were not exposed to negative pretrial publicity (73% and 56% respectively). Negative pretrial publicity also resulted in greater distortion of the evidence in favour of the prosecution in relation to five of the seven testimonies.

Evaluation

Although the research was limited by a lack of ecological validity in comparison to genuine pretrial publicity and an actual trial, it allowed for the influence of pretrial publicity to be examined in a controlled setting.

Expert testimony

Expert testimony about a particular scientific, technical or specialized area is provided by a qualified expert on the basis of training, experience and knowledge (Clifford, 2008). Various issues have been examined, including the presence or absence of expert testimony, the style and content of the testimony, and the extent to which the testimony is challenged (Devine et al., 2001). In the context of eyewitness evidence, expert testimony appears to provide a useful safeguard against jurors' overreliance on witness confidence (Cutler et al., 1989). Not only has it been shown to improve jurors' awareness of factors that influence the accuracy of eyewitness testimony, it has also been found to reduce the influence of witness confidence on jury verdict decisions.

However, research generally suggests that expert testimony has little impact on jury verdict decisions, especially when it is not tailored to the specific case (Devine et al., 2001). Furthermore, the perceived motivations of expert witnesses have been shown to influence the effectiveness of their testimony. For example, Cooper and Nehaus (2000) found that mock jurors were less likely to be persuaded by the testimony of highly paid expert witnesses from prestigious universities than moderately paid expert witnesses from less well-known universities. This finding was explained with reference to the 'hired gun effect', whereby the highly paid experts were thought to be motivated by the money while the moderately paid experts were thought to be motivated by their expertise and knowledge.

Summary

There are a number of procedural and case factors that may influence jury verdict decisions. Strength of evidence appears to be the most important, while inadmissible evidence and pretrial publicity have been found to bias the jury against both the prosecution and the defence. Although expert testimony is increasingly used during trials, research suggests that it has only a limited impact on jury decision making.

Participant factors

In addition to the aforementioned procedural and case factors are a number of participant factors that may influence jury decision making, including defendant, victim and witness characteristics.

Defendant characteristics

Defendant characteristics include race, sex, socioeconomic status, attractiveness and the presence or absence of a criminal record (Devine et al., 2001). Research into the influence of race and socioeconomic status has revealed an interaction between jury–defendant similarity and strength of evidence. When evidence against the defendant is weak, jurors who display similar characteristics to the defendant tend to be lenient in sentencing, but when evidence is strong, jurors tend to be harsher. The presence of a criminal record has also been shown to increase the likelihood of the defendant being convicted, especially when the previous conviction is for a similar crime (Devine et al., 2001; Lloyd-Bostock, 2000).

With regard to attractiveness, research has shown that unattractive defendants are generally more likely to be convicted and to receive harsher sentences than attractive defendants (Darby and Jeffers, 1988). However, the direction of this effect may vary according to the nature of the crime. For example, Sigall and Ostrove (1975) found that unattractive defendants received harsher sentences than attractive defendants for a burglary, but the reverse was true for a swindle. Thus, jurors were more lenient with attractive defendants in the context of an attractiveness-*unrelated* crime (that is, a burglary), but harsher in the context of an attractiveness-*related* crime (that is, a swindle).

Victim and witness characteristics

Victim and witness characteristics include age, attractiveness, victim suffering and witness confidence. Research into the influence of attractiveness and victim suffering have shown them to have little effect on jury decision making, although longer deliberation times were apparent when potential sentences did not 'fit' the degree of victim suffering (Davis et al., 1977; MacCoun, 1990). There is also evidence to suggest that the likelihood of guilty verdicts is higher when the victim is young (Devine et al., 2001). With regard to witness confidence, research has shown that it can influence jury decision making, despite research to suggest that confidence is a poor indicator of testimony accuracy (Cutler and Penrod, 1989; Cutler et al., 1990). Witness confidence was discussed in more detail in Chapter 7.

Child witnesses

The increasing use of **protective shields** and **videolink procedures** with child witnesses to help alleviate the trauma and stress associated with testifying in court represents an additional factor that may influence jury decision making (Sandler, 2006). Proponents of the value of protective shields and videolink procedures argue that reducing the amount of trauma and stress child witnesses experience enables them to provide the best testimony possible. Opponents claim that the use of these procedures biases the jury against the defence (Goodman et al., 1998).

Overall, research suggests that while the use of videolinks may be beneficial to child witnesses, they may limit the impact of their testimony and bias the jury against the prosecution (Goodman et al., 1998). For example, Ross et al. (1994) found that mock jurors were less likely to find a defendant guilty of child sexual abuse when the child witness testified via videolink than when he or she testified in court. This apparent effect may reflect the indirect nature of videolink testimony compared to testimony delivered in the courtroom.

Summary

Various defendant, victim and witness characteristics may influence jury decision making. Defendants are generally more likely to be convicted if they have a criminal record or are unattractive, although attractive defendants receive harsher sentences when crimes are attractiveness-related.

Child witnesses offer an additional issue with regard to jury decision making, as the use of protective shields and videolink procedures may reduce the impact of their testimony.

Countering biases within jury decision making

It is widely assumed that jury trials contain three procedural safeguards against the biasing effects of information that has not been formally admitted into evidence: voir dire, judicial admonitions and jury deliberation. Although it is sometimes argued that **continuance** can be used to reduce the impact of prejudicial pretrial publicity, a meta-analysis of 44 studies indicated that longer delays may actually increase its biasing effect (Steblay, Besirevic, Fulero and Jimenez-Lorente, 1999).

Voir dire

Voir dire is one of the most common approaches used by the court system and involves the exclusion of any jurors who are identified as impartial (that is, have any preconceived notions of the defendant's guilt or innocence) (Kerr, Kramer, Carroll and Alfini, 1991; Kramer, Kerr and Carroll, 1990). However, research utilizing mock jurors, as well as actual jurors, suggests that any confidence judges and lawyers may have in the effectiveness of voir dire is misplaced (Dexter, Cutler and Moran, 1992). As Kerr et al. (1991) pointed out, the assertions made by prospective jurors regarding their impartiality or partiality may indicate very little about their actual level of bias. In the end, it is a self-report measure of attitudes and experiences that is susceptible to intentional and/or unintentional deception (Lieberman and Ardnt, 2000).

Judicial admonitions

Judicial admonitions consist of specific guidance to jurors, usually provided by the judge, directing them to base their verdict decision on the information formally admitted into evidence and to disregard any non-evidentiary information (Bornstein et al., 2002). Reliance on judge's instructions may be unwarranted, however, as research suggests that admonitions do not effectively eliminate jurors' use of defence-slanted or prosecution-slanted inadmissible evidence (Carlson and Russo, 2001; Steblay, Hosch, Culhane and McWethy, 2006).

A number of explanations have been put forward for the ineffectiveness of judicial admonitions to disregard non-evidentiary information (Fein et al., 1997). These include:

- Jurors may not fully understand or agree with the explanations given for disregarding the information.
- The judge's instructions may actually draw attention to the information.
- Jurors may find it difficult to ignore the information even if they want to comply with the judge's instructions.
- Jurors' use of the information may be influenced by the extent to which they believe it is reliable and valid.
- Jurors may find it difficult to discount the information even if they believe it is unreliable and invalid.

Furthermore, jurors often listen to days or weeks of testimony before receiving the judge's instructions and then have the task of integrating the evidence with the legal requirements in order to reach a verdict (Smith, 1991). This task may be particularly difficult once a coherent story has been generated to account for the evidence relevant to the case (Steblay et al., 2006). Similarly, if jurors predecisionally distort the evidence as it is presented during the trial, and are largely unaware of doing so, it might be impossible for them to reconstruct an unbiased version of that information. Therefore, judicial admonitions provided prior to the trial may have a greater chance of success (Carlson and Russo, 2001). In line with this argument, research investigating the effectiveness of judge's instructions regarding the requirement of proof has shown that they are more effective when delivered at the start rather than at the end of the trial (Kassin and Wrightsman, 1979). Also, judge's instructions to disregard prejudicial pretrial publicity have been found to be effective when presented before and after the evidence, but not when only presented after the evidence (Bornstein et al., 2002).

Reliability and suspicion

Taken as a whole, it is clear that judicial instructions do not effectively eliminate jurors' use of inadmissible evidence. Juror non-compliance is particularly likely when inadmissible evidence is rejected due to an unexplained technicality or **due process** concerns. Therefore, the judicial system must develop a means to persuade jurors that such information is not only unfair, but irrelevant to their decisions if it wishes to limit jurors' use of inadmissible evidence (Steblay et al., 2006).

In a mock criminal trial, Kassin and Sommers (1997) found that jurors' verdict decisions were influenced by evidence when it was deemed inadmissible on due process grounds, but not when it was ruled inadmissible on the grounds that it was unreliable (see 'thinking scientifically' box for further details). Fein et al. (1997) also reported that judicial admonitions were more effective at countering the influence of prejudicial pretrial publicity and inadmissible evidence detrimental to the defendant when it was accompanied by suspicion concerning the underlying motives for the introduction of the information. In this instance, suspicion was generated by stating what the prosecution had to gain from the introduction of the inadmissible information.

Thinking scientifically → **Inadmissible testimony, instructions to disregard, and the jury: Substantive versus procedural considerations**

(Kassin and Sommers, 1997)

The research investigated whether the nature of judges' instructions to disregard inadmissible evidence influences the effectiveness of these instructions at countering biases within jury decision making. The research used an experimental design.

Eighty-one students were presented with a trial summary in which a man was accused of murdering his estranged wife and male neighbour. Participants were randomly assigned to one of four conditions that provided different judge's instructions regarding a critical item of incriminating evidence: a wiretap from an unrelated case that contained a recording of the defendant confessing to the murders. In Condition 1 the wiretap evidence was ruled *admissible*, in Condition 2 the evidence was ruled inadmissible on *due process* grounds, and in Condition 3 the evidence was ruled inadmissible on the grounds that it was *unreliable*. Condition 4 was a control condition in which there was no wiretap evidence. Participants provided ratings of how incriminating evidence items were as they were presented, as well as verdict decisions (guilty or not guilty) and justifications for these decisions after the presentation of the trial summary.

Participant ratings of evidence items were consistently more incriminating in the admissible and due process conditions than the unreliable and control conditions. Furthermore, participants in the admissible (79%) and due process (55%) conditions were more likely to provide guilty verdicts than participants in the unreliable (24%) and control (24%) conditions. With regard to verdict justifications, 63 per cent of participants in the admissible condition claimed that the wiretap evidence influenced their verdict decision compared to 15 per cent in the due process condition and 14 per cent in the unreliable condition. It is apparent therefore that participants in the due process condition were largely unaware of the influence the wiretap evidence was having on their verdict decisions.

Evaluation

The ecological validity of the research was limited by the use of a trial summary and the fact that mock jurors participated individually rather than in groups. It was also possible that the ratings of evidence items increased the processing of this evidence compared to actual trials, although the pattern of ratings was not apparent in other research using the same procedure.

Jury deliberation

Finally, it has been argued that although individual jurors may succumb to memory errors and biases, jury deliberation serves to mitigate these biases (Fein et al., 1997; Ruva, McEvoy and Bryant, 2007). With reference to the influence of inadmissible evidence, London and Nunez (2000) suggested that jury deliberations may help moderate biases by raising the jurors' awareness of alternative stories or accounts relevant to the case. Research findings have varied however. Some studies have reported fewer memory errors in groups while others have found that deliberations are more likely to intensify biases through the process of **group polarization** (Fein et al., 1997). For example, Ruva et al. (2007) found that group deliberations increased juror bias, with mock jurors who deliberated viewing the defendant as less credible than those who did not.

Juror training and accountability

Offering jurors training and making them accountable for their verdict decisions may help prevent them from succumbing to memory errors and biases. Shaw and Skolnick (2004) found that while untrained mock jurors' opinions were affected by prejudicial pretrial publicity, the opinions of 'trained' jurors were not (training consisted of completing a university 'psychology and law' course). Content analysis of jurors' deliberations revealed that trained jurors were more focused on the relevant evidence and legal issues than untrained jurors. With respect to accountability, juries do not currently have to provide reasons for their verdict decisions in England and Wales. However, it may be argued that judges should be permitted to ask juries to expose their reasoning and justify their verdict decisions. By announcing that participants may be held accountable for their judgements, Krahé, Temkin and Bieneck (2007) were able to reduce reliance on pre-existing conceptions about rape, including ratings of victim blame and perpetrator responsibility.

Summary

There are three main procedural safeguards against the biasing effects of non-evidentiary information: voir dire, judicial admonitions and jury deliberation. However, none of these safeguards appears to be very effective. Research suggests that judicial instructions are more effective when they question the reliability or raise suspicions about the inadmissible evidence, while jury deliberations are less biased when jurors are required to justify their verdict decisions.

Further reading

Devine, D.J., Clayton, L.D., Dunford, B.B., Seying, R. and Pryce, J. (2001) Jury decision making: 45 years of empirical research on deliberating groups. *Psychology, Public Policy, and Law*, 7, 622–727.

Kassin, S.M. and Sommers, S.R. (1997) Inadmissible testimony, instructions to disregard, and the jury: Substantive versus procedural considerations. *Personality and Social Psychology Bulletin*, 23, 1046–54.

Section Four

Psychology and the Penal System

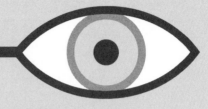

Chapter 11

The punishment of offenders

Introduction

Punishment is a consequence of breaking the law in almost all countries (Andrews and Bonta, 2006). In the UK, punishments are imposed by the judicial system in accordance with the law and are managed by various enforcement agencies including the National Offender Management Service (NOMS). The purpose of NOMS is to provide the effective management of offenders while protecting the public and reducing reoffending (Home Office, 2005a).

This chapter will consider the justifications offered for the use of punishment, as well as the effectiveness of various types of punishment in reducing reoffending. It will first summarize three justifications for the punishment of offenders (retribution, deterrence and confinement) before discussing the roles of rehabilitation and restorative justice (an alternative approach to punishment). The use of prison and probation will then be discussed, including the introduction of NOMS, along with a range of alternative punishments. Finally, the Stanford prison experiment will be summarized and two aspects of prison life will be considered: prison officer stress and prisoner suicide.

This chapter will examine:

- Punishment, rehabilitation and restorative justice
- Prison and probation
- Alternative punishments
- Prison life

Punishment, rehabilitation and restorative justice

Three distinct yet interconnected justifications are offered for the punishment of offenders: retribution, deterrence and confinement. Rehabilitation has also been offered as a separate justification for the use of punishment providing it incorporates effective treatment, while restorative justice has emerged as an alternative to traditional approaches to punishment.

Retribution

Advocates of retribution believe that there is a fundamental principle at stake and that offenders deserve to be punished. Furthermore, punishment is considered to be necessary in order to correct the imbalance caused by crime (McGuire, 2008). Contrary to popular belief, retribution does not support the use of extreme punishments, but adheres to the idea that punishment should fit the crime (Andrews and Bonta, 2006; Cavadino and Digman, 2007). This perspective dates back to the classical school, which asserted that the role of any punishment system should be to deter people from offending through swift, certain and proportionate punishments (a brief overview of the classical school was provided in Chapter 3) (Curran and Renzetti, 2001). However, critics have argued that it is difficult to justify the principle of retribution or see how it relates to the notion of right and wrong (Cavadino and Digman, 2007).

Deterrence

A second justification offered for the use of punishment is that it deters people from offending in two ways (McGuire, 2008):

- **Specific deterrence** refers to a person being less likely to reoffend once he or she has been punished.
- **General deterrence** refers to people being less likely to offend if they are aware that crime is punished.

Although research has shown that punishment deters some offenders, a large proportion continue to reoffend (Hollin, 1992). Furthermore, in some instances the punishment of offenders can reverse any specific deterrent effects by labelling offenders as criminal and producing a self-fulfilling prophecy (labelling theory was discussed in Chapter 3) (Becker,

1963; Cavadino and Digman, 2007). It is also unlikely that punishment is an effective general deterrent, as people are often ignorant as to specific punishments and believe that they will 'get away with it' (Cavadino and Digman, 2007). Consistent with this argument, evidence suggests that increasing the chances of being punished has more of a deterrent effect than increasing the severity of the punishment.

Thinking scientifically → **Zero tolerance in policing**

Zero tolerance is a strict non-discretionary approach to policing that targets minor crimes, such as public drinking, vandalism and vagrancy (that is, having no permanent residence or means of financial support) (J. Marshall, 1999). The approach stems from **broken windows theory**, which asserts that areas characterized by public disorder and incivility 'invite' serious crime (Kelling and Wilson, 1982). Consequently, strict policing (that is, increasing the chances of being punished for minor crimes) and regeneration can help prevent areas from creating an atmosphere that is conducive to crime.

Significant reductions in crime rates in certain areas of the UK and the US have been attributed to the use of zero tolerance approaches (J. Marshall, 1999), including reforms made by the Police Commissioner of New York in 1994 that led to a 37 per cent reduction in the crime rate over a three-year period (Bratton, 1997). However, it has been argued that the reforms went beyond zero tolerance, incorporating **intelligence-led policing**, improvements to police morale (in the UK) and the restructuring of the police department (in the US) (J. Marshall, 1999). The effectiveness of the zero tolerance approach has also been questioned on the grounds that it overemphasizes the importance of short-term policing rather than long-term law enforcement (J. Marshall, 1999). As Grabosky (1999) highlighted, effective law enforcement requires the police to have a trusting relationship with the community, and the use of an overly strict non-discretionary approach may not only destroy any existing trust but also prevent the development of trust in the future.

Death penalty

Although no longer used in the UK, the death penalty is still legal in other countries including certain states of the US (for example California, Florida and Texas). Although it may be argued that the death penalty represents the ultimate deterrent, its use has not been found to influence crime rates for homicide or other violent crimes (Andrews and

Bonta, 2006). Furthermore, the morality of sentencing a person to death has been questioned, particularly in light of miscarriages of justice (Hollin, 1992). It has also been demonstrated that cases involving black perpetrators and white victims are more likely to result in the use of the death penalty than other racial combinations (that is, black–black, white–black or white–white) even when non-racial factors are controlled for (Eberhardt, Davies, Purdie-Vaughns and Johnson, 2006). Thus, race clearly matters and prejudicial beliefs can influence whether or not a person is sentenced to death.

Confinement

A third justification offered for the use of punishment, in particular imprisonment, is that it reduces crime by taking offenders out of circulation either temporarily or permanently (McGuire, 2008). Advocates of confinement believe that crime will decrease as the number of offenders in prison increases (Andrews and Bonta, 2006). However, research has found little evidence to support the association between the size of the prison population and crime rates. This lack of association may be accounted for by the fact that criminal careers are generally short and a large proportion of offenders would naturally reduce their criminal involvement even if they were not in prison. Also, imprisoned offenders are often quickly replaced by the next generation of offenders (Cavadino and Digman, 2007).

Rehabilitation

Finally, rehabilitation has been offered as a separate justification for the punishment of offenders. Although the aforementioned justifications imply that punishment would lead to a reduction in crime, advocates of rehabilitation believe that effective treatment is required in order to reduce the risk of reoffending (McGuire, 2008). The effectiveness of general and specific offending behaviour programmes is discussed in detail in Chapter 12.

Rehabilitation in the US

During the 1970s there was a dramatic shift in the underlying philosophy of the criminal justice system in the US, with punishment being justified on the basis of confinement and retribution rather than rehabilitation (Haney and Zimbardo, 1998). Many states replaced **indeterminate**

sentencing models that allowed for the release or retention of prisoners depending on their level of rehabilitation with **determinate sentencing** models. The length of prison sentences was also increased on a regular basis. Consequently, the prison population increased dramatically and overcrowding became a serious problem. Attempts to build additional prisons were ineffective and many state and federal prisons were forced to operate at nearly double their intended capacity. At the same time, many prisons stopped providing prisoners with any form of meaningful education, training, employment or treatment.

The increased use of imprisonment had a disproportionate effect on certain racial minorities, especially black offenders, and impacted on the communities where they lived (Haney and Zimbardo, 1998). Although this disproportionate effect was partially caused by the increased use of prison sentences for drug crimes, black drug offenders were more likely to be imprisoned than white drug offenders. Haney and Zimbardo concluded:

> There has never been a more critical time at which to begin the intellectual struggle with those who would demean human nature by using prisons exclusively as agencies of social control that punish without attempting to rehabilitate, that isolate and oppress instead of educating and elevating, and that tear down minority communities rather than protecting and strengthening them. (p. 722)

Restorative justice

Restorative justice emerged over the last 25 years as an alternative to traditional approaches to punishment (McGuire, 2008). It aims to restore relations between the offender, the victim, and the community in which the crime occurred: thus, improving the experience of the victim, encouraging the offender to accept responsibility for his or her crime, and repairing the harm caused to the respective parties (Andrews and Bonta, 2006; Cavadino and Digman, 2007). Although restorative justice programmes can be used as an alternative to the criminal justice system, they are more often used to supplement it, particularly in the case of serious crimes involving adult offenders (Sherman and Strang, 2007).

A certain level of cooperation is required from the offender, the victim and the community, otherwise the effectiveness of the restorative justice programmes is reduced. While this requirement is a potential limitation, evidence suggests that the majority of offenders and victims agree to be involved when given the opportunity (T.F. Marshall, 1999). Programmes may use face-to-face meetings, **mediation**, or **indirect mediation** depending on the willingness of the offender and the victim (Andrews and Bonta, 2006; Sherman and Strang, 2007).

Research has shown that the majority of victims who participate in restorative justice programmes are satisfied with them, although a proportion are sceptical about the offenders' motives and find direct contact unsettling and/or intimidating (Miers et al., 2001). Offenders are also generally satisfied and find the experience beneficial. Research conducted by the Smith Institute in the UK and internationally has shown that involvement in restorative justice programmes generally leads to a reduction in offenders' reoffending compared to traditional approaches to punishment (Sherman and Strang, 2007). However, the extent of this reduction has been shown to vary according to the type and seriousness of the crime. For example, programmes were more effective at reducing recidivism for serious and violent crimes than less serious and property crimes.

Overall, restorative justice programmes have been shown to be more effective at improving victim and offender satisfaction, increasing offender compliance with the programme, and reducing reoffending compared to traditional approaches to punishment (Latimer, Dowden and Muise, 2005). These findings should be interpreted with caution, however, as the effectiveness of restorative justice programmes is confounded by a **selection bias**. Participation is voluntary so the effectiveness of restorative justice programmes may be the result of offenders' motivation to be involved rather than the programme per se.

Summary

The punishment of offenders has been justified on the grounds that offenders deserve to be punished (retribution), that it deters people from offending (deterrence) and that it takes offenders out of circulation (confinement). Rehabilitation has also been offered as a separate justification for the punishment of offenders providing it incorporates effective treatment. Restorative justice developed as an alternative to traditional approaches to punishment, and aims to provide a resolution that is acceptable to the offender, the victim and the community.

Prison and probation

The prison service aims to protect the public through the physical holding of prisoners in custody while the probation service aims to protect the public through the assessment and management of offender risk in the community (HM Prison Service, 2004; National Probation Service, 2003). Both services also aim to reduce the risk of reoffending through the provision of effective treatment programmes (general and specific offending behaviour programmes are discussed in detail in Chapter 12).

Despite these aims, rises in the use of custodial and non-custodial sentences have increased the demands placed on the prison and probation services. Consequently, the prison service is struggling to provide effective treatment for prisoners while the probation service is struggling to care for, and control, the increasing number of offenders (Easton and Piper, 2005; UK Parliament, 2010). Although recent reconviction data suggests that rates of reoffending following time in prison or on probation are falling, there is concern that this trend will stop if expansion continues without an increase in funding (UK Parliament, 2010).

The National Offender Management Service

NOMS was created in 2004 in order to improve the integration of correctional services across the prison and probation service in the UK. It aims to provide the effective 'end-to-end' management of offenders (Home Office, 2005a). NOMS replaced the separate prison and probation management systems with an integrated system, whereby offenders are supervised by a single offender manager for the duration of their sentence (National Audit Office, 2009). It was believed that the use of an integrated system would increase the sharing of information about offenders and improve the continuity of treatment with offenders as they progress 'through the gate', from prison to probation.

NOMS has the following principle aims (Home Office, 2005a):

- To protect the public.
- To reduce reoffending.
- To punish offenders.
- To develop offender awareness of the detrimental effects of crime.
- To rehabilitate offenders.

To meet the aims of protecting the public and reducing reoffending, NOMS ensures that the prison and probation services coordinate the management of offenders. It also works with local governments and other relevant agencies to secure services (for example housing, health care, training and employment opportunities) to improve offender rehabilitation and reintegration into the community (Home Office, 2005a; Ministry of Justice, 2008).

Although the rationale of a single system for the management of offenders is generally accepted, some have questioned whether it necessitated the organizational disruption that the creation of NOMS caused (Cavadino and Digman, 2007).

Summary

The prison and probation services aim to protect the public and reduce the risk of reoffending. Although rates of reoffending following time in prison or on probation are falling, there is concern that this trend will stop if expansion continues without an increase in funding. NOMS was created in order to provide the effective management of offenders as they progress from prison to probation. It aims to protect the public and reduce reoffending through the effective punishment and rehabilitation of offenders.

Alternative punishments

For many years, there were essentially two extremes of punishment available to the criminal justice system: prison and probation (Cavadino and Digman, 2007). However, there are now a range of alternative punishments available, including compensatory penalties, punishment orders, intensive supervision programmes, shock incarceration, scared straight programmes, and electronic monitoring.

Compensatory penalties and punishment orders

Compensatory penalties represent a flexible non-intrusive means for the offender to return something to the victim and help make amends for the suffering caused (Cavadino and Digman, 2007). Generally used for less serious crimes, the use of compensatory penalties has declined as a result of many offenders lacking the resources to make the payments. There has also been a reluctance to use compensatory penalties when the amount the offender can afford appears insulting to the victim.

Punishment orders, previously referred to as community service, involve offenders performing between 40 and 240 hours of unpaid work over a one-year period (Ellis and Winstone, 2002). They are generally used as an alternative to short-term prison sentences for less serious crimes (Tonry and Lynch, 1996). Overall, research suggests that punishment orders can provide a cost-effective alternative to prison that does not increase the risk of reoffending (Tonry and Lynch, 1996).

Intensive supervision programmes

Intensive supervision programmes use prison-like controls to monitor offenders in the community (Paparozzi and Gendreau, 2005). Their purpose is to either divert offenders from prison or intensify routine parole and probation (Petersilia and Turner, 1993). Such programmes aim to improve offenders' circumstances by offering educational and treatment services, maintain public safety by monitoring offenders' behaviour, and reinforce offenders' positive behaviour by providing appropriate rewards and punishments (Fulton, Gendreau and Paparozzi, 1995). However, only a minority of supervision programmes include any form of treatment programme (Tonry and Lynch, 1996).

Research has shown that intensive supervision programmes alone are no more effective at reducing reoffending than routine parole and probation (Lane, Turner, Fain and Sehgal, 2005; Tonry and Lynch, 1996). It has also been found that offenders on intensive supervision programmes are more likely to violate technical conditions as a consequence of increased levels of surveillance. Nevertheless, intensive supervision programmes have been found to be effective at reducing reoffending when closer supervision is accompanied by some form of treatment programme (Andrews and Bonta, 2006; Tonry and Lynch, 1996).

Shock incarceration and scared straight programmes

Shock incarceration and scared straight programmes are directed at young offenders, now referred to as young adults in the UK, and attempt to discourage them from entering into a life of crime. Shock incarceration involves exposing young adults to the reality of prison life (Andrews and Bonta, 2006). Most utilize a highly structured military-style boot camp approach, characterized by strict rules and discipline, military-style drills, frequent inspections, hard labour and physical exercise (Hollin, 1992; MacKenzie, Brame, McDowall and Souryal, 1995). Some shock incarceration programmes also offer a treatment element (for example New York's shock incarceration program) (Clark, Aziz and MacKenzie, 1994). Scared straight programmes involve young adults meeting prisoners to discuss prison life (Andrews and Bonta, 2006). The rationale being that the realistic depictions provided by prisoners will deter them from further criminal involvement (Petrosino, Turpin-Petrosino and Buehler, 2003).

Evaluation studies suggest that shock incarceration alone is insufficient to reduce reoffending (MacKenzie et al., 1995). Research has also shown that scared straight programmes are ineffective, with some actually increasing the likelihood of young adults engaging in further crime (Petrosino et al., 2003). However, both programmes have been shown to reduce reoffending when accompanied by some form of treatment programme (Andrews and Bonta, 2006; MacKenzie et al., 1995).

Electronic monitoring

Electronic monitoring involves wearing a device that emits a signal indicating the offender's location (Bonta, Wallace-Capretta and Rooney, 2000). The offender is monitored in the community and is required to remain in a particular area at certain times (Andrews and Bonta, 2006). Leaving this area without permission sounds an alarm and results in the offender's detention and/or arrest. Electronic monitoring is usually used with offenders who present a low risk to the community and may form part of an offender's licence conditions upon release from prison.

In principle, electronic monitoring can improve the enforceability of community monitoring without having to rely on the trustworthiness of offenders or the reliability of supervisors (Cavadino and Digman, 2007). Furthermore, it allows offenders to remain in the community where they can continue to work and interact with family and friends (Nellis, 1991). When compared to prison, however, electronic monitoring increases the risk of exposing the community to crime, as confinement is limited to certain times (Nellis, 2006; Renzema and Mayo-Wilson, 2005). Research has also demonstrated that it does not reduce reoffending any more than prison or probation (Bonta et al., 2000; Renzema and Mayo-Wilson, 2005). Similar to the aforementioned alternative punishments, electronic monitoring has only been found to reduce reoffending when it incorporates a treatment element (Renzema and Mayo-Wilson, 2005).

Summary

Alternative punishments to prison and probation include compensatory penalties, punishment orders, intense supervision programmes, shock incarceration, scared straight programmes, and electronic monitoring. Overall, evidence suggests that alternative punishments have little effect in terms of reducing reoffending, unless they are accompanied by some form of treatment programme.

Prison life

The Stanford prison experiment investigated the dehumanizing effect of prison conditions on prison officers and prisoners (see 'thinking scientifically' box for further details). More recently, two aspects of prison life to have received interest are prison officer stress and prisoner suicide.

Thinking scientifically → **A study of prisoners and guards in a simulated prison (Haney, Banks and Zimbardo, 2004)**

The research attempted to provide an explanation for poor prison conditions and the dehumanizing effect these had on prison officers and prisoners through the use of direct non-participant observation. Previous attention focused on the **dispositional hypothesis**, whereby the poor conditions and dehumanization were thought to result from the 'nature' of prison officers and prisoners.

Twenty-two 'normal' students were randomly assigned to the role of prison officer or prisoner. The intention was for these roles to be enacted over a two-week period within an environment that was physically constructed to resemble a prison. Prison officers were free to implement procedures for the induction and custody of prisoners within certain limits. For example, the use of physical punishment or physical aggression was forbidden.

Although prison officers and prisoners were free to engage in any form of interaction, it tended to be negative, hostile and dehumanizing. Prisoners adopted a generally passive demeanour while prison officers assumed a more dominant role. Prison officers also engaged in various forms of indirect aggression, including control of when prisoners were allowed to eat, sleep or go to the toilet. Five prisoners were released after a few days because of extreme anxiety, depression, crying and rage. Furthermore, the research was terminated after only six days because of concerns over the detrimental impact the research was having on the students who acted as prison officers and prisoners. In contrast to the dispositional hypothesis, it was concluded that poor conditions and dehumanization are a result of the prison environment.

Evaluation

Questions have been raised as to whether the prison officers and prisoners did anything more than act out their roles convincingly, despite the vivid nature of the observations made during the research. In response, it has been claimed that virtually all students experienced reactions that went beyond role-playing. For example, 90 per cent of conversations related to the immediate situation while only 10 per cent related to life outside the 'prison'. Furthermore, prison officers were found to be more aggressive when alone with prisoners than when in groups. Irrespective, it is accepted that the minimal prison-like conditions were insufficient to provide a meaningful representation of the real prison situation. Whether this limitation undermines or strengthens the significance of the observations is less certain.

Prison officer stress

Working in a prison is very challenging and inherently stressful. In a review of the literature, Schaufeli and Peeters (2000) identified ten risk factors associated with increased levels of prison officer stress:

- *High workload*. Includes having a lot to do in a short period of time as well as having to perform a number of different tasks at the same time.
- *Lack of autonomy*. Includes not having much control over the performance of tasks (that is, skill discretion) or involvement in decision making (that is, decision authority).
- *Underutilization of knowledge and skills*. Relates to a lack of opportunity to use knowledge and skills learned during training.
- *Lack of variety*. Relates to the often dull and repetitive nature of daily tasks.
- *Role problems*. Includes a lack of sufficient information to perform tasks efficiently (that is, role ambiguity) and the requirement to meet conflicting demands (that is, role conflict).

- *Demanding social contacts.* Relates to the inherent conflict between the role of the prison officer (that is, 'the keeper') and the role of the prisoner (that is, 'the kept').
- *Uncertainty.* Includes uncertainty regarding job security and career prospects.
- *Health and safety risks.* Concerns the constant threat of having to deal with violent confrontations.
- *Inadequate pay.* Relates to the fairness of pay rather than the actual amount of pay.
- *Poor social status.* Concerns the poor social status associated with working in a prison.

Of these risk factors, research suggests that high workload, lack of autonomy, role problems, demanding social contracts, health and safety risks, and poor social status are the leading risk factors in terms of prison officer stress (Dowden and Tellier, 2004; Schaufeli and Peeters, 2000).

With regard to role conflict, prison officers often find it difficult to maintain a balance between the opposing demands of custody and rehabilitation (Schaufeli and Peeters, 2000). Generally, prison officers with a rehabilitation orientation experience considerably lower levels of stress compared to those with a custody orientation (Dowden and Tellier, 2004). However, the country of study has a dramatic impact on the direction of this effect. For example, prison officers in Canada who possessed a rehabilitation orientation experienced lower levels of stress, but the opposite was true for prison officers in the US. This apparent inconsistency can be explained by the differing philosophies of the Canadian and American prison services: the Canadian prison service endorses rehabilitation while the American prison service emphasizes custody.

Prisoner suicide

Suicide is a serious problem, with death rates in prisons being much higher than death rates in the community (Crighton, 2006b). Furthermore, up until recently there has been a steady increase in the number of suicides committed by prisoners in the UK (Crighton and Towl, 2008). Overcrowding and low staffing levels have been cited as contributing factors, due to their association with a lack of access to medical services, an increase in the incidence of physical assault and a lack of opportunity for activity (Daniel, 2006). Research has also revealed that the first 30 days in prison represents a high-risk period with regard to suicide attempts (Daniel, 2006). Consequently, moving prisoners from one prison to the next is likely to increase the risk of suicide, while interventions during this high-risk time period are likely to decrease the risk of suicide (Crighton and Towl, 2008).

Although the specific causes of suicide and self-harm are poorly understood, it is now accepted that prisoners who attempt suicide are often different in nature to prisoners who engage in self-harm (Snow, 2006). Prisoners who attempt suicide tend to exhibit passive moods (for example depression, loneliness and boredom) while prisoners who engage in self-harm tend to exhibit active moods (for example anger, anxiety and stress). Furthermore, the decision to attempt suicide is more likely to be influenced by specific events or experiences while the decision to self-harm is more likely to be influenced by negative feelings or emotions. It is important therefore that suicide and self-harm are understood in terms of a dual-path model that reflects these differences, and that generic management approaches to treatment are replaced by behavioural-specific approaches.

Summary

Prison life can have a significant impact on the health of prison officers and prisoners. High demands, poor control and conflicting roles lead to increased levels of prison officer stress. Meanwhile, overcrowding and low staffing levels contribute to the comparatively high rates of prisoner suicide. It is now apparent that suicide and self-harm are different in nature so it is important that behavioural-specific approaches to treatment are used.

Further reading

Andrews, D.A. and Bonta, J. (2006) *The Psychology of Criminal Conduct* (4th edn). Newark, NJ: LexisNexis.

McGuire, J. (2008) What's the point of sentencing? Psychological aspects of crime and punishment. In G. Davies, C. Hollin and R. Bull (eds) *Forensic Psychology* (pp. 265–91). Chichester: John Wiley & Sons.

Towl, G.J. (ed.) (2006) *Psychological Research in Prisons*. Oxford: Blackwell Publishing.

Chapter 12

The treatment of offenders

Introduction

The treatment of offenders has been an area of much debate within criminal justice settings over the last 30 years with the **nothing works** doctrine relenting to the principles of **what works** during the 1990s (Hollin and Palmer, 2006). Currently, there is evidence to suggest that accredited offending behaviour programmes can produce small effects in the reduction of reoffending (McGuire, 2004).

Chapter 11 discussed the justifications offered for the use of punishment, the effectiveness of different types of punishment and the effect of prison life on prison officer stress and prisoner suicide. This chapter will consider the effectiveness of different types of treatment in reducing reoffending. It will first provide an overview of the 'what works' debate including the role of meta-analysis. The effectiveness of general and specific offending behaviour programmes will then be examined in the context of violent and sex reoffending. Finally, token economy programmes and drug and alcohol programmes will be considered.

This chapter will examine:

- What works
- General offending behaviour programmes
- Specific offending behaviour programmes
- Other treatment programmes

What works

In the 1960s and early 1970s, many researchers and practitioners were confident that treatment could facilitate a reduction in reoffending (Redondo, Sánchez-Meca and Garrido, 1999). This rehabilitative ideal was replaced by the nothing works doctrine in the mid-1970s as a consequence of a number of **narrative reviews** questioning the utility of various forms of treatment (Andrews and Bonta, 2006; McGuire, 2004). A review by Robert Martinson, published in 1974, was particularly influential with respect to policy, despite vigorous rebuttals on the grounds that positive evidence for the effectiveness of treatment was simply ignored (Hollin and Palmer, 2006; McGuire, 2004). Although Martinson withdrew his initial claim that nothing works in an article published in 1979, his retraction was largely ignored. This was accompanied by a marked shift in the ethos of the criminal justice system during the 1980s, away from rehabilitation, towards retribution and confinement (Andrews and Bonta, 2006; Hollin and Palmer, 2006).

Undeterred by the widespread acceptance of the nothing works doctrine, a number of critics responded to Martinson's initial article by systematically reviewing the literature concerning the effectiveness of treatment (Goggin and Gendreau, 2006). The development of meta-analysis, a statistical alternative to traditional narrative reviews, enabled the reviewers to consolidate trends across studies, and led to the conclusion that certain forms of treatment can be effective at reducing reoffending (Goggin and Gendreau, 2006; McGuire, 2004). Ultimately, the combination of these meta-analytic reviews informed the development of the principles of effective practice in offender treatment; commonly referred to as the principles of what works (Andrews and Bonta, 2006; Hollin and Palmer, 2006).

During the mid-1990s, a number of countries, including the UK and Canada, introduced comprehensive accreditation systems founded on the principles of what works (Goggin and Gendreau, 2006). The accreditation process aimed to maximize the effectiveness of treatment in reducing reoffending, through the establishment of standards for the design, delivery and evaluation of offending behaviour programmes (Goggin and Gendreau, 2006; Jennings, 2003). There are currently more than 40 accredited programmes in the UK (Home Office, 2007).

It is important to note that the development of an accreditation system has not gone without criticism. It has been argued that financial resources should target societal factors known to increase crime rates, such as poverty, restricted educational opportunities and poor housing provision, rather than the development of offending behaviour programmes 'after the fact' (Crighton, 2006a). It has also been suggested that a wider range of activities are required to address offenders' needs (Willmot, 2003). For example, vocational training can play an integral role in reducing reoffending provided it is linked to prospects of employment upon release (McGuire, 2002).

The role of meta-analysis

A fundamental problem that researchers and practitioners have had to contend with is how to interpret the countless research findings concerning the effectiveness of the treatment of offenders (Hollin, 1992). The narrative reviews associated with the nothing works doctrine were essentially 'evaluations of evaluations', judged by the proportion of findings that reached **statistical significance** (Blackburn, 1993). Consequently, they were influenced by the selective inclusion of studies and the subjective interpretation of the findings (Hollin and Palmer, 2006). The development of meta-analysis went some way towards overcoming these problems by offering reviewers the opportunity to quantify the findings of a large number of studies (Hollin, 1992). Furthermore, this statistical technique allowed researchers to search for the characteristics that differentiate effective from non-effective treatment, and to better understand what works and for whom (Goggin and Gendreau, 2006; Redondo et al., 1999).

However, meta-analytic reviews are not without their own methodological shortcomings. For example, the reviews are only as reliable as the original studies included in the analysis, and as such can be compromised by the use of studies with small samples and/or poor methodologies (Hollin and Palmer, 2006; McGuire, 2002, 2004). The utility of this statistical technique may also be limited by **publication bias**, whereby research with non-significant findings is less likely to be submitted or accepted for publication (McGuire, 2002). Nevertheless, there is evidence that research methodologies are improving. Coding systems can be used to control for differences between studies, and researchers can ensure that reviews include both published and unpublished research (Hollin and Palmer, 2006; McGuire, 2004).

Collectively, meta-analytic reviews of the effectiveness of treatment suggest that the completion of offending behaviour programmes can have a small yet significant effect in reducing reoffending (McGuire 2004). In brief, the principles of what works recommend that programmes have a strong theoretical and empirical foundation; target medium- to high-risk offenders (offender risk); focus on **dynamic risk factors** rather than **static risk factors** (offender needs); use social learning or **cognitive-behavioural** styles of delivery (treatment delivery); address barriers to treatment (treatment responsivity); and are implemented as intended (treatment integrity) (McGuire, 2004).

Cognitive-behavioural styles of delivery

As noted in the principles of what works, cognitive-behavioural styles of delivery have the potential to reduce reoffending. Cognitive-behavioural therapy is an umbrella term that incorporates elements of social learning (that is, behavioural) and cognitive theories (social learning theory was outlined in Chapter 3 and cognitive theories of offending were discussed in Chapter 4) (Hansen, 2008; McGuire, 2006). These theories and corresponding therapies target, treat and evaluate different aspects of offending behaviour:

- *Behavioural therapy*. Targets the contingencies of reinforcement and punishment that led to the development and maintenance of maladaptive behaviour (Pearson, Lipton, Cleland and Yee, 2002). Interventions focus on the removal of this maladaptive behaviour and often incorporate relaxation training, thought stopping and assertion training (Lipton, Pearson, Cleland and Yee, 2002; Pearson et al., 2002). The effectiveness of therapy is then evaluated on the basis of changes in behaviour (Kendall and Hollon, 1979).
- *Cognitive therapy*. Targets the distorted and dysfunctional thinking patterns that are common to all psychological problems including maladaptive behaviour (Moster, Wnuk and Jeglic, 2008). Interventions focus on the alteration or replacement of these dysfunctional thinking patterns with particular attention to negative thoughts, tendencies to draw inappropriate conclusions and 'all-or-nothing' thinking (Lipton et al., 2002; Moster et al., 2008). The effectiveness of therapy is then evaluated on the basis of changes in

thinking patterns (and corresponding behaviour) (Kendall and Hollon, 1979).

Interpersonal skills training and anger management

Cognitive-behavioural styles of delivery are often used to provide interpersonal skills training and anger management. Interpersonal skills training forms an integral part of many offending behaviour programmes and aims to improve and develop prisoners' cognitive skills (Bourke and Van Hasselt, 2001). These include:

- Social skills and assertiveness.
- Stress management and coping skills.
- Empathy.
- Problem-solving skills.
- Anger and impulse control.

Most of these programmes involve a combination of direct instruction, modelling, rehearsal and role-play (Bourke and Van Hasselt, 2001; Lipton et al., 2002). Thus, the use of a skills-oriented approach allows prisoners to learn specific skills and practise them in a controlled setting.

Although interpersonal skills training often incorporates anger and impulse control, specific anger management programmes are also available. These generally offer a version of Novaco's (1979) stress inoculation model, an adaptation of the model developed by David Meichenbaum (Polaschek, 2006). Central to this model is the assumption that violence is caused and modified by experiences of aggression, which in turn represent maladaptive responses to stressful situations.

Therefore, the aim of anger management programmes is to help prisoners regulate their aggression by providing them with a range of cognitive-behavioural skills. The stress inoculation model comprises three stages (Novaco, 1979, 2000):

1. *Cognitive preparation*. Prisoners learn about anger and how to distinguish adaptive and non-adaptive uses of aggression. They also identify triggers for their own aggression and learn a variety of anger management techniques (for example self-regulation and cognitive flexibility).
2. *Skill acquisition*. Prisoners learn to prepare for provocative and confrontational situations. They also learn how to control their aggression and resolve conflicts in a non-aggressive manner.

3 *Application training.* Prisoners practise the new techniques they have learned in imaginary and realistic role-play situations.

In combination, the three stages of the stress inoculation model provide prisoners with the skills to identify aggression-provoking situations and respond to them non-aggressively.

Thinking scientifically → **Measuring the effectiveness of treatment**

Evaluation research has considered the effectiveness of many types of treatment, but there is no definitive measure of success (Hollin, 1992). For example, the majority of evaluation studies in the UK utilize reconviction as an outcome variable, compared to the US where **recidivism** is most frequently used (Friendship and Falshaw, 2003). It is generally accepted that reconviction and recidivism data is, at best, a proxy for actual reoffending behaviour. Reconviction measures depend on the accurate recording of convictions, which is unlikely to reflect the true level of offending, while recidivism measures rarely access offending beyond that which is officially recorded (Friendship, Falshaw and Beech, 2003b).

The validity of these outcome variables as measures of success has also been questioned as they dichotomize reoffending behaviour, and as such conceal variations in the incidence and seriousness of any crimes committed (Blackburn, 1993). Other drawbacks of reconviction data include the inevitably long lag-time between the charge and the conviction of an offender, the associated high attrition rates, and the likelihood that programmes will have been modified prior to the completion of the evaluation research (Blud, Travers, Nugent and Thornton, 2003; Friendship and Falshaw, 2003).

In the context of intimate partner violence, determining the effectiveness of treatment programmes is especially problematic due to the difficulties associated with defining suitable measures of success (Geffner and Rosenbaum, 2001; Gilchrist and Kebbell, 2005). High attrition rates in securing a conviction for intimate partner violence are well documented, so reconviction data is unlikely to provide an accurate measure of reoffending (Lindsay, Brady and McQueirns, 2005). Furthermore, it has been debated whether a reduction in violence is a satisfactory outcome variable. As Gilchrist and Kebbell (2005, p. 235) commented, 'Is cessation of physical violence enough? If a man has beaten his partner up once and then stops, but the threat is always there, is her quality of life enhanced in any way?'

Factors affecting reoffending in the community

Although attention is often given to the effectiveness of treatment programmes in isolation, it is important to acknowledge that many other factors influence the risk of reoffending. Visher and Travis (2003) describe four transitions that influence the success or failure of the transition from prison to the community and the corresponding risk of reoffending:

1. *Pre-prison circumstances*. Includes demographic factors, drug addiction, employment history, employment-related skills and family situation.
2. *Prison experiences*. Includes length of sentence, completion of treatment and contact with family and friends.
3. *Short-term post-prison experiences*. Includes housing, social support from family and friends, and support with the transition from prison to the community.
4. *Long-term post-prison experiences*. Includes employment, social support from family and friends, criminal associations, and supervision by the criminal justice system.

There is considerable evidence to suggest that these factors influence the risk of ex-prisoners reoffending (Social Exclusion Unit, 2002). For example, research has shown that ex-prisoners are more likely to reoffend if they lack employment opportunities and social support, or suffer from drug addiction and continue to have criminal associations (Brown, St Amand and Zamble, 2009; DeJong, 1997; Uggen, 2000). Consequently, it is important that mechanisms are available to help ex-prisoners with this transition from prison to the community (Graffam, Shinkfield and Hardcastle, 2008).

Summary

The principles of what works were introduced during the 1990s on the understanding that completion of offending behaviour programmes can have a small yet significant effect in reducing reoffending. The principles of what works recommend that programmes should target offender risk and need, as well as treatment responsivity, delivery and integrity. Cognitive-behavioural styles of delivery have the potential to reduce reoffending and are often used to provide interpersonal skills training and anger management.

General offending behaviour programmes

There are three prominent accredited general offending behaviour programmes that draw on social cognitive theory: Reasoning and Rehabilitation (R&R), Enhanced Thinking Skills (ETS) and Think First. In the UK, ETS and Think First are currently being replaced by Thinking Skills Programme (TSP). At the time of writing TSP was being rolled out across the prison and probation services. Collectively, these programmes target offenders' maladjusted thinking and behaviour by teaching self-management and problem-solving skills to promote prosocial behaviour (Hatcher, 2008; Home Office, 2007):

- *Reasoning and Rehabilitation*. Designed for use with higher risk offenders, R&R utilizes a combination of tutoring, role-play, discussions and exercises to promote the acquisition and rehearsal of a range of interpersonal skills. These include problem solving, social interaction, self-control, emotional management, creative thinking and moral reasoning.
- *Enhanced Thinking Skills*. Developed to compliment R&R with medium- to high-risk offenders, ETS focuses on a similar range of interpersonal skills. Particular attention is given to problem solving, and social and moral reasoning skills through the use of prosocial modelling (that is, the modelling of positive behaviour).
- *Think First*. Think First also focuses on the acquisition and rehearsal of a range of interpersonal skills, but differs from R&R and ETS in that it is crime specific and only offered in the community. As such, offenders are encouraged to analyse their criminal involvement in order to change their behaviour.

Evaluation of general offending behaviour programmes

According to Friendship et al. (2003a), prison service reconviction data concerning R&R and ETS programmes suggests that they have a beneficial impact for medium-low- and medium-high-risk offenders. Research in both prison and community settings has also shown that these programmes can produce positive results in terms of reducing reoffending (Jennings, 2003). With specific reference to R&R, Tong and Farrington (2006) found there was a decrease in reoffending based on reconviction data for offenders who received treatment compared to those who did not. Furthermore, this effect was evident in all countries where the programme had been evaluated extensively, including the UK, the US and Canada.

However, not all reviews have found general offending behaviour programmes to be effective in reducing reoffending. For example, two evaluations of cognitive skills programmes in the UK found no difference in the reconviction rates of offenders according to whether they had participated in R&R or ETS while in prison (Cann, Falshaw, Nugent and Friendship, 2003; Falshaw, Friendship, Travers and Nugent, 2003). Research has also shown that the effectiveness of general offending behaviour programmes may not be consistent for all types of offender. In Canada, Robinson (1995) found that cognitive skills training was most effective for sex offenders, followed by violent and drug offenders, but was not effective for non-violent property or robbery offenders. Consequently, it suggests that general offending behaviour programmes can incorporate components of anger management effectively (Jennings, 2003; Thomas and Jackson, 2003).

Programme completion versus non-completion

Many studies have demonstrated a positive effect for programme completion, and a negative effect for programme non-completion (that is, dropping out of the programme), in terms of a reduction in reconviction rates compared to no treatment (Palmer, 2007). For example, Palmer et al. (2008) found that offenders who completed R&R, ETS or Think First had lower reconviction rates compared to offenders who had not attended the programme, while offenders who failed to complete the programme had the highest reconviction rates.

It is apparent therefore that the relationship between non-completion and increased reconviction rates has important implications for evaluation research (Palmer et al., 2008). Only a third of offenders allocated to one of the offending behaviour programmes evaluated in Hollin et al.'s (2004) study actually completed the programme so the lack of a significant treatment effect could reflect a failure to complete, rather than a failure of the programme per se. Consequently, it appears that general offending behaviour programmes are associated with a reduction in reconviction when completed by appropriate offenders. It is the responsibility of the National Offender Management Service (NOMS) to ensure the appropriate selection of offenders for programmes is not compromised by attempts to achieve the completion targets set by the prison and probation services (Palmer et al., 2008).

Summary

There are a number of general offending behaviour programmes including R&R, ETS and Think First that target the maladjusted thinking and behaviour of offenders through the teaching of a range of interpersonal skills. Although evaluations of the effectiveness of general offending behaviour programmes have been mixed, it appears that programme completion can lead to a reduction in reoffending. However, programme non-completion is associated with increased rates of reoffending.

Specific offending behaviour programmes

There are a range of accredited programmes that target specific types of offender, including those convicted for violent and sex crimes. These programmes use a combination of cognitive-behavioural and **psycho-educational** styles of delivery (Hatcher, 2008).

Violent offending behaviour programmes

There are two distinct types of violent offending behaviour programmes, those that target general violent offending and those that target intimate partner violence (Hatcher, 2008). In the UK, current accredited programmes include Aggression Replacement Training (ART), Controlling Anger and Learning to Manage it (CALM), the Cognitive Self-Change Programme (CSCP) and the Integrated Domestic Violence Programme (IDAP) (Home Office, 2007):

- *Aggression Replacement Training*. Designed for use with medium- to high-risk offenders, ART aims to reduce aggressive behaviour by targeting anger management, self-control, self-awareness and moral reasoning (Palmer, 2005; Hatcher, 2008). Offenders learn to control their anger by identifying the triggers of their aggression and developing alternative prosocial coping strategies (Hatcher, 2008).
- *Controlling Anger and Learning to Manage it*. CALM targets medium- to high-risk offenders with an emotional element to their

criminal behaviour. It focuses on a similar range of issues to ART: social skills, self-control and moral reasoning (Home Office, 2004).

- *The Cognitive Self-Change Programme.* CSCP targets high-risk offenders with a history of instrumental violence. It aims to identify and change thinking patterns associated with violence (Home Office, 2004).
- *The Integrated Domestic Violence Programme.* In contrast to ART, CALM and CSCP, IDAP targets intimate partner violence. It aims to challenge dysfunctional attitudes and beliefs, enhance victim empathy and teach self-control strategies (Home Office, 2007).

Sex offending behaviour programmes

The Sex Offender Treatment Programme (SOTP) represents a 'family' of programmes that address the different risks associated with sex offending (Home Office, 2004). They include the Core, Extended, Rolling and Adapted Programmes, and the Better Lives Booster (BLB) Programme (Hatcher, 2008):

- *Sex Offender Treatment Programme.* The core SOTP targets medium-risk offenders and focuses on the dynamic risk factors related to sex offending via the use of structured exercises, role-play and non-aggressive challenges. Dynamic risk factors include deviant sex interests and a range of social issues (for example problems with intimacy, self-esteem, anxiety and feelings of inadequacy).
- *Extended Programme.* Offers additional treatment for high-risk offenders who have completed the core programme.
- *Rolling Programme.* Offers alternative treatment for low-risk offenders, allowing them to join and leave the programme when appropriate.
- *Adapted Programme.* Offers an adapted programme for offenders with learning difficulties and/or social functioning problems (for example personality disorders).
- *Better Lives Booster Programme.* Offers additional treatment for offenders who are close to release, focusing on their particular treatment needs.

Cognitive aspects of SOTPs involve the identification of the maladaptive thoughts that cause offenders to contemplate inappropriate sexual behaviour, while behavioural aspects focus on reducing the levels of arousal experienced by offenders in order to prevent them from engaging in inappropriate sexual behaviour in the future (Beech, Fisher and Beckett, 1998).

Evaluation of specific offending behaviour programmes

Dowden and Andrews (2000) found that the largest reductions in violent reoffending were achieved when programmes adhered to the principles of what works. Furthermore, research utilizing the **Offender Group Reconviction Scale (OGRS)** has found completion of ART and/or CALM to be associated with a significant reduction in predicted reconviction rates over a period of two years (Hollis, 2007). In relation to intimate partner violence programmes, the findings of evaluation research are mixed. Research utilizing OGRS failed to find significant reductions in predicted reconviction rates, while other evaluation research suggests that partner abuse programmes have a small yet significant effect (Babcock, Green and Robie, 2004; Gilchrist and Kebbell, 2005). On the basis of research in the US, Gadd and Jefferson (2007) argued that, at best, intimate partner violence programmes have a modest impact on a minority of the offenders who complete them.

The findings of evaluation research for the effectiveness of SOTP have also been mixed (Hatcher, 2008). Research examining post-completion measures has shown that completion of the core SOTP is associated with significant reductions in pro-offending attitudes and significant improvements in relapse prevention skills (Beech et al., 1998). When reconviction rates are considered, research has found that although completion of SOTP is associated with a slight reduction in sex reconvictions, it is not significant (Friendship, Mann and Beech, 2003d; Friendship and Debidin, 2006). However, significant reductions have been found when reconviction rates for medium- and low-risk sex and violent crimes are combined. When considering the lack of statistical significance for sex crimes, it is important to note that reconviction rates are generally low (about 5% for untreated offenders) so any reduction due to treatment is small and therefore difficult to demonstrate statistically (Friendship, Mann and Beech, 2003c).

Thinking scientifically → **The treatment of women and psychopathic offenders**

A wider range of programmes are available to male offenders compared to female offenders at present, and programme development is primarily based on the needs of men (Carney, Buttell and Dutton, 2007). However, it is well documented that the number of women serving custodial sentences is increasing (Home Office, 2002). It is therefore important to determine whether practice should be based on the assumption that women are the same as, or different to, men (Mosson, 2003). Evaluation research is also required to determine whether the adaptation of traditionally male-oriented treatments can account for the causes of female aggression (Carney et al., 2007).

With regard to the effectiveness of programmes with **psychopathic offenders**, research suggests that offending behaviour programmes may actually increase their risk of reoffending (Hodgins, 2007; Rice, 1997). Polaschek (2006) commented that the 'here and now' focus of psychopathic offenders, together with their inability to feel remorse or distress, hinders self-reflection and personal responsivity. As such, psychopathic offenders only participate in treatment in order to create the impression that they can change their behaviour (Polaschek, 2006). Although the origins of psychopathy remain poorly understood, Dangerous and Severe Personality Disorder (DSPD) units have been developed for the treatment of the most dangerous violent offenders within the prison service in England and Wales (Maden, 2005). The Chromis programme has been specifically designed to meet the responsivity needs of highly psychopathic offenders. Treatment focuses on the identification, reduction and management of a number of risk factors with an emphasis on the development of relapse prevention techniques (Home Office, 2007).

Summary

There are a range of specific offending behaviour programmes in addition to the general programmes that are intended for use with particular types of offender. These include violent offending behaviour programmes that target general violent offending and intimate partner violence, and sex offending behaviour programmes that address the sex offending of low- through to high-risk offenders. Evaluations of the specific offending behaviour programmes suggest that they are more effective at reducing reoffending for general violence than intimate partner violence or sex offending.

Other treatment programmes

In addition to the aforementioned accredited offending behaviour programmes are a number of treatment programmes that target offenders' behaviour and substance (drug and alcohol) misuse.

Token economy programmes

Token economy programmes utilize reinforcement systems to modify offenders' behaviour. Programmes usually involve offenders receiving tokens for the performance of certain desirable behaviours (for example cleaning living areas and assisting other offenders) which can later be exchanged for certain privileges or goods (for example television rights and confectionary) (Lipton et al., 2002). Punishment systems can also be incorporated, whereby tokens are deducted if offenders engage in certain undesirable behaviours (for example testing positive for drugs or alcohol). As such, token economy programmes provide a means of immediately reinforcing desirable behaviours (or punishing undesirable behaviours) in an unambiguous manner as tokens have a clear exchange value (Lipton et al., 2002).

Early research indicated that token economy programmes offer an effective alternative to traditional punishment systems. For example, they have been used to effectively reduce the need for aversive control procedures with young offenders in short-term detention facilities (Gambrill, 1976). Programmes have also been used successfully with adult offenders to reduce the frequency of rule violations (Milan, Throckmorton, McKee and Wood, 1979).

Drug and alcohol programmes

Prisons employ a three-stage approach to address the problem of substance misuse (Crighton and Towl, 2008):

1. Reduce availability through the use of intelligence-led interceptions.
2. Reduce demand through the delivery of effective treatments.

3 Increase the long-term effectiveness of treatment through the development of community-based services.

Cognitive-behavioural programmes

In the UK there are a number of treatment programmes that target substance misuse, including FOCUS in high-security prisons, and STOP and Action on Drugs in medium-security prisons. These cognitive-behavioural programmes focus on six areas (McMurran, 2006):

- *Motivation enhancement*. Motivational interviewing is used to increase offenders' desire for change by drawing attention to the discrepancy between their current situation and a more desirable or less problematic one.
- *Behavioural self-control*. Offenders identify the triggers for their substance misuse, and develop alternative coping strategies. Successful self-control is rewarded while relapses are treated as learning experiences.
- *Cognitive coping skills*. Offenders construct scripts that incorporate self-statements and self-instructions to support the implementation of new coping strategies.
- *Interpersonal skills*. Offenders develop a range of skills to help them refrain from using drugs or alcohol as well as cope with the disbelief and discouragement of others.
- *Relapse prevention*. Offenders identify high-risk situations on the basis of past relapses and learn to anticipate future difficulties. Consideration is also given to the broader issues of social support and stress management.
- *Lifestyle change*. Offenders develop positive substitute behaviours that meet the needs originally satisfied through substance misuse.

Overall, research suggests that the effectiveness of cognitive-behavioural treatment programmes in reducing offender substance misuse is limited by its implementation in prison and probation settings. Consequently, it is important that programmes are oriented towards offenders' lives outside these settings (McMurran, 2006).

Acupuncture programmes

Acupuncture programmes offer an alternative to cognitive-behavioural programmes in the treatment of substance misuse (Gottfredson and Exum, 2002). Acupuncture is a Chinese medical art that involves inserting fine needles into the skin in order to reduce pain and/or disability. It is non-addictive, quick to administer and relatively inexpensive (Latessa and Moon, 1992). Acupuncture programmes generally embrace a rehabilitative philosophy, and treat offenders through a combination of acupuncture and therapy (Latessa and Moon, 1992). Acupuncture is used to break the addiction while therapy is used to address the underlying social and psychological problems.

An acupuncture programme implemented in the US offered three phases of treatment (Latessa and Moon, 1992). The first phase provided five treatment sessions a week, the second phase provided three treatment sessions a week, and the third offered thirty days of aftercare. Progression from one phase to the next was contingent on three weeks of negative drug testing. Offenders were removed from the programme if they failed to attend, failed consecutive drug tests, or were convicted for new crimes. When the programme was evaluated, there was no treatment effect for offenders who received acupuncture compared to those who received an acupuncture simulation (that is, a placebo) or no acupuncture.

Summary

Token economy programmes utilize reinforcement systems to modify offenders' behaviour. Evaluations have shown that they can be used to reduce the frequency of rule violations and the need for aversive control procedures. Cognitive-behavioural programmes and acupuncture programmes represent two approaches to the treatment of substance misuse. Neither has been found to be particularly effective.

Further reading

Crighton, D.A. and Towl, G.J. (2008) *Psychology in Prisons* (2nd edn). Oxford: Blackwell Publishing.

Hatcher, R. (2008) Psychological skills in working with offenders. In G.M. Davies, C.R. Hollin and R. Bull (eds) *Forensic Psychology* (pp. 293–322). Chichester: John Wiley & Sons.

Hollin, C.R. and Palmer, E.J. (eds) (2006) *Offending Behaviour Programmes: Development, Application and Controversies*. Chichester: John Wiley & Sons.

Glossary

Adolescence-limited offenders Those who develop antisocial behaviours during adolescence, which then desist in early adulthood.

Antisocial behaviour A broad range of behaviour that causes or is likely to cause members of the public alarm, harassment or distress. Antisocial behaviour may involve the misuse of public areas and environmental damage, as well as acts that negatively impact upon other members of the public.

Behavioural consistency hypothesis Asserts that the same offender will behave and perpetrate crimes in a similar manner.

Bottom-up approach An approach to profiling that relies on psychological theory and research to interpret information and develop conclusions in relation to a particular crime.

Broken windows theory Asserts that a high concentration of petty crimes leads to a higher incidence of serious crimes.

Cambridge study in delinquent development Initiated by Donald J. West in 1961, and continued by David P. Farrington, this longitudinal survey originally followed the lives of 411 males born in an urban area of South London for 24 years, from the age of 8 through to 32. This was subsequently extended with a reinvestigation of the men at age 46. Employing both qualitative and quantitative methods, the study tested and examined factors influencing delinquency and criminal behaviour.

Chicago School University of Chicago based theorists who developed theories about human behaviour within the sociological framework of the social structure and urban environment.

Classical conditioning A type of behavioural learning discovered by Ivan P. Pavlov in which a stimulus gains the ability to elicit a response that was originally elicited by another stimulus through the process of learning by association.

Coerced-compliant false confessions False confessions provided by innocent suspects in order to escape the police interview despite knowing that the confession is untrue.

Coerced-internalized false confessions False confessions provided by innocent suspects who have come to believe they committed the crime with which they are accused despite having no memory of it.

Cognitive-behavioural Styles of delivery that focus on changing the maladaptive thoughts of offenders in order to change their maladaptive behaviour.

Cognitive interview An interviewee-led interviewing procedure developed to enhance memory recall; often used with victims, witnesses, and cooperative suspects.

Cognitive load The amount of mental activity required to store and process information in the short-term memory.

Compliance behaviour Involves a public but not a private change in opinion towards that of the group. Usually associated with majority influence.

Concurrent validity The level of agreement between two different measures of the same underlying concept.

Conditionability The extent to which a child is able to learn that antisocial behaviour elicits negative consequences and thus develops the self-restraint necessary for conventional socialization.

Confederates People who pretend to be naive participants but are actually involved with the research and are aware of its aims.

Confirmation bias The search for and interpretation of information so that it confirms preconceptions.

Confounding variables Variables that have not been controlled for and influence the independent and dependent variables.

Continuance Involves delaying the start of the trial.

Control condition Provides a measure of behaviour in the absence of experimental manipulations that can be used for comparison purposes.

Conversation management An interviewer-led interviewing procedure developed to enhance memory recall; often used with uncooperative suspects.

Conversion behaviour Involves a public and a private change in opinion towards that of the group. Usually associated with minority influence.

Crime rates The aggregate number of crimes per person in a particular population.

Cross-sectional designs The study of one group at one particular time, generally involving a representative sample of a larger social group. This form of research produces a 'snapshot' illustration of certain social trends.

Dark figure The difference between the amount of crime committed and the amount of crime officially recorded.

Decision rule The amount of agreement required for a guilty or not guilty verdict.

Determinate sentencing Prison sentences that have a specified duration or release date. Release only occurs at the end of the sentence.

Differential social organization Relates to the prevalence of crime within particular social areas and the degree to which they are organized favourably or unfavourably towards breaking the law.

Disorganized offender Offenders who are not in control and do not plan their crimes. The crimes are usually spontaneous and the crime scenes are chaotic (for example no attempts to hide the victim's body or remove forensic evidence).

Dispositional hypothesis Asserts that behaviour is caused by internal (that is, individual) characteristics rather than external (that is, situational) characteristics.

DNA The abbreviation for deoxyribonuleic acid. DNA provides a 'genetic blueprint' that contains information on the unique genetic characteristics of people.

Due process The principle that laws should be fair and legal proceedings should adhere to the accepted legal procedures and safeguards.

Dunedin multidisciplinary health and development study A New Zealand cohort study of 1037 people born in the city of Dunedin between April 1972 and March 1973. Study members have been and will continue to be assessed at regular intervals. Due to its multidisciplinary objectives, participants provide investigators with a vast array of information from surveys and interviews through to medical examinations.

Dyads Two people who are regarded as a pair (for example husband and wife).

Dynamic risk factors Risk factors that can potentially be changed during treatment (for example alcohol and drug use).

Ecological validity The degree to which behaviours observed in research settings can be generalized to behaviours occurring in natural settings.

Estimator variables Factors that influence the accuracy of eyewitness testimony and are not under the control of the criminal justice system.

False confessions Occur when an innocent suspect confesses to a crime he or she did not commit.

False memory debate Relates to whether the extensive use of memory recovery techniques increases the risk of fabricated allegations of childhood abuse among people who were not abused.

False memory syndrome The recovery of memories that are shown to be false.

Flashbulb memories Highly detailed and accurate memories that are created during significant and unexpected events.

Foils People in a police lineup who are not the suspect.

General deterrence Occurs when people are less likely to offend as a consequence of the threat of punishment.

Genetic propensity To have a natural or biological inclination toward particular behaviours or conditions.

GRIMACE An approach to investigative interviewing that involves the *G*athering of *R*eliable *I*nformation, *M*otivating a free recall *A*ccount, and *C*hallenging *E*ffectively.

Group polarization The tendency for people to be more extreme in their views when they are in a group than when they are alone.

Hedonistic The gaining of pleasure as the primary goal of human behaviour.

Homology assumption Asserts that different offenders who commit similar crimes will have similar demographic characteristics.

Hung jury Occurs when a jury is unable to agree on a verdict and results in a retrial at a later date.

Incidence The number of crimes committed per person.

Indeterminate sentencing Prison sentences that do not have a specified duration or release date. Release is determined by the parole board.

Indirect mediation Occurs when the offender and/or the victim do not want to meet face to face and an independent person is used to convey messages between the interested parties in an attempt to reach an agreement.

Intelligence-led policing The use of intelligence gathering to ensure that policies address persistent as well as developing problems in the community.

Judicial admonitions Involve the judge informing jurors to reach a verdict on the basis of information formally admitted into evidence during the trial and to ignore or disregard any non-evidentiary information.

Jury deliberation Occurs at the end of the trial when jurors retire to discuss the case and reach a verdict.

Life-course-persistent offenders Those who develop antisocial behaviours during childhood, which then continue through adolescence and adulthood.

Longitudinal designs The study of the same group over a given time that examines changes within and between groups.

Majority influence A form of social influence in which a minority conforms to the views of a majority.

Mass murder The killing of four or more people in one location over a short period of time.

Maternal deprivation Refers to a number of situations in which a warm, intimate and continuous relationship between a child and his or her primary caregiver is lacking. Deprivation can vary from temporary disruptions to the child–caregiver relationship (that is, partial deprivation) to the complete absence of any child–caregiver relationship (that is, complete deprivation).

Mating effort Refers to the energy or resources expended to find and secure a mate.

Mediation Occurs when an independent person is present during a face-to-face meeting in an attempt to help the offender and victim reach an agreement.

Memory distrust syndrome The gradual distrust of recollections and beliefs.

Memory recovery techniques Techniques employed during therapy to 'recover' memories of childhood abuse. Examples include hypnosis, guided imagery, journalling and dream interpretation.

Meta-analysis A quantitative method that allows the findings of similar studies to be combined into a single statistical analysis.

Method of operation (MO) The choices and behaviours that are intended to assist the offender in the completion of their crime. It is the functional aspect of an offence and may change over time due to experience and learning.

Minority influence A form of social influence in which a majority conforms to the views of a minority.

Miscarriages of justice Involve the conviction of an innocent person, while the guilty person goes unpunished.

Munchausen syndrome by proxy Involves a person deliberately causing another person injury or illness in order to gain attention or some other benefit (for example financial gain).

Narrative reviews Qualitative summaries of research that present the proportion of findings that reached statistical significance.

Nothing works The dominant belief during the 1970s that offending behaviour programmes are ineffective at reducing reoffending.

Notifiable offences Offences that are recorded by the police, the totals of which are forwarded to the Home Office.

Offender Group Reconviction Scale (OGRS) Uses information regarding the offender and the offence (for example age, sex, time since first conviction and type of offence) to estimate the probability that he or she will receive one or more reconvictions during the next two years.

Official statistics Statistics produced by the government that are restricted to the number of crimes that have been reported and recorded by the police.

Operant conditioning A type of behavioural learning developed by Burrhus F. Skinner in which people learn particular behaviours as a consequence of the rewards and punishments they receive in response to these behaviours.

Organized offender Offenders who are in control and carefully plan their crimes. The crimes are usually prepared in advance and the crime scenes are orderly (for example the victim's body is hidden and forensic evidence has been removed).

Parenting effort Refers to the energy or resources expended to raise children.

PEACE The interview model for investigative interviewing that comprises five stages: *P*reparation and planning, *E*ngage and explain, *A*ccount, *C*losure and *E*valuation.

Peterborough adolescent development study A longitudinal study overseen by Per-Olf Wikström at the University of Cambridge. The study collected data from over 700 youths on an annual basis from 2002 to 2007. It aimed to identify the main individual and environmental factors that increase and decrease offending during adolescence.

Pittsburgh youth study A longitudinal study undertaken by David P. Farrington and Rolf Loeber. This study focused on the lives of over 1500 First, Fourth and Seventh grade boys attending public schools in Pittsburgh. Beginning in 1987, the study investigated the developmental experience of the boys in relation to delinquency. In addition to the boys themselves, interviews were conducted with their primary caregivers and teacher reports were consulted.

Police and Criminal Evidence (PACE) Act Provides the core framework of police practice, and offers safeguards for stop and search, arrest, detention, investigation, identification and interviewing procedures.

Post-admission narrative Everything a suspect says after an initial admission of guilt; often provides details of the crime.

Predecisional distortion The biased interpretation and evaluation of new evidence to support the current leading verdict (guilty or not guilty).

Prevalence The number of people committing crime at any one time.

Protective shields The use of screens to shield vulnerable victims and witnesses (for example children) from the accused while they testify in court.

Psycho-educational Styles of delivery that focus on educating offenders about the causes of their maladaptive behaviour while offering alternative prosocial coping strategies.

Psychopathic personality/offenders Characterized by a lack of remorse and apathy to others. Often manipulative and controlling.

Publication bias Occurs because research is more likely to be submitted and accepted for publication when the findings are statistically significant.

Recidivism A relapse into criminal behaviour by an offender.

Reconstructive nature of memory The active reconstruction of memories during the process of recall. It contrasts with the common view that memories are like video recordings that can be stored and replayed.

Sampling bias The tendency to underrepresent some members of the population while overrepresenting other members of the population.

Schemas Cognitive systems that help organize and make sense of information.

Selection bias The non-random selection of participants for different conditions of research.

Self-fulfilling prophecy When beliefs or expectations affect a situation or the way a person behaves in manner that is consistent with these beliefs or expectations.

Self-report surveys Surveys that ask people about their involvement in delinquent and criminal activities.

Serial murder The killing of three or more people in different locations over a prolonged period of time with a cooling-off period between each of the murders.

Sheffield pathways out of crime study A longitudinal desistence study overseen by Sir Anthony Bottom at the University of Sheffield. The study collected data from more than 100 persistent young offenders over a period of four years. It aimed to develop an understanding of the process of reduction in, or cessation of, offending in early adulthood.

Signature The distinctive behaviours that are unnecessary for the completion of the crime but serve to fulfil the psychological and/or emotional needs of the offender. It remains the same over time and can be used to link crimes.

Social Contexts of Pathways in Crime (SCoPiC) Started in 2002 as an Economic and Social Research Council funded research consortium based in the UK. SCoPiC comprised four UK research sites in London, Cambridge, Sheffield and Huddersfield. Its main aim was to investigate the causes of change and stability in offending behaviour over time.

Social disorganization The development of areas that are marked by conflict and competitiveness, and therefore lack the communal bonds necessary for the control of crime.

Source monitoring errors The misattribution of information to a different source.

Specific deterrence Occurs when a person is less likely to reoffend as a consequence of being punished.

Spiritualism A belief that people who commit crimes are possessed by evil spirits or act under the influence of a god or god-like figures.

Spree murder The killing of two or more people in different locations over a short period of time with no cooling-off period between each of the murders.

Static risk factors Risk factors that cannot be changed during treatment (for example age and sex).

Statistical significance Occurs when there is less than a five per cent probability that a difference or relationship happened by chance.

Stereotypes Widely shared generalizations about members of social groups that are often prejudicial.

Story model An explanation model of jury decision making that asserts that jurors incorporate trial information into one or more plausible stories and select the verdict decision that represents the best match to the accepted story.

Strategic use of evidence (SUE) An interviewing technique that involves the late disclosure of evidence.

System variables Factors that influence the accuracy of eyewitness testimony and are under the control of the criminal justice system.

Top-down approach An approach to profiling that utilizes previous knowledge and experience to interpret information and develop conclusions in relation to a particular crime.

Tunnel vision The tendency to focus on particular aspects of an investigation (for example the presumption that a suspect is guilty) to the detriment of other legitimate lines of inquiry.

Validity The extent to which a particular measure reflects the meaning of the underlying concept being investigated.

Victim surveys Surveys that ask people about their experiences of crime.

Videolink procedures The use of video technology to enable vulnerable victims and witnesses (for example children) to testify from outside the courtroom.

Voir dire Involves judges and, in some instances, lawyers questioning prospective jurors to determine whether they have any preconceived notions of the defendant's guilt or innocence. Any jurors identified as impartial are removed from the jury.

Voluntary false confessions False confessions provided by innocent suspects in the absence of external pressure from the police.

Weapon focus effect The attention witnesses give to a perpetrator's weapon during the commission of a crime and the associated reduction in their ability to identify other aspects of the crime including the perpetrator.

What works The current belief that offending behaviour programmes can be effective in reducing reoffending providing they target offender risk and need, as well as treatment responsivity, delivery and integrity.

References

Aichhorn, A. (1965) *Wayward Youth*. New York, NY: The Viking Press. (Original work published 1935)

Ainsworth, P.B. (1998) *Psychology, Law and Eyewitness Testimony*. Chichester: John Wiley & Sons.

Akers, R.L. (1973) *Deviant Behavior: A Social Learning Approach*. Belmont, CA: Wadsworth Publishing Company Inc.

Akers, R.L. (1999) *Criminological Theories: Introduction and Evaluation* (2nd edn). London: Fitzroy Dearborn Publishers.

Alarid, L.F., Burton, V.S., Jr. and Cullen, F.T. (2000) Gender and crime among felony offenders: Assessing the generality of social control and differential association theories. *Journal of Research in Crime and Delinquency*, 37, 171–99.

Alison, L., McLean, C. and Almond, L. (2007) Profiling suspects. In T. Newburn, T. Williamson and A. Wright (eds) *Handbook of Criminal Investigation* (pp. 493–516). Cullompton: Willan Publishing.

Alison, L., Smith, M.D. and Morgan, K. (2003) Interpreting the accuracy of offender profiles. *Psychology, Crime & Law*, 9, 185–95.

Allen, W.D. (2007) The reporting and underreporting of rape. *Sourthern Economic Journal*, 73, 623–41.

Andrews, D.A. and Bonta, J. (2006) *The Psychology of Criminal Conduct* (4th edn). Newark, NJ: LexisNexis.

Anderson, G.S. (2007) *Biological Influences on Criminal Behavior*. London: Taylor & Francis Group.

Asch, S.E. (1952) *Social Psychology*. Englewood Cliffs, NJ: Prentice-Hall.

Babcock, J.C., Green, C.E. and Robie, C. (2004) Does batterers' treatment work? A meta-analytic review of domestic violence treatment. *Clinical Psychology Review,* 23, 1023–53.

Babinski, L.M., Hartsough, C.S. and Lambert, N.M. (2001) A comparison of self-report of criminal involvement and official arrest records. *Aggressive Behavior*, 27, 44–54.

Baldwin, J. (1992) *Video Taping Police Interviews with Suspects: An Evaluation* (Police Research Series: Paper 1) London: Home Office.

Baldwin, J. (1993) Police interview techniques: Establishing truth or proof? *The British Journal of Criminology,* 33, 325–52.

Bandura, A. (1977) *Social Learning Theory*. Englewood Cliffs, NJ: Prentice-Hall.

Bandura, A. (1986) *Social Foundations of Thought and Action: A Social Cognitive Theory*. Englewood Cliffs, NJ: Prentice-Hall.

Bartol, A.M. and Bartol, C.R. (2006) Overview of forensic psychology. In C.R. Bartol and A.M. Bartol (eds) *Current Perspectives in Forensic Psychology and Criminal Justice* (pp. 1–10). London: Sage Publications.

Bartol, C.R. (1991) *Criminal Behavior: A Psychosocial Approach* (3rd edn). Englewood Cliffs, NJ: Prentice-Hall.

Becker, H.S. (1963) *Outsiders: Studies in the Sociology of Deviance*. New York, NY: The Free Press.

Beech, A., Fisher, D. and Beckett, R. (1998, November). *Step 3: An Evaluation of the Prison Sex Offender Treatment Programme*. London: Home Office.

Bekerian, D.A. and Jackson, J.L. (1997) Critical issues in offender profiling. In J.L. Jackson and D.A. Bekerian (eds) *Offender Profiling: Theory, Research and Practice* (pp. 221–33). Chichester: John Wiley & Sons.

Bernard, T.J. and Snipes, J.B. (1996) Theoretical integration in criminology. In M. Tonry (ed.) *Crime and Justice: A Review of Research Vol. 20* (pp. 301–48). Chicago, IL: University of Chicago Press.

Blackburn, R. (1993) *The Psychology of Criminal Conduct: Theory, Research and Practice*. Chichester: John Wiley & Sons.

Blair, J.P. (2007) The roles of interrogation, perception, and individual differences in producing compliant false confessions. *Psychology, Crime & Law,* 13, 173–86.

Blud, L., Travers, R., Nugent, F. and Thornton, D. (2003) Accreditation of offending behaviour programmes in HM Prison Service: 'What works' in practice. *Legal and Criminological Psychology,* 8, 69–81.

Bonta, J., Wallace-Capretta, S. and Rooney, J. (2000) Can electronic monitoring make a difference? An evaluation of three Canadian programs. *Crime and Delinquency*, 46, 61–75.

Bornstein, B.H. (1999) The ecological validity of jury simulations: Is the jury still out? *Law and Human Behavior*, 23, 75–91.

Bornstein, B.H., Whisenhunt, B.L., Nemeth, R.J. and Dunaway, D.L. (2002). Pretrial publicity and civil cases: A two-way street? *Law and Human Behavior*, 26, 3–17.

Bourke, M.L. and Van Hasselt, V.B. (2001) Social problem-solving skills training for incarcerated offenders: A treatment manual. *Behavior Modification*, 25, 163–88.

Bowlby, J. (1944) Forty-four juvenile thieves: Their character and home-life. *International Journal of Psychoanalysis*, 25, 19–52.

Bowlby, J. (1965) *Child Care and the Growth of Love* (2nd edn). Harmondsworth: Penguin Books.

Bratton, W.J. (1997) Crime is down in New York City: Blame the police. In Dennis, N. (ed.) *Zero Tolerance: Policing a Free Society* (2nd edn, pp. 29–43). London: Institute of Economic Affairs.

Brown, R. and Kulik, J. (1977) Flashbulb memories. *Cognition*, 5, 73–99.

Brown, S.L., St Amand, M.D. and Zamble, E. (2009) The dynamic prediction of criminal recidivism: A three-wave prospective study. *Law and Human Behavior*, 33, 25–45.

Browne, K. and Pennell, A. (1998) *The Effects of Video Violence on Young Offenders* (Research Findings No. 65). London: Home Office.

Browning, J. and Dutton, D. (1986) Assessment of wife assault with the Conflict Tactics Scale: Using couple data to quantify the differential reporting effect. *Journal of Marriage and the Family*, 48, 375–9.

Bruce, V., Burton, M. and Hancock, P. (2007) Remembering faces. In R.C.L. Lindsay, D.F. Ross, J.D. Read and M.P. Toglia (eds) *The Handbook of Eyewitness Psychology: Volume II Memory for People* (pp. 87–100). London: Lawrence Erlbaum Associates.

Bruce, V., Ness, H., Hancock, P.J.B., Newman, C. and Rarity, J. (2002) Four heads are better than one: Combining face composites yields improvements in face likeness. *Journal of Applied Psychology*, 87, 894–902.

Buckle, A. and Farrington, D.P. (1994) Measuring shoplifting by systematic observation: A replication study. *Psychology, Crime & Law*, 1, 133–41.

Buckley, J.P. (2006) The Reid Technique of interviewing and interrogation. In T. Williamson (ed.) *Investigative Interviewing: Rights, Research, Regulation* (pp. 190–206). Cullompton: Willan Publishing.

Bull, R. (2007, June) Interviewing suspects: To detect deception. Paper presented at the Forensic Psychology: Investigating, Identifying and Interviewing Conference, Leicester, UK.

Bull, R. (2009, September) What really works in interviewing suspects by police. Key note presented at the 19th conference of the European Association of Psychology and Law, Sorrento, Italy.

Bull, R. and Milne, R. (2004) Attempts to improve the police interviewing of suspects. In Lassiter, G.D. (ed.) *Interrogations, Confessions, and Entrapment* (pp. 181–96). New York, NY: Plenum Press.

Burgess, E.W. (1984) The growth of the city: An introduction to a research project. In R.E. Park and E.W. Burgess (eds) *The City: Suggestions for Investigation of Human Behavior in the Urban Environment* (pp. 47–62). Chicago, IL: University of Chicago Press. (Original work published 1925)

Cann, J., Falshaw, L., Nugent, F. and Friendship, C. (2003) *Understanding What Works: Accredited Cognitive Skills Programmes for Adult Men and Young Offenders* (Findings 226). London: Home Office.

Canter, D.V., Alison, L.J., Alison, E. and Wentink, N. (2004) The organized/disorganized typology of serial murder: Myth or model? *Psychology, Public Policy, and Law*, 10, 293–320.

Canter, D.V. and Youngs, D. (2008) Geographical offender profiling: Origins and principles. In D.V. Canter and D. Youngs (eds) *Principles of Geographical Offender Profiling* (pp. 1–18). Aldershot: Ashgate Publishing Limited.

Canter, D.V. and Wentink, N. (2004) An empirical test of Holmes and Holmes's serial murder typology. *Criminal Justice and Behavior*, 31, 489–515.

Carlson, K.A. and Russo, J.E. (2001) Biased interpretation of evidence by mock jurors. *Journal of Experimental Psychology: Applied*, 7, 91–103.

Carney, M., Buttell, F. and Dutton, D. (2007) Women who perpetrate intimate partner violence: A review of the literature with recommendations for treatment. *Aggression and Violent Behavior*, 12, 108–15.

Caspi, A. (2000) The child is father of the man: Personality continuities from childhood to adulthood. *Journal of Personality and Social Psychology*, 78, 158–72.

Catalano, R.F. and Hawkins, J.D. (1996) The social development model: A theory of antisocial behaviour. In J.D. Hawkins (ed.) *Delinquency and Crime: Current Theories* (pp. 149–97). Cambridge: Cambridge University Press.

Catalano, S.M. (2006, September) *Criminal Victimization, 2005* (Bureau of Justice Statistics Bulletin, NCJ-214644). Washington, DC: US Department of Justice.

Cavadino, M. and Digman, J. (2007) *The Penal System: An Introduction* (4th edn). London: Sage Publications.

Ceci, S.J. and Bruck, M. (1995) *Jeopardy in the Courtroom: A Scientific Analysis of Children's Testimony*. Washington, DC: American Psychological Association.

Centerwall, B.S. (1993) Television and violent crime. *Public Interest*, 111, 56–71.

Chilton, R. and Jarvis, J. (1999) Victims and offenders in two crime statistics programs: A comparison of the National Incident-Based Reporting System (NIBRS) and the National Crime Victimization Survey (NCVS). *Journal of Quantitative Criminology*, 15, 193–205.

Clark, C.L., Aziz, D.W. and MacKenzie, D.L. (1994, August) *Shock Incarceration in New York: Focus on Treatment*. Washington, DC: National Institute of Justice.

Clarke, C. and Milne, R. (2001) *National Evaluation of the PEACE Investigative Interviewing Course* (Police Research Award Scheme, Report). London: Home Office.

Clay-Warner, J. and Burt, C.H. (2005) Rape reporting after reforms: Have times really changed? *Violence Against Women*, 11, 150–76.

Clifford, B.R. (2008) Role of the expert witness. In G.M. Davies, C.R. Hollin and R. Bull (eds) *Forensic Psychology* (pp. 235–61). Chichester: John Wiley & Sons.

Clifford, B.R. and Scott, J. (1978) Individual and situational factors in eyewitness testimony. *Journal of Applied Psychology*, 63, 352–9.

Cloward, R.A. and Ohlin, L.E. (1960) *Delinquency and Opportunity: A Theory of Delinquent Gangs*. New York, NY: The Free Press.

Cohen, A.K. (1955) *Delinquent Boys: The Culture of the Gang*. New York, NY: The Free Press.

Connors, E., Lundregan, T., Miller, N. and McEwen, T. (1996, June) *Convicted by Juries, Exonerated by Science: Case Studies in the Use of DNA Evidence to Establish Innocence After Trial*. Washington, DC: US Department of Justice.

Cook, P.J. (1980) Research in criminal deterrence: Laying the groundwork for the second decade. In N. Morris and M. Tonry (eds) *Crime and Justice: A Review of Research Vol. 2* (pp. 211–68). Chicago, IL: University of Chicago Press.

Cooper, J. and Neuhaus, I.M. (2000) The 'hired gun' effect: Assessing the effect of pay, frequency of testifying, and credentials on the perception of expert testimony. *Law and Human Behavior,* 24, 149–71.

Cornish, D.B. and Clarke, R.V. (1987) Understanding crime displacement: An application of rational choice theory. *Criminology,* 25, 933–47.

Côté, S.M., Vaillancourt, T., LeBlanc, J.C., Nagin, D.S. and Tremblay, R.E. (2006) The development of physical aggression from toddlerhood to pre-adolescence: A nation wide longitudinal study of Canadian children. *Journal of Abnormal Child Psychology,* 34, 71–85.

Coyne, S.M. (2007) Does media violence cause violent crime? *European Journal on Criminal Policy,* 13, 205–11.

Crighton D.A. (2006a) Methodological issues in psychological research in prisons. In G.J. Towl (ed.) *Psychological Research in Prisons* (pp. 7–23). Oxford: Blackwell Publications Ltd.

Crighton, D.A. (2006b) Psychological research into reducing suicides. In G.J. Towl (ed.) *Psychological Research in Prisons* (pp. 54–69). Oxford: Blackwell Publishing.

Crighton, D.A. and Towl, G.J. (2008) *Psychology in Prisons* (2nd edn). Oxford: Blackwell Publishing.

Crisanti, A., Laygo, R. and Junginger, J. (2003) A review of the validity of self-reported arrests among persons with mental illness. *Current Opinion in Psychiatry,* 16, 565–9.

Crowther, C. (2007) *An Introduction to Criminology and Criminal Justice*. Basingstoke: Palgrave Macmillan.

Curran, D.J. and Renzetti, C.M. (2001) *Theories of Crime* (2nd edn). London: Allyn & Bacon.

Cutler, B.L. and Penrod, S.D. (1988) Improving the reliability of eyewitness identification: Lineup construction and presentation. *Journal of Applied Psychology,* 73, 281–90.

Culter, B.L. and Penrod, S.D. (1989) Forensically relevant moderators of the relation between eyewitness identification accuracy and confidence. *Journal of Applied Psychology*, 74, 650–2.

Cutler, B.L. and Penrod, S.D. (1995) *Mistaken Identification: The Eyewitness, Psychology, and the Law*. Cambridge: Cambridge University Press.

Cutler, B.L., Penrod, S.D. and Dexter, H.R. (1989) The eyewitness, the expert psychologist, and the jury. *Law and Human Behavior,* 13, 311–32.

Cutler, B.L., Penrod, S.D. and Dexter, H.R. (1990) Juror sensitivity to eyewitness identification evidence. *Law and Human Behavior,* 14, 185–91.

Daly, K. (2006) Aims of the criminal justice system. In A. Goldsmith, M. Israel and K. Daly (eds) *Crime and Justice: A Guide to Criminology* (3rd edn, pp. 265–82). Sydney, NSW: Thomson Legal & Regulatory Limited.

Daly, M. and Wilson, M. (1988) Evolutionary social psychology and family homicide. *Science,* 242, 519–24.

Daly, M. and Wilson, M. (1990) Killing the competition: Female/female and male/male homicide. *Human Nature,* 1, 81–107.

Daly, M. and Wilson, M. (1994) Some differential attributes of lethal assaults on small children by stepfathers versus genetic fathers. *Ethology and Sociobiology,* 15, 207–17.

Daly, M. and Wilson, M. (1996) Violence against stepchildren. *Current Directions in Psychological Science,* 5, 77–81.

Daly, M. and Wilson, M. (1997) Crime and conflict: Homicide in evolutionary psychological perspective. *Crime and Justice,* 22, 51–100.

Daly, M. and Wilson, M. (1999) An evolutionary psychological perspective on homicide. In M.D. Smith and M.E. Zahn (eds) *Homicide Studies: A Sourcebook of Social Research* (pp. 58–71). Thousand Oaks, CA: Sage Publications.

Daly, M. and Wilson, M. (2007) Is the 'Cinderella effect' controversial? A case study of evolution-minded research and critiques thereof. In C. Crawford and D. Krebs (eds) *Foundations of Evolutionary Psychology* (pp. 383–400). Mahwah, NJ: Erlbaum.

Daniel, A.E. (2006) Preventing suicide in prison: A collaborative responsibility of administrative, custodial, and clinical staff. *Journal of the American Academy of Psychiatry and the Law,* 34, 165–75.

Dannerbeck, A.M. (2005) Differences in parenting attributes, experiences, and behaviors of delinquent youth with and without a parental history of incarceration. *Youth Justice and Juvenile Justice,* 3, 199–213.

Darby, B.W. and Jeffers, D. (1988) The effects of defendant and juror attractiveness on simulated courtroom trial decisions. *Social Behavior and Personality,* 16, 39–50.

Davies, G.M. and Valentine, T. (2007) Facial composites: Forensic utility and psychological research. In R.C.L. Lindsay, D.F. Ross, J.D. Read and M.P. Toglia (eds) *The Handbook of Eyewitness Psychology: Volume II Memory for People* (pp. 59–83). London: Lawrence Erlbaum Associates.

Davis, D. and Leo, R. (2006) Strategies for preventing false confessions and their consequences. In M.R. Kebbell and G.M. Davies (eds) *Practical Psychology for Forensic Investigations and Prosecutions* (pp. 121–49). Chichester: John Wiley & Sons.

Davis, D. and Loftus, E.F. (2007) Internal and external sources of misinformation in adult witness memory. In M.P. Toglia, J.D. Read, D.F. Ross and R.C.L. Lindsay (eds) *The Handbook of Eyewitness Psychology: Volume I Memory for Events* (pp. 195–237). London: Lawrence Erlbaum Associates.

Davis, J.D., Kerr, N.L., Stasser, G., Meek, D. and Holt, R. (1977) Victim consequences, sentence severity, and decision processes in mock juries. *Organizational Behavior and Human Performance,* 18, 346–65.

Davis, M.R., McMahon, M. and Greenwood, K.M. (2005) The efficacy of mnemonic components of the cognitive interview: Towards a shortened variant for time-critical investigations. *Applied Cognitive Psychology,* 19, 75–93.

Davison, S.E. and Forshaw, D.M. (1993) Retracted confessions: Through opiate withdrawal to a new conceptual framework. *Medicine, Science and the Law,* 33, 285–90.

DeJong, C. (1997) Survival analysis and specific deterrence: Integrating theoretical and empirical models of recidivism. *Criminology,* 35, 561–75.

Deutsch, M. and Gerard, H.B. (1955) A study of normative and informational social influences upon individual judgment. *Journal of Abnormal and Social Psychology,* 51, 629–36.

Devine, D.J., Clayton, L.D., Dunford, B.B., Seying, R. and Pryce, J. (2001) Jury decision making: 45 years of empirical research on deliberating groups. *Psychology, Public Policy, and Law,* 7, 622–727.

Dexter, H.R., Cutler, B.L. and Moran, G. (1992) A test of voir dire as a remedy for the prejudicial effects of pretrial publicity. *Journal of Applied Social Psychology,* 22, 819–32.

DiIulio, J.J., Jr. (1996) Help wanted: Economists, crime and public policy. *The Journal of Economic Perspectives,* 10, 3–24.
Dobash, R.E. and Dobash, R.P. (1984) The nature and antecedents of violent events. *British Journal of Criminology,* 24, 269–90.
Dobash, R.P., Dobash, R.E., Wilson, M. and Daly, M. (1992) The myth of sexual symmetry in marital violence. *Social Problems,* 39, 71–91.
Dowden, C. and Andrews, D.A. (2000) Effective correctional treatment and violent offending: A meta-analysis. *Canadian Journal of Criminology,* 42, 449–76.
Dowden, C. and Tellier, C. (2004) Predicting work-related stress in correctional officers: A meta-analysis. *Journal of Criminal Justice,* 32, 31–47.
Dull, R.T. (1983) Friend's use and adult drug and drinking behavior: A further test of differential association theory. *The Journal of Criminal Law and Criminology,* 74, 1608–19.
Dunning, D. and Perretta, S. (2002) Automaticity and eyewitness accuracy: A 10- to 12-second rule for distinguishing accurate from inaccurate positive identifications. *Journal of Applied Psychology,* 87, 951–62.
Dupuis, P.R. and Lindsay, R.C.L. (2007) Radical alternatives to traditional lineups. In R.C.L. Lindsay, D.F. Ross, J.D. Read and M.P. Toglia (eds) *The Handbook of Eyewitness Psychology: Volume II Memory for People* (pp. 179–200). London: Lawrence Erlbaum Associates.
Easton, S. and Piper, C. (2005) *Sentencing and Punishment: The Quest for Punishment*. Oxford: Oxford University Press.
Eberhardt, J.L., Davies, P.G., Purdie-Vaughns, V.J. and Johnson, S.L. (2006) Looking deathworthy: Perceived stereotypicality of black defendants predicts capital-sentencing outcomes. *Psychological Science,* 17, 383–6.
Egger, S.A. (1999) Psychological profiling: Past, present, and future. *Journal of Contemporary Criminal Justice,* 15, 242–61.
Eklund, J.M. and af Klinteberg, B. (2006) Stability of and change in criminal behavior: A prospective study of young male lawbreakers and controls. *International Journal of Forensic Mental Health,* 5, 83–95.
Elliott, D.S. (1985) The assumption that theories can be combined with increased explanatory power. In R.F. Meier (ed.) *Theoretical Methods in Criminology.* Beverly Hills, CA: Sage Publications.
Elliott, D.S. (1994) Serious violent offenders: Onset, developmental course and termination – The American Society of Criminology 1999 presidential address. *Criminology,* 32, 1–21.

Elliott, D.S., Ageton, S.S. and Canter, R.J. (1979) An integrated theoretical perspective on delinquent behavior. *Journal of Research in Crime and Delinquency,* 16, 3–27.

Ellis, T. and Winstone, J. (2002) The policy impact of a survey of programme evaluations in England and Wales. In J. McGuire (ed.) *Offender Rehabilitation and Treatment: Effective Programmes and Policies to Reduce Reoffending* (pp. 333–58). Chichester: John Wiley & Sons.

Ellison, K.W. and Buckhout, R. (1981) *Psychology and Criminal Justice.* New York, NY: Harper & Row.

Eron, L.D. (1982) Parent–child interaction, television violence, and aggression of children. *American Psychologist,* 37, 197–211.

Eron, L.D., Huesmann, L.R., Lefkowitz, M.M. and Walder, L.O. (1972) Does television violence cause aggression? *American Psychologist,* 27, 253–63.

Ewen, R.B. (1993) *An Introduction to Theories of Personality* (4th edn). Hove: Psychology Press.

Eysenck, H.J. (1964) *Crime and Personality.* London: Routledge & Kegan Paul Ltd.

Eysenck, H.J. (1976) The biology of morality. In T. Lickona (ed.) *Moral Development and Behaviour: Theory, Research, and Social Issues* (pp. 108–23). London: Holt, Rinehart and Winston.

Eysenck, H.J. and Gudjonsson, G.H. (1989) *The Causes and Cures of Criminality.* New York, NY: Plenum Press.

Falshaw, L., Friendship, C., Travers, R. and Nugent, F. (2003) *Searching for 'What Works': An Evaluation of Cognitive Skills Programmes* (Findings 206). London: Home Office.

Farrington, D.P. (1994) Introduction. In D.P. Farrington (ed.) *Psychological Explanations of Crime* (pp. xiii–xxxvi). Aldershot: Dartmouth Publishing Company Limited.

Farrington, D.P. (1995) The development of offending and antisocial behaviour from childhood: Key findings from the Cambridge Study in delinquent development. *Journal of Child Psychology,* 36, 929–64.

Farrington, D.P. (1996) The explanation and prevention of youthful offending. In J.D. Hawkins (ed.) *Delinquency and Crime: Current Theories* (pp. 68–148). Cambridge: Cambridge University Press.

Farrington, D.P. (2002) Developmental criminology and risk-focused prevention. In M. Maguire, R. Morgan and R. Reiner (eds) *The Oxford Handbook of Criminology* (3rd edn, pp. 657–701). Oxford: Oxford University Press.

Farrington, D.P., Coid, J.W., Harnett, L.M., Jolliffe, D., Soteriou, N., Turner, R.E. and West, D.J. (2006, September) *Criminal Careers up to Age 50 and Life Success up to Age 48: New findings from the Cambridge Study in Delinquent Development* (Home Office Research Study 299). London: Home Office.

Farrington, D.P., Ohlin, L.E. and Wilson, J.Q. (1986) *Understanding and Controlling Crime: Toward a New Research Strategy*. New York, NY: Springer-Verlag.

Federal Bureau of Investigation (2006a, September) *About the UCR Program* (US Department of Justice – Federal Bureau of Investigation). Retrieved 12 December 2009 from http://www.fbi.gov/ucr/05cius/about/about_ucr.html.

Federal Bureau of Investigation (2006b, September) *Table 1: Crime in the United States* (US Department of Justice – Federal Bureau of Investigation). Retrieved 8 January 2010 from http://www.fbi.gov/ucr/05cius/data/table_01.html.

Fein, S., McCloskey, A.L. and Tomlinson, T.M. (1997) Can the jury disregard that information? The use of suspicion to reduce the prejudicial effects of pretrial publicity and inadmissible testimony. *Personality and Social Psychology Bulletin,* 23, 1215–26.

Feldman, P. (1993) *The Psychology of Crime: A Social Science Textbook*. Cambridge: Cambridge University Press.

Felson, R.B. (1996) Mass media effects on violent behavior. *Annual Review of Sociology,* 22, 103–28.

Finkelhor, D. and Ormrod, R. (1999, November) *Reporting Crimes Against Juveniles* (Juvenile Justice Bulletin, NCJ-178887). Washington, DC: US Department of Justice.

Fishbein, D.H. (1990) Biological perspectives in criminology. *Criminology,* 28, 27–72.

Fisher, R.P., Geiselman, R.E. and Amador, M. (1989) Field test of the cognitive interview: Enhancing the recollection of actual victims and witnesses of crime. *Journal of Applied Psychology,* 74, 722–7.

Fisher, R.P. and Schreiber, N. (2007) Interview protocols to improve eyewitness memory. In M.P. Toglia, J.D. Read, D.F. Ross and R.C.L. Lindsay (eds) *The Handbook of Eyewitness Psychology: Volume I Memory for Events* (pp. 53–80). London: Lawrence Erlbaum Associates.

Fleury, R.E., Sullivan, C.M., Bybee, D.I. and Davidson, W.S. II. (1998) What happened depends on whom you ask: A comparison of police records and victim reports regarding arrests for woman battering. *Journal of Criminal Justice,* 26, 53–9.

Forrest, K.D., Wadkins, T.A. and Larson, B.A. (2006) Suspect personality, police interrogations, and false confessions: Maybe it is not just the situation. *Personality and Individual Differences,* 40, 621–8.

Friendship, C. and Debidin, M. (2006) Probation and prison interventions. In A.E. Perry, C. McDougall and D.P. Farrington (eds) *Reducing Crime: The Effectiveness of Criminal Justice Interventions* (pp. 73–93). Chichester: John Wiley & Sons.

Friendship, C. and Falshaw, L. (2003) Evaluating groupwork in prisons. In G. Towl (ed.) *Psychology in Prisons* (pp. 52–63). Oxford: Blackwell Publishing Ltd.

Friendship, C., Blud, L., Erikson, M., Travers, R. and Thornton, D. (2003a) Cognitive-behavioural treatment for imprisoned offenders: An evaluation of HM Prison Service's cognitive skills programmes. *Legal and Criminological Psychology,* 8, 103–14.

Friendship, C., Falshaw, L. and Beech, A.R. (2003b) Measuring the real impact of accredited offending behaviour programmes. *Legal and Criminological Psychology,* 8, 115–27.

Friendship, C., Mann, R.E. and Beech, A.R. (2003c) Evaluation of a national prison-based treatment program for sexual offenders in England and Wales. *Journal of Interpersonal Violence,* 18, 744–59.

Friendship, C., Mann, R.E. and Beech, A.R. (2003d) *The Prison-based Sex Offender Treatment Programme – An Evaluation* (Findings 205). London: Home Office.

Fulton, B., Gendreau, P. and Paparozzi, M. (1995) APPA's prototypical intensive supervision program: ISP as it was meant to be. *Perspectives,* 19, 25–41.

Gadd, D. and Jefferson, T. (2007) *Psychosocial Criminology: An Introduction*. London: Sage Publications.

Gambrill, E.D. (1976) The use of behavioral methods in a short-term detention setting. *Criminal Justice and Behavior,* 3, 53–66.

Geffner, R.A. and Rosenbaum, A. (2001) Domestic violence offenders: Treatment and intervention standards. *Journal of Aggression, Maltreatment and Trauma,* 5, 1–9.

Geiselman, R.E. (1999) Commentary on recent research with the cognitive interview. *Psychology, Crime & Law,* 5, 197–202.

Gilchrist, E. and Kebbell, M. (2005) Domestic violence: Current issues in definitions and interventions with perpetrators in the UK. In J.R.

Adler (ed.) *Forensic Psychology: Concepts, Debates and Practice* (pp. 219–44). Cullompton: Willan Publishing.

Glueck, S. and Glueck, E. (1950) *Unraveling Juvenile Delinquency*. Cambridge, MA: Harvard University Press.

Glueck, S. and Glueck, E. (1968) *Delinquents and Nondeliquents in Perspective*. Cambridge, MA: Harvard University Press.

Glueck, S. and Glueck, E. (1970) *Toward a Typology of Juvenile Offenders: Implications for Therapy and Prevention*. London: Grune & Stratton.

Godwin, M. (2002) Reliability, validity, and utility of criminal profiling typologies. *Journal of Police and Criminal Psychology*, 17, 1–18.

Goggin, C. and Gendreau, P. (2006) The implementation and maintenance of quality services in offender rehabilitation programmes. In C.R. Hollin and E.J. Palmer (eds) *Offending Behaviour Programmes: Development, Application, and Controversies* (pp. 209–47). Chichester: John Wiley & Sons.

Goodman, G.S., Tobey, A.E., Batterman-Faunce, J.M., Orcutt, H., Thomas, S., Shapiro, C. and Sachsenmaier, T. (1998) Face-to-face confrontation: Effects of closed-circuit technology on children's eyewitness testimony and jurors' decisions. *Law and Human Behavior*, 22, 165–203.

Gordon, N.J. and Fleisher, W.L. (2006) *Effective Interviewing and Interrogation Techniques* (2nd edn). London: Elsevier.

Gottfredson, D.C. and Exum, M.L. (2002) The Baltimore city drug treatment court: One-year results from a randomised study. *Journal of Research in Crime and Delinquency*, 39, 337–56.

Gottfredson, M.R. and Hirschi, T. (1990) *A General Theory of Crime*. Stanford, CA: Stanford University Press.

Gove, W.R., Hughes, M. and Geerken, M. (1985) Are uniform reports a valid indicator of the index crimes? An affirmative answer with minor qualifications. *Criminology*, 23, 451–501.

Grabosky, P.N. (1999, January) *Zero Tolerance Policing* (Trends and Issues in Crime and Criminal Justice, No. 102). Canberra, ACT: Australian Institute of Criminology.

Graffam, J., Shinkfield, A.J. and Hardcastle, L. (2008) The perceived employability of ex-prisoners and offenders. *International Journal of Offender Therapy and Comparative Criminology*, 52, 673–85.

Granhag, P.A., Strömwall, L.A. and Hartwig, M. (2007) The SUE technique: The way to interview to detect deception. *Forensic Update*, 88, 25–9.

Greene, E., Heilbrun, K., Fortune, W.H. and Nietzel, M.T. (2007) *Wrightsman's Psychology and the Legal System* (6th edn). Belmont, CA: Thomson Wadsworth.

Gresswell, D.M. and Hollin, C.R. (1994) Multiple murder: A review. *The British Journal of Criminology,* 34, 1–14.

Griffiths, A. and Milne, B. (2006) Will it all end in tiers? Police interviews with suspects in Britain. In T. Williamson (ed.) *Investigative Interviewing: Rights, Research, Regulation* (pp. 167–89). Cullompton: Willan Publishing.

Gudjonsson, G.H. (1984) Attribution of blame for criminal acts and its relationship with personality. *Personality and Individual Differences,* 5, 53–8.

Gudjonsson, G.H. (1997) Crime and personality. In H. Nyborg (ed.) *The Scientific Study of Human Nature* (pp. 142–64). London: Pergamon Press.

Gudjonsson, G.H. (2003) *The Psychology of Interrogations and Confessions: A Handbook*. Chichester: John Wiley & Sons.

Gudjonsson, G.H. (2006) The psychology of interrogations and confessions. In T. Williamson (ed.) *Investigative Interviewing: Rights, Research, Regulation* (pp. 123–46). Cullompton: Willan Publishing.

Gudjonsson, G.H. (2007) Investigative interviewing. In T. Newburn, T. Williamson and A. Wright (eds) *Handbook of Criminal Investigation* (pp. 466–92). Cullompton: Willan Publishing.

Gudjonsson, G.H. and MacKeith, J.A.C. (2003) The 'Guildford four' and the 'Birmingham six'. In G.H. Gudjonsson, *The Psychology of Interrogations and Confessions: A Handbook* (pp. 443–57). Chichester: John Wiley & Sons.

Gudjonsson, G.H. and Singh, K.K. (1988) Attribution of blame for criminal acts and its relationship with type of offence. *Medicine, Science and the Law,* 28, 301–3.

Gudjonsson, G.H. and Singh, K.K. (1989) The revised Gudjonsson blame attribution inventory. *Personality and Individual Differences,* 10, 67–70.

Halwani, S. and Krupp, D.B. (2004) The genetic defence: The impact of genetics on the concept of criminal responsibility. *Health Law Journal,* 12, 35–70.

Haney, C., Banks, C. and Zimbardo, P. (2004) A study of prisoners and guards in a simulated prison. In M. Balfour (ed.) *Theatre in Prisons: Theory and Practice* (pp. 19–33). Bristol: Intellect Books.

Haney, C. and Zimbardo, P. (1998) The past and future of US prison policy: Twenty-five years after the Stanford prison experiment. *American Psychologist*, 53, 709–27.

Hansen, C. (2008) Cognitive-behavioral interventions: Where they come from and what they do. *Federal Probation*, 72, 43–9.

Hartl, E.M., Monnelly, E.P. and Elderkin, R.D. (1982) *Physique and Delinquent Behavior: A Thirty-year Follow-up of William H. Sheldon's Varieties of Delinquent Youth*. London: Academic Press.

Hartwig, M., Granhag, P.A., Strömwall, L.A. and Kronkvist, O. (2006) Strategic use of evidence during police interviews: When training to detect deception works. *Law and Human Behavior*, 30, 603–19.

Hartwig, M., Granhag, P.A., Strömwall, L.A. and Vrij, A. (2005) Detecting deception via strategic disclosure of evidence. *Law and Human Behavior*, 29, 469–84.

Hasel, L.E. and Wells, G.L. (2007) Catching the bad guy: Morphing composite faces helps. *Law and Human Behavior*, 31, 193–207.

Hastie, R. (1993) Introduction. In R. Hastie (ed.) *Inside the Juror: The Psychology of Juror Decision Making* (pp. 3–41). Cambridge: Cambridge University Press.

Hatcher, R. (2008) Psychological skills in working with offenders. In G.M. Davies, C.R. Hollin and R. Bull (eds) *Forensic Psychology* (pp. 293–322). Chichester: John Wiley & Sons.

Hennigan, K.M., Del Rosario, M.L., Heath, L., Cook, T.D., Wharton, J.D. and Calder, B.J. (1982) Impact of the introduction of television crime in the United States: Empirical findings and theoretical implications. *Journal of Personality and Social Psychology*, 42, 461–77.

Hindelang, M.J. (1973) Causes of delinquency: A partial replication and extension. *Social Problems*, 20, 471–87.

Hirschi, T. (1969) *Causes of Delinquency*. Berkeley and Los Angeles, CA: University of California Press.

HM Prison Service (2004) *About the Service*. Retrieved 2 April 2010 from http://www.hmprisonservice.gov.uk/abouttheservice/statementofpurpose/.

Hodgins, S. (2007) Persistent violent offending: What do we do? *British Journal of Psychiatry*, 190 (Suppl. 49), 12–14.

Hollin, C.R. (1992) *Criminal Behaviour: A Psychological Approach to Explanation and Prevention*. Hove: Psychology Press.

Hollin, C.R., Browne, D. and Palmer, E.J. (2002) *Delinquency and Young Offenders*. Oxford: Blackwell Publishing Ltd.

Hollin, C.R. and Palmer, E.J. (2006) Offending behaviour programmes: History and development. In C.R. Hollin and E.J. Palmer (eds) *Offending Behaviour Programmes: Development, Application, and Controversies* (pp. 1–32). Chichester: John Wiley & Sons.

Hollin, C.R., Palmer, E., McGuire, J., Hounsome, J., Hatcher, R., Bilby, C. and Clark, C. (2004) *Pathfinder Programmes in the Probation Service: A Retrospective Analysis* (Home Office Online Report 66/04). London: Home Office.

Hollis, V. (2007, December) *Reconviction Analysis of Programme Data Using Interim Accredited Programmes Software (IAPS)*. London: Ministry of Justice.

Holmberg, U. and Christianson, S.-A. (2002) Murderers' and sexual offenders' experiences of police interviews and their inclination to admit or deny crimes. *Behavioral Sciences and the Law*, 20, 31–45.

Holmes, R.M. and DeBurger, J. (1988) *Serial Murder*. London. Sage Publications.

Holmes, S.T., Hickey, E. and Holmes, R.M. (1991) Female serial murderesses: Constructing differentiating typologies. *Journal of Contemporary Criminal Justice*, 7, 245–56.

Holmes, R.M. and Holmes, S.T. (2002) *Profiling Violent Crimes: An Investigative Tool* (3rd edn). London: Sage Publications.

Home Office (2002) *Statistics on Women and the Criminal Justice System: A Home Office Publication under Section 95 of the Criminal Justice Act 1991*. London: Home Office.

Home Office (2004, July) *Reducing Reoffending: National Action Plan Reference Document*. London: Home Office.

Home Office (2005a) *National Offender Management Service – Corporate Plan 2005–06 to 2007–08*. London: Home Office.

Home Office (2005b) *Police and Criminal Evidence (PACE) Act 1984: Code of Practice E* (Revised Edition, HMSO). London: Home Office.

Home Office (2006a) *Changes in How Police Record Crime*. London: Home Office.

Home Office (2006b) *Police and Criminal Evidence (PACE) Act 1984: Codes of Practice C and H* (Revised Edition, HMSO). London: Home Office.

Home Office (2007) *The Correctional Services Accreditation Panel Report 2006/07* (National Offender Management Service). London: Home Office.

Hope, L., Memon, A. and McGeorge, P. (2004) Understanding pretrial publicity: Predecisional distortion of evidence by mock jurors. *Journal of Experimental Psychology: Applied,* 10, 111–19.

Hope, L. and Wright, D. (2007) Beyond unusual? Examining the role of attention in the weapon focus effect. *Applied Cognitive Psychology,* 21, 951–61.

Horney, J. and Spohn, C. (1991) Rape law reform and instrumental change in six urban jurisdictions. *Law and Society Review,* 25, 117–54.

Horselenberg, R., Merckelbach, H. and Josephs, S. (2003) Individual differences and false confessions: A conceptual replication of Kassin and Kiechel (1996). *Psychology, Crime & Law,* 9, 1–8.

House, J.C. (1997) Towards a practical application of offender profiling: The RNC's criminal suspect prioritization system. In J.L. Jackson and D.A. Bekerian (eds). *Offender Profiling: Theory, Research and Practice* (pp. 1–7). Chichester: John Wiley & Sons.

Howitt, D. (2006) *Introduction to Forensic and Criminal Psychology* (2nd edn). Harlow: Pearson Education Limited.

Huesmann, L.R., Moise-Titus, J., Podolski, C.-L. and Eron, L.D. (2003) Longitudinal relations between children's exposure to TV violence and their aggressive and violent behaviour in young adulthood: 1977–1992. *Developmental Psychology,* 39, 201–22.

Huntley, J.E. and Costanzo, M. (2003) Sexual harassment stories: Testing a story-mediated model of juror decision-making in civil litigation. *Law and Human Behavior,* 27, 29–51.

Inbau, F.E., Reid, J.E. and Buckley, J.P. (1986) *Criminal Interrogation and Confessions* (3rd edn). Baltimore: Williams & Wilkins.

Israel, M. (2006) What is crime? Who is the criminal? In A. Goldsmith, M. Israel and K. Daly (eds) *Crime and Justice: A Guide to Criminology* (3rd edn, pp. 3–14). Sydney: Lawbrook Co.

Jackson, E.F., Tittle, C.R. and Burke, M.J. (1986) Offense-specific models of the differential association process. *Social Problems,* 33, 335–56.

Jackson, J.L. and Bekerian, D.A. (1997) Does offender profiling have a role to play? In J.L. Jackson and D.A. Bekerian (eds) *Offender Profiling: Theory, Research and Practice* (pp. 1–7). Chichester: John Wiley & Sons.

Jeffery, C.R. (1965) Criminal behavior and learning theory. *The Journal of Criminal Law, Criminology and Police Science,* 56, 294–300.

Jennings, M. (2003) Anger-management groupwork. In G. Towl (ed.) *Psychology in Prisons* (pp. 93–101). Oxford: Blackwell Publishing Ltd.

Jensen, G.F. and Karpos, M. (1993) Managing rape: Exploratory research on the behavior of rape statistics. *Criminology,* 31, 363–85.

Johnson, M.K., Hashtroudi, S. and Lindsay, D.S. (1993) Source monitoring. *Psychological Bulletin,* 114, 3–28.

Jungar-Tas, J. and Marshall, I.H. (1999) The self-report methodology in crime research. *Crime and Justice,* 25, 291–367.

Kalven, H., Jr. and Zeisel, H. (with Callahan, T. and Ennis, P.) (1966) *The American Jury*. Chicago, IL: University of Chicago Press.

Kapardis, A. (2003) *Psychology and Law: A Critical Introduction* (2nd edn). Cambridge: Cambridge University Press.

Kassin, S.M. (1997) The psychology of confession evidence. *American Psychologist,* 52, 221–33.

Kassin, S.M. (2006) A critical appraisal of modern police interrogations. In T. Williamson (ed.) *Investigative Interviewing: Rights, Research, Regulation* (pp. 207–28). Cullompton: Willan Publishing.

Kassin, S.M., Goldstein, C.C. and Savitsky, K. (2003) Behavioral confirmation in the interrogation room: On the dangers of presuming guilt. *Law and Human Behavior,* 27, 187–203.

Kassin, S.M. and Gudjonsson, G.H. (2004) The psychology of confessions: A review of the literature and issues. *Psychological Science in the Public Interest,* 5, 33–67.

Kassin, S.M. and Kiechel, K.L. (1996) The social psychology of false confessions: Compliance, internalization, and confabulation. *Psychological Science,* 7, 125–8.

Kassin, S.M., Leo, R.A., Meissner, C.A., Richman, K.D., Colwell, L.H., Leach, A.-M. and Fon, D.L. (2007) Police interviewing and interrogation: A self-report survey of police practices and beliefs. *Law and Human Behavior,* 31, 381–400.

Kassin, S.M. and Sommers, S.R. (1997) Inadmissible testimony, instructions to disregard, and the jury: Substantive versus procedural considerations. *Personality and Social Psychology Bulletin*, 23, 1046–54.

Kassin, S.M. and Wrightsman, L.S. (1979) On the requirements of proof: The timing of judicial instruction and mock juror verdicts. *Journal of Personality and Social Psychology,* 37, 1877–87.

Kassin, S.M. and Wrightsman L.S. (1985) Confession evidence. In S.M. Kassin and L.S. Wrightsman (eds) *The Psychology of Evidence and Trial Procedures* (pp. 67–94). London: Sage Publications.

Kelling, G.L. and Wilson, J.Q. (1982, March) Broken windows: The police and neighborhood safety. *The Atlantic*. Retrieved 12 December 2009 from http://www.theatlantic.com.

Kebbell, M.R. and Hurren, E. (2006) Improving the interviewing of suspected offenders. In M.R. Kebbell and G.M. Davies (eds) *Practical Psychology for Forensic Investigations and Prosecutions* (pp. 103–19). Chichester: John Wiley & Sons.

Kellam, S.G., Ensminger, M.E. and Simon, M.B. (1980) Mental health in first grade and teenage drug, alcohol and cigarette use. *Drug and Alcohol Dependence*, 5, 273–304.

Kelley, B.T., Loeber, R., Keenan, K. and DeLamatre, M. (1997, December) *Developmental Pathways in Boys' Disruptive and Delinquent Behavior* (Juvenile Justice Bulletin, NCJ-165692). Washington, DC: US Department of Justice.

Kendall, P.C. and Hollon, S.D. (1979) Cognitive-behavioral interventions: Overview and current status. In P.C. Kendall and S.D. Hollon (eds) *Cognitive-behavioral Interventions: Theory, Research, and Procedures* (pp. 1–9). London: Academic Press.

Keppel, R.D. and Walter, R. (1999) Profiling killers: A revised classification model for understanding sexual murder. *International Journal of Offender Therapy and Comparative Criminology*, 43, 417–37.

Kerr, N.L., Kramer, G.P., Carroll, J.S. and Alfini, J.J. (1991) On the effectiveness of voir dire in criminal cases with prejudicial pretrial publicity: An empirical study. *American University Law Review*, 40, 665–701.

Kindermann, C., Lynch, J. and Cantor, D. (1997, April) *Effects of Redesign on Victimization Estimates* (Bureau of Justice Statistics National Crime Victimization Survey, NCJ-164381). Washington, DC: US Department of Justice.

Kirk, D.S. (2006) Examining the divergence across self-report and official data sources on inferences about the adolescent life-course of crime. *Journal of Quantitative Criminology*, 22, 107–29.

Knight, R.A. and Prentky, R.A. (1987) The developmental antecedents and adult adaptations of rapist subtypes. *Criminal Justice and Behavior*, 14, 403–26.

Kocsis, R.N. and Palermo, G.B. (2007) Contemporary problems in criminal profiling. In R.N. Kocsis (ed.) *Criminal Profiling: International Theory, Research, and Practice* (pp. 327–45). Totowa, NJ: Humana Press Inc.

Kohlberg, L. (1976) Moral stages and moralization: The cognitive-developmental approach. In T. Lickona (ed.) *Moral Development and Behavior: Theory, Research, and Social Issues* (pp. 31–53). London: Holt, Rinehart and Winston.

Kohlberg, L. (1981) *Essays on Moral Development: Volume 1. The Philosophy of Moral Development*. Cambridge: Harper & Row.

Koocher, G.P., Goodman, G.S., White, C.S., Friedrich, W.N., Sivan, A.B. and Reynolds, C.R. (1995) Psychological science and the use of anatomically detailed dolls in child sexual-abuse assessments. *Psychological Bulletin,* 118, 199–222.

Koss, M.P., Gidycz, C.A. and Wisniewski, N. (1987) The scope of rape: Incidence and prevalence of sexual aggression and victimization in a national sample of higher education students. *Journal of Consulting and Clinical Psychology,* 55, 162–70.

Krahé, B., Temkin, J. and Bieneck, S. (2007) Schema-driven information processing in judgements about rape. *Applied Cognitive Psychology,* 21, 601–19.

Krakowski, M. (2003) Violence and serotonin: Influence of impulse control, affect regulation, and social functioning. *The Journal of Neuropsychiatry and Clinical Neurosciences,* 15, 294–305.

Kramer, G.P. and Kerr, N.L. (1989) Laboratory simulation and bias in the study of juror behaviour: A methodological note. *Law and Human Behavior,* 13, 89–99.

Kramer, G.P., Kerr, N.L. and Carroll, J.S. (1990) Pretrial publicity, judicial remedies, and jury bias. *Law and Human Behavior,* 14, 409–38.

Lab, S.P. and Allen, R.B. (1984) Self-report and official measures: A further examination of the validity issue. *Journal of Criminal Justice,* 12, 445–55.

Lane, J., Turner, S., Fain, T. and Sehgal, A. (2005) Evaluating an experimental intensive juvenile probation program: Supervision and official outcomes. *Crime and Delinquency,* 51, 26–52.

Latessa, E.J. and Moon, M.M. (1992) The effectiveness of acupuncture in an outpatient drug treatment program. *Journal of Contemporary Criminal Justice,* 8, 317–31.

Latimer, J., Dowden, C. and Muise, D. (2005) The effectiveness of restorative justice practices: A meta-analysis. *The Prison Journal,* 85, 127–44.

Laub, J.H., Nagin, D.S. and Sampson, R.J. (1998) Trajectories of change in criminal offending: Good marriages and the desistance process. *American Sociological Review,* 63, 225–38.

Leippe, M.R. and Eisenstadt, D. (2007) Eyewitness confidence and the confidence–accuracy relationship in memory for people. In R.C.L. Lindsay, D.F. Ross, J.D. Read and M.P. Toglia (eds) *The Handbook of Eyewitness Psychology: Volume II Memory for People* (pp. 377–425). London: Lawrence Erlbaum Associates.

Lemert, E.M. (1972) *Human Deviance, Social Problems, and Social Control* (2nd edn). Englewood Cliffs, NJ: Prentice-Hall.

Levitt, S.D. (1998) The relationship between crime reporting and police: Implications for the use of Uniform Crime Reports. *Journal of Quantitative Criminology,* 14, 61–81.

Lieberman, J.D. and Arndt, J. (2000) Understanding the limits of limiting instructions: Social psychological explanations for the failures of instructions to disregard pretrial publicity and other inadmissible evidence. *Psychology, Public Policy, and Law,* 6, 677–711.

Lilly, J.R., Cullen, F.T. and Ball, R.A. (2007) *Criminological Theory: Context and Consequences* (4th edn). London: Sage Publications.

Lindsay, D.S. and Read, J.D. (1994) Psychotherapy and memories of childhood sexual abuse: A cognitive perspective. *Applied Cognitive Psychology,* 8, 281–338.

Lindsay, J., Brady, D. and McQueirns, D. (2005) Domestic violence work with male offenders. In D. Crighton and G. Towl (eds) *Psychology in Probation Services* (pp. 115–37). Oxford: Blackwell Publishing Ltd.

Lindsay, R.C.L. and Bellinger, K. (1999) Alternatives to the sequential lineup: The importance of controlling the pictures. *Journal of Applied Psychology,* 84, 315–21.

Lindsay, R.C.L. and Wells, G.L. (1985) Improving eyewitness identifications from lineups: Simultaneous versus sequential lineup presentation. *Journal of Applied Psychology,* 70, 556–64.

Lipton, D.S., Pearson, F.S., Cleland, C.M. and Yee, D. (2002) The effectiveness of cognitive-behavioural treatment methods on offender recidivism: Meta-analytic outcomes from the CDATE project. In J. McGuire (ed.) *Offender Rehabilitation and Treatment: Effective Programmes and Policies to Reduce Re-offending* (pp. 79–112). Chichester: John Wiley & Sons.

Lloyd-Bostock, S. (2000) The effects on juries of hearing about the defendant's previous criminal record: A simulation study. *Criminal Law Review,* September, 734–55.

Loeber, R. (1996) Developmental continuity, change, and pathways in male juvenile problem behaviors and delinquency. In J.D. Hawkins (ed.). *Delinquency and Crime: Current Theories* (pp. 1–27). Cambridge: Cambridge University Press.

Loeber, R., Pardini, D., Homish, D.L., Wei, E.H., Crawford, A.M., Farrington, D.P., Stouthamer-Loeber, M., Creemers, J., Koehler, S.A. and Rosenfeld, R. (2005) The prediction of violence and homicide in young men. *Journal of Consulting and Clinical Psychology,* 73, 1074–88.

Loeber, R. and Stouthamer-Loeber, M. (1996) The development of offending. *Criminal Justice and Behavior*, 23, 12–24.

Loeber, R., Wung, P., Keenan, K., Giroux, B., Stouthamer-Loeber, M., Van Kammen, W.B. and Maughan, B. (1993) Developmental pathways in disruptive child behavior. *Development and Psychopathology,* 5, 103–33.

Loftus, E.F. (1975) Leading questions and the eyewitness report. *Cognitive Psychology,* 7, 560–72.

Loftus, E.F. (2003) Our changeable memories: Legal and practical implications. *Neuroscience,* 4, 231–4.

Loftus, E.F., Loftus, G.R. and Messo, J. (1987) Some facts about 'weapon focus'. *Law and Human Behavior,* 11, 55–62.

Loftus, E.F., Miller, D.G. and Burns, H.J. (1978) Semantic integration of verbal information into a visual memory. *Journal of Experimental Psychology: Human Learning and Memory,* 4, 19–31.

Loftus, E.F. and Palmer, J.C. (1974) Reconstruction of automobile destruction: An example of the interaction between language and memory. *Journal of Verbal Learning and Verbal Behavior,* 13, 585–9.

Lombroso, C. (1911) Introduction. In G. Lombroso-Ferrero (1911). *Criminal Man: According to the Classification of Cesare Lombroso* (pp. xi–xx). London: G.P. Putman's Sons.

Lombroso-Ferrero, G. (1911) *Criminal Man: According to the Classification of Cesare Lombroso*. London: G.P. Putman's Sons.

London, K. and Nunez, N. (2000) The effect of jury deliberations on jurors' propensity to disregard inadmissible evidence. *Journal of Applied Psychology,* 85, 932–9.

MacCoun, R.J. (1990) The emergence of extralegal bias during jury deliberation. *Criminal Justice and Behavior,* 17, 303–14.

MacDonald, Z. (2000) The impact of under-reporting on the relationship between unemployment and property crime. *Applied Economics Letters,* 7, 659–63.

MacDonald, Z. (2001) Revisiting the dark figure: A microeconomic analysis of the under-reporting of property crime and its implications. *British Journal of Criminology,* 41, 127–49.

MacDonald, Z. (2002) Official crime statistics: Their use and interpretation. *The Economic Journal,* 112, 85–106.

MacKenzie, D.L., Brame, R., McDowall, D. and Souryal, C. (1995) Boot camp prisons and recidivism in eight states. *Criminology,* 33, 327–57.

Maden, T. (2005) Dangerous and severe personality disorder: Clinical and legal implications. *Psychiatry,* 4, 23–5.

Maguire, M. (2002) Crime statistics: The 'data explosion' and its implications. In M. Maguire, R. Morgan and R. Reiner (eds) *The Oxford Handbook of Criminology* (3rd edn, pp. 322–75). Oxford: Oxford University Press.

Marshall, J. (1999, March) *Zero Tolerance Policing* (Information Bulletin: Issue No. 9). Adelaide, SA: Office of Crime Statistics.

Marshall, T.F. (1999) *Restorative Justice: An Overview*. London: Home Office.

Maxfield, M.G., Weiler, B.L. and Widom, C.S. (2000) Comparing self-reports and official records of arrests. *Journal of Quantitative Criminology,* 16, 87–110.

Mayhew, P. and Elliott, D. (1990) Self-reported offending, victimization, and the British Crime Survey. *Violence and Victims,* 5, 83–96.

McGuire, J. (2002) Integrating findings from research reviews. In J. McGuire (ed.), *Offender Rehabilitation and Treatment: Effective Programmes and Policies to Reduce Re-offending* (pp. 3–38). Chichester: John Wiley & Sons.

McGuire, J. (2004) *Understanding Psychology and Crime: Perspectives on Theory and Action*. Maidenhead: Open University Press.

McGuire, J. (2006) General offending behaviour programmes: Concept, theory, and practice. In C.R. Hollin and E.J. Palmer (eds), *Offending Behaviour Programmes: Development, Application, and Controversies* (pp. 69–111). Chichester: John Wiley & Sons.

McGuire, J. (2008) What's the point of sentencing? Psychological aspects of crime and punishment. In G.M. Davies, C.R. Hollin and R. Bull (eds) *Forensic Psychology* (pp. 265–91). Chichester: John Wiley & Sons.

McGurk, B.J., Carr, M.J. and McGurk, D. (1993) *Investigative Interviewing Courses for Police Officers: An Evaluation* (Police Research Group, Police Research Series: Paper No. 4). London: Home Office.

McMurran, M. (2006) Drug and alcohol programmes: Concept, theory, and practice. In C.R. Hollin and E.J. Palmer (eds) *Offending Behaviour Programmes: Development, Application, and Controversies* (pp. 179–207). Chichester: John Wiley & Sons.

Meeus, W., Branje, S. and Overbeek, G.J. (2004) Parents and partners in crime: A six-year longitudinal study on changes in supportive relationships and delinquency in adolescence and young adulthood. *Journal of Child Psychology and Psychiatry,* 45, 1288–98.

Melnyk, L., Crossman, A.M. and Scullin, M.H. (2007) The suggestibility of children's memory. In M.P. Toglia, J.D. Read, D.F. Ross and R.C.L. Lindsay (eds) *The Handbook of Eyewitness Psychology: Volume I Memory for Events* (pp. 401–27). London: Lawrence Erlbaum Associates.

Memon, A., Vrij, A. and Bull, R. (2003) *Psychology and Law: Truthfulness, Accuracy and Credibility* (2nd edn). Chichester: John Wiley & Sons.

Memon, A., Wark, L., Bull, R. and Koehnken, G. (1997) Isolating the effects of cognitive interview techniques. *British Journal of Psychology,* 88, 179–97.

Merton, R.K. (1938) Social structure and anomie. *American Sociological Review,* 3, 672–82.

Messner, S.F. (1986) Television violence and violent crime: An aggregate analysis. *Social Problems,* 33, 218–35.

Miers, D., Maguire, M., Goldie, S., Sharpe, K., Hale, C., Netten, A., Uglow, S., Doolin, K., Hallam, A., Enterkin, J. and Newburn, T. (2001) *An Exploratory Evaluation of Restorative Justice Schemes* (Crime Reduction Research Series: Paper 9). London: Home Office.

Milan, M.A., Throckmorton, W.R., McKee, J.M. and Wood, L.F. (1979) Contingency management in a cellblock token economy: Reducing rules violations and maximizing the effects of token reinforcement. *Criminal Justice and Behavior,* 6, 307–25.

Milne, R. and Bull, R. (1999) *Investigative Interviewing: Psychology and Practice*. Chichester: John Wiley & Sons.

Ministry of Justice (2008, July) *National Offender Management Service: Agency Framework Document*. London: Ministry of Justice.

Moffitt, T.E. (1993) Adolescence-limited and life-course-persistent antisocial behavior: A developmental taxonomy. *Psychological Review*, 100, 674–701.

Moffitt, T.E. and Caspi, A. (2001) Childhood predictors differentiate life-course persistent and adolescence-limited antisocial pathways among males and females. *Development and Psychopathology*, 13, 355–75.

Moffitt, T.E. and Harrington, H.L. (1996) Delinquency: The natural history of antisocial behaviour. In P.A. Silva and W.R. Stanton (eds) *From Child to Adult: The Dunedin Multidisciplinary Health and Development Study* (pp. 163–85). Oxford: Oxford University Press.

Moscovici, S. (1985) Innovation and minority influence. In S. Moscovici, G. Mugny and E. Van Avermaet (eds) *Perspectives on Minority Influence* (pp. 9–51). Cambridge: Cambridge University Press.

Moscovici, S. and Lage, E. (1976) Studies in social influence III: Majority versus minority influence in a group. *European Journal of Social Psychology*, 6, 149–74.

Mosson, L. (2003) Working with women prisoners. In G. Towl (ed.) *Psychology in Prisons* (pp. 124–37). Oxford: Blackwell Publishing Ltd.

Moster, A., Wnuk, D.W. and Jeglic, E.L. (2008) Cognitive behavioral therapy interventions with sex offenders. *Journal of Correctional Health Care*, 14, 109–21.

Muller, D.A. (2000) Criminal profiling: Real science or just wishful thinking? *Homicide Studies*, 4, 234–64.

Murray, J.M. and Farrington, D.P. (2005) Parental imprisonment: Effect on boys' antisocial behaviour and delinquency through the life-course. *Journal of Child Psychology and Psychiatry*, 46, 1269–78.

National Audit Office (2009, March) *The National Offender Management Information System*. London: The Stationery Office.

National Probation Service (2003) *About us*. Retrieved 2 April 2010 from http://www.probation.homeoffice.gov.uk/output/page2.asp.

Nellis, M. (1991) The electronic monitoring of offenders in England and Wales: Recent developments and future prospects. *British Journal of Criminology*, 31, 165–85.

Nellis, M. (2006) Surveillance, rehabilitation, and electronic monitoring: Getting the issues clear. *Criminology and Public Policy*, 5, 103–8.

Nemeth, C.J. (1986) Differential contributions of majority and minority influence. *Psychological Review*, 93, 23–32.

Nemeth, C.J. (1987) Interactions between jurors as a function of majority vs. unanimity decision rules. In L.S. Wrightsman, S.M. Kassin and C.E. Willis (eds) *In the Jury Box: Controversies in the Courtroom* (pp. 235–55). London: Sage Publications.

Newburn, T. (2007) *Criminology*. Cullompton: Willan Publishing.

Novaco, R.W. (1979) The cognitive regulation of anger and stress. In P.C. Kendall and S.D. Hollon (eds) *Cognitive-behavioral Interventions: Theory, Research, and Procedures* (pp. 241–85). London: Academic Press.

Novaco, R.W. (2000) Anger. In A.E. Kazdin (ed.) *Encyclopedia of Psychology: Volume 1* (pp. 170–4). Oxford: Oxford University Press.

O'Brien, R.M. (1996) Police productivity and crime rates: 1973–1992. *Criminology*, 34, 183–207.

Ofshe, R.J. and Leo, R.A. (1997) The decision to confess falsely: Rational choice and irrational action. *Denver University Law Review*, 74, 979–1122.

Ogloff, J.R.P. and Vidmar, N. (1994) The impact of pretrial publicity on jurors: A study to compare the relative effects of television and print media in a child sex abuse case. *Law and Human Behavior*, 18, 507–25.

Owen, D. (2004) *Crime Psych: Get Inside the Criminal Mind*. Sydney, NSW: ABC Books.

Owen, D.R. (1972) The 47, XYY male: A review. *Psychological Bulletin*, 78, 209–33.

Palmer, E.J. (2005) The relationship between moral reasoning and aggression, and the implications for practice. *Psychology, Crime & Law*, 11, 353–61.

Palmer, E.J. (2007, December) Methods of evaluating psychological interventions. Paper presented at the Intervening Psychologically with Offenders Conference, Leicester, UK.

Palmer, E.J., McGuire, J., Hatcher, R.M., Hounsome, J.C., Bilby, C.A.L. and Hollin, C.R. (2008) The importance of appropriate allocation to offending behavior programs. *International Journal of Offender Therapy and Comparative Criminology*, 52, 206–21.

Paparozzi, M.A. and Gendreau, P. (2005) An intensive supervision program that worked: Service delivery, professional orientation, and organizational supportiveness. *The Prison Journal*, 85, 445–66.

Park, R.E. (1984) The city: Suggestions for the investigation of human behavior in the urban environment. In R.E. Park and E.W. Burgess (eds) *The City: Suggestions for Investigation of Human Behavior in the Urban Environment* (pp. 1–46). Chicago, IL: University of Chicago Press. (Original work published 1925)

Pearse, J. and Gudjonsson, G.H. (1996) Police interviewing techniques at two South London police stations. *Psychology, Crime & Law,* 3, 63–74.

Pearson, F.S., Lipton, D.S., Cleland, C.M. and Yee, D.S. (2002) The effects of behavioral/cognitive-behavioral programs on recidivism. *Crime and Delinquency,* 48, 476–96.

Pennington, N. and Hastie, R. (1986) Evidence evaluation in complex decision making. *Journal of Personality and Social Psychology,* 51, 242–58.

Pennington, N. and Hastie, R. (1988) Explanation-based decision making: Effects of memory structure on judgment. *Journal of Experimental Psychology: Learning, Memory, and Cognition,* 14, 521–33.

Pennington, N. and Hastie, R. (1992). Explaining the evidence: Tests of the story model for juror decision making. *Journal of Personality and Social Psychology*, 62, 189–206.

Petersilia, J. and Turner, S. (1993) Intensive probation and parole. *Crime and Justice,* 17, 281–335.

Petherick, W.A. and Turvey, B.E. (2008) Nomethic methods of criminal profiling. In B.E. Turvey, *Criminal Profiling: An Introduction to Behavioral Evidence Analysis* (3rd edn, pp. 75–111). London: Elsevier Inc.

Petrosino, A., Turpin-Petrosino, C. and Buehler, J. (2003) Scared straight and other juvenile awareness programs for preventing juvenile delinquency: A systematic review of the randomized experimental evidence. *The ANNALS of the American Academy of Political and Social Science,* 589, 41–62.

Phillips, S.D., Erkanli, A., Keeler, G.P., Costello, E.J. and Angold, A. (2006) Disentangling the risks: Parent criminal justice involvement and children's exposure to family risks. *Criminology and Public Policy,* 5, 677–702.

Pino, N.W. and Meier, R.F. (1999) Gender differences in rape reporting. *Sex Roles,* 40, 979–90.

Polaschek, D.L.L. (2006) Violent offender programmes: Concept, theory, and practice. In C.R. Hollin and E.J. Palmer (eds) *Offending Behaviour Programmes: Development, Application, and Controversies* (pp. 113–54). Chichester: John Wiley & Sons.

Raine, A. (1993) *The Psychopathology of Crime: Criminal Behavior as a Clinical Disorder*. London: Academic Press.

Rand, M.R. and Rennison, C.M. (2005) Bigger is not necessarily better: An analysis of violence against women estimates from the National Crime Victimization Survey and the National Violence Against Women Survey. *Journal of Quantitative Criminology*, 21, 267–91.

Rankin, J.H. and Kern, R. (1994) Parental attachments and delinquency. *Criminology*, 32, 495–515.

Redlich, A.D. (2004) Mental illness, police interrogations, and the potential for false confession. *Psychiatric Services*, 55, 19–21.

Redondo, S., Sánchez-Meca, J. and Garrido, V. (1999) The influence of treatment programmes on the recidivism of juvenile and adult offenders: A European meta-analytic review. *Psychology, Crime & Law*, 5, 251–78.

Renzema, M. and Mayo-Wilson, E. (2005) Can electronic monitoring reduce crime for moderate to high-risk offenders? *Journal of Experimental Criminology*, 1, 215–37.

Ressler, R.K., Burgess, A.W. and Douglas, J.E. (1988) *Sexual Homicide: Patterns and Motives*. New York, NY: Lexington Books.

Rice, M.E. (1997) Violent offender research and implications for the criminal justice system. *American Psychologist*, 52, 414–23.

Robertson, J. (2003, 7 October) Murder suspect tells court vampire queen ordered him to kill friend. *The Scotsman*. Retrieved 22 March 2010 from http://news.scotsman.com.

Robinson, D. (1995, August) *The Impact of Cognitive Skills Training on Post-release Recidivism Among Canadian Federal Offenders*. Ottawa, ON: Correctional Service Canada.

Ross, D.F., Hopkins, S., Hanson, E., Lindsay, R.C.L., Hazen, K. and Eslinger, T. (1994) The impact of protective shields and videotape testimony on conviction rates in a simulated trial of child sexual abuse. *Law and Human Behavior*, 18, 553–66.

Rossmo, D.K. (1997) Geographic profiling. In J.L. Jackson and D.A. Bekerian (eds) *Offender Profiling: Theory, Research and Practice* (pp. 177–90). Chichester: John Wiley & Sons.

Rutter, M. (1979) Maternal deprivation, 1972–1978: New findings, new concepts, new approaches. *Child Development*, 50, 283–305.

Ruva, C., McEvoy, C. and Bryant, J.B. (2007) Effects of pre-trial publicity and jury deliberation on juror bias and source memory errors. *Applied Cognitive Psychology*, 21, 45–67.

Salfati, C.G. and Canter, D.V. (1999) Differentiating stranger murders: Profiling offender characteristics from behavioural styles. *Behavioral Sciences and the Law,* 17, 391–406.

Sampson, R.J. and Laub, J.H. (1990) Crime and deviance over the life course: The salience of adult social bonds. *American Sociological Review,* 55, 609–27.

Sampson, R.J. and Laub, J.H. (1992) Crime and deviance in the life course. *Annual Review of Psychology,* 18, 63–84.

Sandler. J.C. (2006) Alternative methods of child testimony: A review of law and research. In C.R. Bartol and A.M. Bartol (eds) *Current Perspectives in Forensic Psychology and Criminal Justice* (pp. 203–12). London: Sage Publications.

Sandys, M. and Dillehay, R.C. (1995) First-ballot votes, predeliberation distortions, and final verdicts in jury trials. *Law and Human Behavior,* 19, 175–95.

Schaufeli, W.B. and Peeters, M.C.W. (2000) Job stress and burnout among correctional officers: A literature review. *International Journal of Stress Management,* 7, 19–48.

Schollum, M. (2005, September) *Investigative Interviewing: The Literature* (New Zealand Police). Wellington: Office of the Commissioner of Police.

SCoPiC. (n.d.a) *The Peterborough Adolescent Development Study (PADS)*. Retrieved 2 April 2010 from http://www.scopic.ac.uk/StudiesPADS.html.

SCoPiC. (n.d.b) *The Sheffield Pathways out of Crime Study (SPooCS)*. Retrieved 2 April 2010 from http://www.scopic.ac.uk/StudiesSPooCS.html.

Sear, L. and Williamson, T. (1999) British and American interrogation strategies. In D.V. Canter and L. Alison (eds) *Interviewing and Deception* (pp. 67–81). Aldershot: Ashgate Publishing Company Limited.

Shader, M. (2003) *Risk Factors for Delinquency: An Overview*. Washington, DC: US Department of Justice.

Shaw, C.R. and McKay, H.D. (1969) *Juvenile Delinquency and Urban Areas: A Study of Delinquency in Relation to Differential Characteristics of Local Communities in American Cities*. Chicago, IL: University of Chicago Press. (Original work published 1942)

Shaw, C.R. and McKay, H.D. (1971a) Juvenile delinquency in urban areas: Research. In H.L. Voss and D.M. Petersen (eds) *Ecology, Crime, and Delinquency* (pp. 79–86). New York, NY: Meredith Corporation.

Shaw, C.R. and McKay, H.D. (1971b) Juvenile delinquency in urban areas: Theory. In H.L. Voss and D.M. Petersen (eds) *Ecology, Crime, and Delinquency* (pp. 87–99). New York, NY: Meredith Corporation.

Shaw, J.I. and Skolnick, P. (2004). Effects of prejudicial pretrial publicity from physical and witness evidence on mock jurors' decision making. *Journal of Applied Social Psychology,* 34, 2132–48.

Shawyer, A., Milne, B. and Bull, R. (2009) Investigative interviewing in the UK. In T. Williamson, B. Milne and S.P. Savage (eds) *International Developments in Investigative Interviewing* (pp. 24–38). Cullompton: Willan Publishing.

Sheldon, W.H. (1971) The New York study of physical constitution and psychotic pattern. *Journal of the History of the Behavioral Sciences,* 7, 115–26.

Sheldon, W.H. (with Dupertuis, C.W. and McDermott, E.) (1954) *Atlas of Men: A Guide and Handbook on Somatotyping the Adult Male at All Ages*. New York, NY: Harper and Brothers.

Sherman, L.W. and Strang, H. (2007) *Restorative Justice: The Evidence*. London: The Smith Institute.

Sigall, H. and Ostrove, N. (1975) Beautiful but dangerous: Effects of offender attractiveness and nature of the crime on juridic judgment. *Journal of Personality and Social Psychology,* 31, 410–14.

Simmons, J. (2000, July) *Review of Crime Statistics: A Discussion Document*. London: Home Office.

Skogan, W.G. (1976) Citizen reporting of crime: Some national panel data. *Criminology,* 13, 535–49.

Smallbone, S. (2009) Psychological explanations. In H. Hayes and T. Prenzler (eds) *An Introduction to Crime and Criminology* (2nd edn, pp. 205–20). Frenchs Forest, NSW: Pearson Education Australia.

Smith, A. (2006, November) *Crime Statistics: An Independent Review*. London: Home Office.

Smith, D.J. (2002) Crime and the life course. In M. Maguire, R. Morgan and R. Reiner (eds) *The Oxford Handbook of Criminology* (3rd edn, pp. 702–45). Oxford: Oxford University Press.

Smith, V.L. (1991) Prototypes in the courtroom: Lay representations of legal concepts. *Journal of Personality and Social Psychology,* 61, 857–72.

Snook, B., Cullen, R.M., Bennell, C., Taylor, P.J. and Gendreau, P. (2008) The criminal profiling illusion: What's behind the smoke and mirrors? *Criminal Justice and Behavior,* 35, 1257–76.

Snow, L. (2006) Psychological understanding of self-injury and attempted suicide in prisons. In G.J. Towl (ed.) *Psychological Research in Prisons* (pp. 70–115). Oxford: Blackwell Publishing.

Social Exclusion Unit (2002, July) *Reducing Re-offending by Ex-prisoners*. London: Social Exclusion Unit.

Soukara, S., Bull, R., Turner, M. and Cherryman, J. (2009) What really happens in police interviews of suspects? Tactics and confessions. *Psychology, Crime & Law*, 15, 493–506.

Spinney, L. (2008) Line-ups on trial. *Nature*, 453, 442–4.

Steblay, N.M., Besirevic, J., Fulero, S.M. and Jimenez-Lorente, B. (1999). The effects of pretrial publicity on juror verdicts: A meta-analytic view. *Law and Human Behavior,* 23, 219–35.

Sporer, S.L., Penrod, S.D., Read, D. and Cutler, B.L. (1995) Choosing, confidence, and accuracy: A meta-analysis of the confidence-accuracy relation in eyewitness identification studies. *Psychological Bulletin*, 118, 315–27.

Steblay, N.M., Dysart, J., Fulero, S. and Lindsay, R.C.L. (2001) Eyewitness accuracy rates in sequential and simultaneous lineup presentations: A meta-analytic comparison. *Law and Human Behavior,* 25, 459–73.

Steblay, N.M., Hosch, H.M., Culhane, S.E. and McWethy, A. (2006) The impact on juror verdicts of judicial instruction to disregard inadmissible evidence: A meta-analysis. *Law and Human Behavior,* 30, 469–92.

Stockdale, J.E. (1993) *Management and Supervision of Police Interviews* (Police Research Group, Police Research Series: Paper No. 5). London: Home Office.

Strachey, J. (1975) Sigmund Freud: A sketch of his life and ideas. In J. Strachey (with A. Richards and A. Tyson) (eds) *Sigmund Freud: The Psychopathology of Everyday Life*. London: Penguin Books.

Studebaker, C.A., Robbennolt, J.K., Penrod, S.D., Pathak-Sharma, M.K., Groscup, J.L. and Devenport, J.L. (2002) Studying pretrial publicity effects: New methods for improving ecological validity and testing external validity. *Law and Human Behavior,* 26, 19–41.

Sullivan, C.J. (2006) Early adolescent delinquency: Assessing the role of childhood problems, family environment, and peer pressure. *Youth Violence and Juvenile Justice,* 4, 291–313.

Sutherland, E.H. and Cressey, D.R. (1970) *Criminology* (8th edn). New York, NY: J.B. Lippincott Company.

Tanford, S. and Penrod, S. (1984) Social influence model: A formal integration of research on majority and minority influence processes. *Psychological Bulletin,* 95, 189–225.

Thomas, M. and Jackson, S. (2003) Cognitive-skills groupwork. In G. Towl (ed.) *Psychology in Prisons* (pp. 83–92). Oxford: Blackwell Publishing Ltd.

Thomson, D.M. (1995a) Allegations of childhood abuse: Repressed memories or false memories? *Psychiatry, Psychology and Law,* 2, 97–105.

Thomson, D.M. (1995b) Eyewitness testimony and identification tests. In N. Brewer and C. Wilson (eds) *Psychology and Policing* (pp. 119–54). Hillsdale, NJ: Lawrence Erlbaum Associates.

Thornberry, T.P. and Krohn, M.D. (2000) The self-report method of measuring delinquency and crime. *Criminal Justice,* 4, 33–83.

Thornberry, T.P., Smith, C.A., Rivera, C., Huizinga, D. and Stouthamer-Loeber, M. (1999, September) *Family Disruption and Delinquency*. Washington, DC: US Department of Justice.

Thornhill, R. and Palmer, C.T. (2000a) *A Natural History of Rape: Biological Bases of Sexual Coercion*. Cambridge, MA: Massachusetts Institute of Technology.

Thornhill, R. and Palmer, C.T. (2000b) Why men rape. *The Sciences*, 40, 30–6.

Tibbitts, C. (1932) Crime. *The American Journal of Sociology,* 37, 963–9.

Tong, L.S.J. and Farrington, D.P. (2006) How effective is the 'Reasoning and Rehabilitation' programme in reducing reoffending? A meta-analysis of evaluations in four countries. *Psychology, Crime & Law,* 12, 3–24.

Tonry, M. and Lynch, M. (1996) Intermediate sanctions. *Crime and Justice,* 20, 99–144.

Tremblay, R.E. (2000) The development of aggressive behaviour during childhood: What have we learned in the past century? *International Journal of Behavioral Development,* 24, 129–41.

Tremblay, R.E. (2007) The development of youth violence: An old story with new data. *European Journal of Criminal Policy and Research,* 13, 161–70.

Trowbridge, B.C. (2003) Suggestibility and confessions. *American Journal of Forensic Psychology,* 21, 5–23.

Turvey, B.E. (2008a) Case linkage: Offender modus operandi and signature. In B.E. Turvey, *Criminal Profiling: An Introduction to Behavioral Evidence Analysis* (3rd edn, pp. 309–56). London: Elsevier Inc.

Turvey, B.E. (2008b) Offender characteristics: Rendering the profile. In B.E. Turvey, *Criminal Profiling: An Introduction to Behavioral Evidence Analysis* (3rd edn, pp. 539–68). London: Elsevier Inc.

Uggen, C. (2000) Work as a turning point in the life course of criminals: A duration model of age, employment and recidivism. *American Sociological Review,* 65, 529–46.

UK Parliament (2010, 14 January) *Cutting Crime: The Case for Justice Reinvestment*. Retrieved 8 April 2010 from http://www.publications.parliament.uk/pa/cm200910/cmselect/cmjust/94/9407.htm.

Vrij, A. (2007) Deception: A social lubricant and a selfish act. In K. Fiedler (ed.) *Social Communication* (pp. 309–42). New York, NY: Psychology Press.

Vrij, A. (2008) *Detecting Lies and Deceit: Pitfalls and Opportunities* (2nd edn). Chichester: John Wiley & Sons.

Vrij, A., Fisher, R., Mann, S. and Leal, S. (2009) Increasing cognitive load in interviews to detect deceit. In T. Williamson, B. Milne and S.P. Savage (eds) *International Developments in Investigative Interviewing* (pp. 176–89). Cullompton: Willan Publishing.

Vrij, A. and Granhag, P.A. (2007) Interviewing to detect deception. In S.Å. Christianson (ed.) *Offenders' Memories of Violent Crimes* (pp. 279–304). Chichester: John Wiley & Sons.

Vrij, A., Mann, S., Kristen, S. and Fisher, R.P. (2007) Cues to deception and ability to detect lies as a function of police interview styles. *Law and Human Behavior,* 31, 499–518.

Visher, C.A. and Travis, J. (2003) Transitions from prison to community: Understanding individual pathways. *Annual Review of Sociology,* 29, 89–113.

Walker, A., Kershaw, C. and Nicholas, S. (2006, July) *Crime in England and Wales 2005/06* (Home Office Statistical Bulletin). London: Home Office.

Walsh, A. and Ellis, L. (2007) *Criminology: An Interdisciplinary Approach*. London: Sage Publications.

Weber, N., Brewer, N., Wells, G.L., Semmler, C. and Keast, A. (2004) Eyewitness identification and response latency: The unruly 10–12-second rule. *Journal of Experimental Psychology: Applied,* 10, 139–47.

Wells, G.L. (1978) Applied eyewitness-testimony research: System variables and estimator variables. *Journal of Personality and Social Psychology,* 36, 1546–57.

Wells, G.L. (1984) The psychology of lineup identifications. *Journal of Applied Social Psychology*, 14, 89–103.

Wells, G.L. (1993) What do we know about eyewitness identification? *American Psychologist*, 48, 553–71.

Wells, G.L., Small, M., Penrod, S., Malpass, R.S., Fulero, S.M. and Brimacombe, C.A.E. (1998) Eyewitness identification procedures: Recommendations for lineups and photospreads. *Law and Human Behavior*, 22, 603–47.

West, D.J. (1982) *Delinquency: Its Roots, Careers and Prospects*. London: Heinemann Educational Books Ltd.

Williamson, T. (2004) USA and UK responses to miscarriages of justice. In J.R. Adler (ed.) *Forensic Psychology: Concepts, Debates and Practice* (pp. 39–57). Cullompton: Willan Publishing.

Williamson, T. (2006) Towards a greater professionalism: Minimizing miscarriages of justice. In T. Williamson (ed.) *Investigative Interviewing: Rights, Research, Regulation* (pp. 147–66). Cullompton: Willan Publishing.

Williamson, T., Milne, B. and Savage, S.P. (2009) Introduction. In T. Williamson, B. Milne and S.P. Savage (eds) *International Developments in Investigative Interviewing* (pp. xxi–xxvi). Cullompton: Willan Publishing.

Willmot, P. (2003) Applying the research on reducing recidivism to prison regimes. In G. Towl (ed.) *Psychology in Prisons* (pp. 35–51). Oxford: Blackwell Publishing Ltd.

Wilson, P., Lincoln, R. and Kocsis, R. (1997) Validity, utility and ethics of profiling for serial violent and sexual offenders. *Psychiatry, Psychology and Law*, 4, 1–11.

Wittebrood, K. and Junger, M. (2002) Trends in violent crime: A comparison between police statistics and victimization surveys. *Social Indicators Research*, 59, 153–73.

Woodhams, J. and Toye, K. (2007) An empirical test of the assumptions of case linkage and offender profiling with serial commercial robberies. *Psychology, Public Policy, and Law*, 13, 59–85.

Woodworth, M. and Porter, S. (1999) Historical foundations and current applications of criminal profiling in violent crime investigations. *Expert Evidence*, 7, 241–64.

Woolnough, P.S. and MacLeod, M.D. (2001) Watching the birdie watching you: Eyewitness memory for actions using CCTV recordings of actual crimes. *Applied Cognitive Psychology,* 15, 395–411.

Yochelson, S. and Samenow, S.E. (1998) Appendix: An overview of the criminal personality. In S.E. Samenow, *Straight Talk about Criminals* (pp. 271–314). London: Jason Aronson Inc.

Yuille, J.C. and Cutshall, J.L. (1986) A case study of eyewitness memory of a crime. *Journal of Applied Psychology,* 71, 291–301.

Zedner, L. (2002) Victims. In M. Maguire, R. Morgan and R. Reiner (eds) *The Oxford Handbook of Criminology* (3rd edn, pp. 419–56). Oxford: Oxford University Press.

Index

T

U, V, W Z

Reading guide

This table identifies where in the book you'll find relevant information for those of you studying or teaching A-level. You should also, of course, refer to the Index and the Glossary, but navigating a book for a particular set of items can be awkward and we found this table a useful tool when editing the book and so include it here for your convenience.

Topic	Edexcel	OCR	WJEC	AQA(B)	Page
Acupuncture		x			193–4
Alternatives to custodial sentencing				x	172–4
Anger management	x	x			183–4, 187
Attribution theory and bias			x		53–4, 95
Behavioural therapy			x		182–4, 188–9
Bottom-up approaches		x	x		83–5
Brain dysfunction		x			44–6
Children giving evidence		x			105–7, 156
Cognitive interview		x			103–5, 131–2
Cognitive skills training		x	x		183
Custodial sentencing				x	171–2
Decision making		x	x		141–7, 157–61
Defining crime	x	x	x	x	8, 9
Depression/suicide		x			177–8
Detecting lies		x			134–7
Differentiation association hypothesis		x			28–30, 60

Topic	Edexcel	OCR	WJEC	AQA(B)	Page
Emotion			x		96–9
Evolution		x			47–9
Expert witness use		x			154
Face perception		x	x		113–15
False confessions		x			120–3
Gender		x			86–7, 191, 48
Genes		x		x	42–4
Inadmissible evidence		x			153–4
Interrogation		x			124–6
Labelling	x				30–1
Learning theory				x	35
Majority influence		x			147–50
Measuring crime				x	9–18
Minority influence		x			147–50
Modelling	x				35
Moral development		x			52–3
Offender profiling	x			x	73–5, 90–2
Peers		x			60
Poverty		x			61
Probation		x			171–2
Psychodynamic theory				x	32–3
Punishment	x				166–74
Recidivism	x	x		x	185
Restorative justice		x			169–70
Self-fulfilling prophecy	x				30–1
Social cognition		x			53–4
Social skills training	x	x		x	183
Stereotyping	x				95–6
Token economy	x				192
Top-down typology		x	x		75–8, 84
Weapons focus		x			98–9
Witness confidence		x			111
Zero tolerance			x		167